DIRECTIVE
DESTINY

A Divine Proclamation

J. MICHAEL FRANKLIN,
CAMERON FALEJCZYK

abbott press®

A DIVISION OF WRITER'S DIGEST

Abbott Press books may be ordered through booksellers or by contacting:

Abbott Press
1663 Liberty Drive
Bloomington, IN 47403
www.abbottpress.com
Phone: 1-866-697-5310

Because of the dynamic nature of the Internet, any web addresses or links contained in this book may have changed since publication and may no longer be valid. The views expressed in this work are solely those of the author and do not necessarily reflect the views of the publisher, and the publisher hereby disclaims any responsibility for them.

Any people depicted in stock imagery provided by Thinkstock are models, and such images are being used for illustrative purposes only. Certain stock imagery © Thinkstock.

ISBN: 978-1-4582-1634-2 (sc)
ISBN: 978-1-4582-1636-6 (hc)
ISBN: 978-1-4582-1635-9 (e)

Library of Congress Control Number: 2014910008

Printed in the United States of America.

Abbott Press rev. date: 8/28/2014

For Mom and Dad

I believe all suffering is caused by ignorance. People inflict pain on others in the selfish pursuit of their happiness or satisfaction. Yet true happiness comes from a sense of peace and contentment, which in turn must be achieved through the cultivation of altruism, of love and compassion, and elimination of ignorance, selfishness, and greed.
—The Dalai Lama

All too often we find ourselves searching for truths and answers to questions we've never asked.
—J. C. Smith

CONTENTS

ACKNOWLEDGMENTS

IF THERE IS ONE THING I now absolutely believe to be true, it's that, as my mentor has told me many times, "Everything happens for a reason." In that respect, many people have helped mold the final contents of this book either directly or indirectly, and to all of you, I offer my sincere thanks and gratitude.

To the very special people who helped turn this work into a life-changing accomplishment, I offer you my deepest gratitude. I especially want to thank Pamela, Pete and Cheryl, Karen, Carol and Annie, and Bob and Ellen And, for your emotional support and your love, a special thank you to my wife, Sarah, and Justin, Jeremiah and Joshua, Terri and Jimmy, and Elizabeth.

Many others have helped in ways you may not even know. Sometimes through moral support and encouragement, and other times through constructive criticism, you helped me to stay on the right track, and to you I also offer my sincere thanks.

I especially extend my warmest thanks to you, Tom and Yong Morgan, for always being there. I know how rare it is to find true friends and how blessed I am for your friendship.

I also want to thank you, Ed, Kelly, and Destini, for giving me a reality check to stay on course. I wish for you much success and happiness in all that you do.

I also want to thank Diane's friend Connie for taking the time to read the manuscript. Even though I could not use any of your suggestions, I do appreciate the time and effort you gave to me in the process.

When a project goes from months to years, one of the most unfortunate consequences, in my opinion, is that some of the people that helped get it started and headed in the right direction early on may be sadly lost through time and left out in the final acknowledgments. If you are one of the people that helped me along the way, I sincerely apologize for my shoddy memory. I thank you again for your input and will appreciatively add your name to these acknowledgments if you contact me.

Finally, I want to thank all those that helped me with my editing and technical support; Joe Falejczyk, Maridel Nirosky, Diane Whalen, Nancy Niedzwiecki, Chelou Hills, and Deborah Bowling. Most of all I want to thank J. C. Smith, Amanda Becher, and Ellen Tanner. Throughout the life of this project, I have asked many friends and family to help, but you are the ones who really helped it all come together. The profound messages brought forward through this book would have still gotten out there one way or another. However, without the insightful, time-consuming editing you all brought into the process to help shape the final product, it surely would not be expressed as clearly or professionally.

Amanda, your career as a writer and editor will no doubt be astonishing, and I look forward to reading your work in the future. I hope we stay in touch. Thank you and never give up on your dreams or your talents. Like Ed and Destini, you are destined to touch the lives of many, and that is a treasured gift indeed!

Jeremiah and Joshua, my sons, I could never put into words how much I appreciate the honor of being your dad, nor could I ever imagine what my life would have been if you two had not been the biggest part of it. You guys have made me the person I am today. Thank you from the bottom of my heart—I love you!

PROLOGUE

ORDINARILY, I CONSIDER MYSELF A relatively content individual, maybe not happy in the usual sense, but content. I can't afford a new car or fancy, expensive clothes, but my kids seem to be happy, and they have never gone to bed hungry or without me telling them that I love them. So, all in all, I think life in general keeps me on par with everyone else, considering. However, I will admit that taking care of my dad, who day by day had grown thinner and weaker from the rapidly progressing bone cancer, clearly left a noticeable scar on my usually relaxed demeanor.

Dad was a good man. Everyone that knew him described him as a relatively quiet person who did a lot of thinking but not a lot of socializing. He always lived by the Golden Rule and went out of his way to help others, even strangers, whenever they needed him. He never wasted time talking about trivial or highly opinioned things like sports or politics but seemed to know all the answers if anyone asked. As a well-respected businessman and highly-spoken-of member of the community, he was well regarded as being very kind and courteous, extremely smart and creative, and honest to a fault.

I appreciated all the kind remarks and condolences of those who knew and respected my father—I really did. But as I stood silently over his casket, my memories and sadness swelled into a simmering pool of emotions that pushed its way to the surface in the form of mounting rage.

He was a good man, I screamed in my head. I couldn't hold back the tears any longer, so I swiftly slipped out the back door to find solitude.

How could God, if he really exists, let this happen to such a warm and loving man? The weight of conflicting emotions and that awful emptiness demanded an answer.

"How could you do this to such a good man? It's not fair. It's just not fair. Why did you decide to pick on our family? It's not right—and you know it. What am I supposed to do now? Can you hear me? I'm talking to you, God! I'm tired of seeing bad things happen to good people while bad people live the good life and get everything they want! Why is there so much more evil than good in the world? If you are real, why aren't you doing something about it? Do you hear me? Are you there? Do you even exist? ... Silence? So, that's your answer? Yeah, that's what I thought! You're a joke, a phony, and I'm not falling for it anymore. If you are real, then I want proof. Do you hear me, God? Is this loud enough for you? I'm not playing your stupid game anymore. I demand answers. I challenge you to prove your existence!"

It's a good thing I stepped outside to have that one-way conversation with God, because by the time I finished my rant, my yelling left my voice nothing but a tattered whisper.

In the weeks following Dad's death, I found myself quite busy between part-time jobs, taking care of my invalid mother, and trying to spend as much time as I could fit in with my two very active children. As the weeks turned into months, I all but forgot about my challenge to God.

But apparently, God did not forget!

CHAPTER 1

ESCAPE

RESCUED FROM THE HOPELESSNESS OF a confinement that until now held me prisoner to its reality, I quickly latched onto the realization that Angela freed all four of us and brought us here to a place only she knew ... a safe place ... an enlightened place.

The night had vanished without any conscious recollection of passing time, and a long overdue feeling of hope and quietness hugged my inner thoughts. The brightness of an awakening sun revealed the splendor of a lush, green hillside. It reminded me of a storybook meadow, far removed from the bonds of colorless nights and the caged existence I gladly abandoned as a shackled memory.

I momentarily closed my eyes and tried to capture the fresh ambiance of the crisp morning air and full solitude of our surroundings. A thick blanket of knee-high grasses, clover, and wildflowers saturated my senses with their refreshing beauty and aromas. The kiss of a light breeze complemented the radiance of the early-morning sun.

Angela gave us a few moments to clear our thoughts and adjust to our new circumstances before summoning us together as a group in preparation for our journey.

"We need to all join as one in a bonding circle," Angela insisted; she would never take us on such a venture without first invoking a prayer of protection around us. She kept it short but effective and knew all the right things to say. I felt very secure and reassured by her peaceful yet authoritative nature.

Leaving the obvious unambiguousness of the open field, I watchfully stayed focused in anticipation of what awaited our group beyond the fringe of the majestic, virgin forest that appeared before us.

"Follow me closely," Angela instructed, "and be keenly aware of all that your senses reveal, both physically and emotionally."

As we neared the edge of the forest, a previously unnoticed pathway guided us through a perimeter of deep-purple flowering shrubs seeping out from the wooded boundary. Approaching the hedged border, I paused and examined the expressive nature of bountiful blood-red, multi-petaled, thorned flowers peering out from beneath the glossy, dark leaves. The shyness of the flowers and theatrical dominance of their protective foliage left me with an unnerving feeling of emotional conflict, as if they represented more of a warning than just a contrasting adornment. This unknowing sent mixed emotional apprehensions threading through my thoughts, urging me not to enter, but Angela and the others continued onward without hesitation, so I had no choice but to follow them.

Stepping prominently onto the mossy forest floor, the transition to this pristine woodland, abundant with evergreen and hardwood trees, awakened all of my senses. Angela and the other two women, Elizabeth and Nancy, led the way, with Ed and me bringing up the rear on the narrow, well-camouflaged trail.

Beneath the giant timbers lay an array of ferns, vines, and wild orchids that would surpass even the greatest painter's vision. With cascades of sunlight rushing through the bright green canopy above, the details of contrasting colors grew ever clearer.

As we ventured deeper into the woods, the tapestry of our environment became more vibrant and alive. I could feel the dynamics of our seclusion calling me to an understanding of crisp solitude found nowhere else. It felt liberating.

We soon joined a well-worn path alongside a smooth, rock-laden, and gently flowing stream. It presented us with a choice of transitioning to the right, into a deeper blend of browns and greens adeptly charging up a sleepy hillside, or to the left, where the stream split into two smaller side-by-side brooks flowing like a painter's brush through the shadows of watchful evergreens. With skillful certainty, our capable guide bypassed the hillside in favor of a pathway paralleling the pleasing brooks.

Reaching a widening of the trail where two fallen trees provided a perfect pair of natural benches, Angela asked us to find a comfortable seat, close our eyes, and relax. After reassuring us that nothing could reach or harm us in this protected place, she instructed us to focus consciously on our breathing by taking in slow, deep breaths beyond the regular capacity of our lungs, until it felt like it filled our stomachs. Then, after holding it as long as we comfortably could, to slowly let it out again. She called it "belly breathing" and said that these full, cleansing breaths would help keep us relaxed and focused while sharpening our physical and mental acuity as well.

"An attribute you will find most helpful in what you are about to experience," Angela claimed.

We followed Angela's instructions as she shared with us some of the sacred beliefs her ancestors passed down concerning the spiritual significance of the trees and animals of these forests. She revealed her personal beliefs in secret and invisible realms, spoken of in legends and ages past, while inviting us to keep our minds open and our thoughts clear. Her words resonated with the depth of her wisdom, and the expanse of her knowledge seemed endless. When she stopped talking, we all sat quietly with our eyes closed and listened to the meticulous sounds of unspoiled nature.

After several minutes, Angela said softly, "Once you feel completely relaxed, both physically and mentally, continue belly breathing and maintain your relaxed state, but, keeping your thoughts clear, open your eyes and shift your awareness to all of your senses, both physical and intuitive. Let the story they tell unveil every aspect of the beauty that surrounds us, not as a passive witness, but as an active participant. Above all, pay special attention to how each of your senses complements the others and remember how that makes you feel. Being acutely aware of your emotions is what helps you to remember. This is because your ability to recall each moment is enhanced by the intensity of the feelings you associate with the memory." She said this to all four of us, but I knew her emphasis was meant for me. Mindful of my inexperience, she wanted to make sure I understood the full significance of her words.

I remained still and at ease, pushing away the usual mind-filling distractions of random thoughts, as best I could, while silently encouraging my mind to take in the full symphony of Mother Nature's backdrop. About twenty feet in front of us, three frisky, red squirrels started playfully chasing one another through the underbrush, bouncing off the trunks of fall-colored oaks and sugar maples, while somewhere up in the branches, the methodical hammering of a determined woodpecker echoed through the leaves.

With another quick reminder of the importance of *all* our senses, Angela again asked us to close our eyes briefly and try to distinguish the diversity of fragrances in the air.

"Your sense of smell is directly linked to your memories," she told us. "It plays an important role in the degree of emotions attached to them."

I turned my head slowly from side to side. The sweet, earthy smell brought back warm childhood memories of kneeling next to my mom as she worked meticulously in her many gardens.

I remember how much patience she had teaching me to recognize and name various plants and understand the differences between the numerous varieties of perennials and herbs and the look-alike "weeds" that grew right alongside them. She explained how some flowers carried a greater worth or importance than others simply because of their color or shape or even just because of tradition. She also pointed out that most of the people who held those beliefs just pulled the other so-called weeds out and threw them away. It seemed plain to me that their vibrant colors and complex designs made them just as beautiful and original as the other plants. So, in her loving way of teaching, she always let me leave many colorful weeds in the garden.

As I transitioned from seeing the world through the eyes of a child to the added perspective of my teenage years, I realized the real life lesson of "the flowers and the weeds" played out in the world around me.

Even to this day, I cannot understand society's reason for its destructive attitude. What gives anyone the right to segregate or destroy any member of "the garden" just because *that person* doesn't feel someone else is worthy enough to be on equal standing with the others? This way of appreciating life remains one of the greatest gifts I received from Mom.

"We need to continue," Angela emphasized in a soft but persuasive voice, summoning me back to the present.

We arose from our seats on the logs and once again proceeded down the trail as Angela pointed out the seemingly endless varieties and colors of delicate blossoms that blanketed the forest floor. With her years of experience, she could describe our landscape with so much detail and clarity it almost seemed as if she created it herself. The sheer magnitude and depth of beauty, as only nature could conceive it, revitalized my soul.

Leaving the soothing sounds of the twin streams, our guide then led us into a much denser area of old-growth hardwoods and a small clearing where three fallen, majestic oak trees formed a semi-circle around an alluring pool of clear, deep-blue water. This rustic, ancient-looking pond, about half the size of a basketball court, immediately captured my imagination. The almost perfectly round shape and single row of bowling-ball-size, smooth, white rocks encircling it reminded me of a giant pearl necklace. I stared at the pool of dark water for quite a while, allowing my mind to wander back and forth, contemplating its origin. I faintly heard Angela say something about leaving us there for a short time, but I never looked up. Reflections of sunbeams skipped across tiny ripples created by a gentle breeze. Like the deepening of a dream, the rest of my world seemed to fade away, and I became totally focused on the shimmering images in the pool. It mesmerized me. As I gazed at the sparkling peaks rolling in perfect rhythm toward me, I felt drawn to them, as if something in the water plucked at my inner desires, beckoning me to learn its secrets. I leaned closer.

Suddenly, a soft but brilliant white light encircled me, eclipsing everything in my view except the water itself. The tunneling effect of the mysterious light forced me to concentrate all my attention on the liquid mirror before me. Kneeling on the rocky bank, I slowly reached out to touch the water with my fingertips.

Then, leaning back in what felt like slow motion, I silently watched as the gentle ripples evolved and grew into massive, tumbling waves filled with millions of pinpoints of light. It was magnificent! They returned in torrents, cascading toward me as if to swallow me up. I suppose I should have instinctively jumped back to safety, but an unexplainable, peaceful feeling kept me still and focused.

Locked in its spell, I watched in awe as the waves morphed into an expanding cloud of churning white light. It silently grabbed me and wrapped me in a cocoon of absolute calm. I felt totally at the mercy of my peaceful captor, yet, instead of feeling imprisoned, I experienced a deep sense of belonging as if a long-awaited reunion was about to take place.

I closed my eyes and let myself go.

CHAPTER 2

THE ARCHWAY

A STRANGE SENSATION RUSHED THROUGH me, that of moving upward. Could I be floating? Flying? I couldn't be sure. I opened my eyes, but with no real reference for speed or distance, my perceived feeling of rising felt more like I somehow just "knew" it.

Without warning, through the brilliance of the misty light, I found myself face to face with an enormous angel standing within arm's reach in front of me. When he came into focus, my first impression was that of a very large body builder or an American football player because of his extremely broad chest and shoulders and sizably smaller waist. This was quite evident even concealed under the bright white, full-length robe, fashionably tied in place with a golden sash. His youthful, clean-shaven, fair-skinned face, medium length, curly black colored hair, and dark brown eyes complemented his massive, very powerful-looking wings.

Unlike the feathery look often portrayed in movies, his wings had a translucent, silky, satin appearance and glistened as if they were made of multi-colored clear ice. A waving, gold-and-magenta-colored aura extended several feet out from his enormous frame, adding a dazzling effect to the already bright white glow reflecting off his robe. It made him somewhat difficult but breathtaking to look at. I felt alarmed but not afraid. He smiled and looked directly into my eyes.

"Peace be with you, Jeremiah," he said in a quiet, calming voice. "I am Metatron. I will guide you."

I guess those must have been just the words I needed to hear, because after he spoke them, I felt very much at ease. However, he did not exactly "speak" them. Though these reassuring words did indeed come from this huge, glowing angel, they did not come from his mouth. He spoke to me only with his mind—telepathically!

I then noticed two other angels with us, one on either side of me. They also stood very large and powerful in appearance, though not as grandiose as Metatron. They also displayed large, folded wings. Their aqua-blue auras set them ablaze in the same manner as a bright white object glowing under the rays of a black light. With my relatively short stature of only five foot seven inches, I barely came up to their chests, yet they filled me with a sense of peace and security that made me feel like I was some sort of dignitary, and they were my bodyguards escorting me to a very important meeting. I felt a strong sense of certainty that while in their company no harm could come to me.

When I looked away from the other two angels and back at Metatron, his wings were no longer visible, and his aura now extended only a few inches from his body, making him appear more like a gladiator in a white choir gown with a silhouetting, gold-tinted, magenta glow. This new perspective also prompted me to look back at the other two angels. Their wings had likewise disappeared, and their auras had dimmed to a resonating delicate hue.

About the same time I became aware of the fact that we no longer seemed to be ascending, something shiny flashed in front of me. As the brilliance of the encircling light subsided, the shiny object became clearer. I found myself gazing upon the superb, golden-armored breastplate of another even bigger angel now standing alongside Metatron. His shoulder-length, wavy dirty-blonde colored hair, sapphire-blue eyes, and light bronze complexion perfectly complemented his dark, double-strapped sandals and the thigh-length, pure white, sleeveless robe he wore under his armor. His enormous wings were also more solid and heavier looking than those of Metatron, and his face more distinct. With his arms outstretched in a welcoming manner, he smiled and proclaimed, "Peace be with you!"

As a child, I learned of the indestructible golden armor worn by Michael, commander of all the angels, so as soon as I saw him, I felt confident it *had* to be him. I briefly admired his incredible protective armor and then asked, "Are you the Archangel Michael?"

"I am," he replied in a commanding voice as his massive, rainbow-tinted, semi-folded wings disappeared behind him, and his rich, dark red, and gold aura diminished to a pleasingly soft level.

"Can you tell me why I am here?" I asked.

"Only to remember," he responded in a decisive tone.

He turned his head to the right and gestured toward a colossal, freestanding arch positioned perhaps twenty-five or thirty feet in front of us. Focusing on it only briefly, I began to look around the room we now occupied. The brilliant light that first surrounded us faded away into a refreshing clearness, and in its place, a delicate, violet glow, like an aura, could be seen everywhere, even emanating from the floor and walls. A feeling of total peacefulness continued to flow through me as I slowly surveyed the room.

Like the arch in front of us, the extraordinary chamber seemed to be completely constructed of smooth, pure-white stone. High above the floor, I noticed a large, triangle-shaped opening, big enough to easily stand up in. Keeping my eyes focused upward, I continued to turn slowly all the way around, noting the walls contained twelve of these large, triangular openings, all spaced equally apart and positioned with the tips of the triangles pointed down. The subtle but noticeably different color of each opening suggested a single pane of faintly stained glass filled the void. The chamber itself was completely round, about half the size of a football field. The room may have had a domed ceiling, but if it existed at all, the ceiling seemed to disappear into its own brightness, rendering it indistinguishable from the walls. A sweet, tantalizing aroma of fresh-ground cinnamon filled the air. I closed my eyes and breathed in deeply through my nose.

"Cinnamon! I love the smell of cinnamon." The appealing fragrance reminded me of the homemade pumpkin pies my brother, my sister, and I used to make every Thanksgiving with our grandma, whom we called Busia, the Polish word for "Grandmother."

Some of my fondest childhood memories involved doing things with her around the house and yard. I clearly remember her telling me the importance of mastering the essentials of life, because one day I would parent children of my own, and they would be depending on me to take care of them.

She taught us that the true secret of happiness is, "To love and take care of each other and remain true to yourself, your family, and your friends no matter what happens in your life or in the world around you."

Could she have somehow known of my fate to become a single parent, or was it simply the wisdom of her years that foretold my future so accurately? I thought to myself. I opened my eyes and continued to survey the room.

Turning around and looking behind me, I discovered the fountain. It was the most exquisite thing I think I've ever seen. (Though referring to it as a fountain is probably a great injustice to its true purpose, not to mention its magnitude and artistry. It reminded me of a fountain because of its outer ring of interlocking crystal angels and a continuous flow of water trickling down the front of them, which originated from somewhere within their mists. So, for lack of a better term, I'll call it a fountain).

Appearing large enough to hold perhaps a hundred people, this sculpted masterpiece seemed to be made entirely of diamond-quality crystal. A soft, wavy, bluish-white light emanated from somewhere within, reflecting through its many gem-like facets. The resulting laser show of vivid prism-like beams lit up the entire area. Even the water itself seemed to carry a light of its own as it soothingly cascaded down the faces of the life-size figures of mighty archangels. These crystalline guardians stood shoulder to shoulder with drawn swords in hand, facing outward.

I excitedly moved closer toward the fountain, and in doing so, I came upon a high spot in the floor, hidden in plain sight by the whiteness that surrounded it. Mounting it with three large steps, I still remained well out of reach of the fountain itself;

however, I could now look over the heads of the crystal sentinels to discover what they protected.

In the center, encased in a shield of bluish-white light, stood an ancient-looking fruit tree, unlike any tree I've ever seen. Having a single large trunk at its base, it branched off into two identical trunks in opposing directions. This in itself struck me as quite unusual. However, after examining the rest of the tree, I discovered an even more intriguing feature. A different fruit grew on each side of the tree.

On one side, it produced an easily accessible and delicious-looking fruit resembling dark red apples, though the leaves and bark resembled those of a fig tree. In contrast, the other side of the tree grew darker heart-shaped leaves and created a fruit similar in appearance to a small, pale-colored coconut. I could see only a few of these fruits in the high branches. They seemed too far to reach and well camouflaged, making the effort it would take to obtain one seem hardly worth the prize. In either case, the circle of crystal guardians protecting the tree left no doubt it was meant to be seen and admired but not touched.

From this vantage point, even though I could not observe the entire base of the main trunk, I could see that the flow of sparkling water originating from the fountain's center seemed to be coming from within the base of the tree itself. The water almost magically flowed out through the junction of the two trunks, down the main trunk, and then appeared again as it came up and over the heads of the ring of crystal angels that protected it. As I watched the glistening flow of the water coating its way down the sculpted bodies of crystalline protectors, I detected something truly puzzling. When the water reached the floor at the feet of the angelic guards, I expected to see it flow either into a drain or into some sort of collecting area, or out across the floor. Instead, as it splashed against the white stone floor, it softened into a beautiful, aqua-green light, like a mystical fog, and simply faded away! Admiring this unanticipated scene, I knew I *had* to be viewing it for the first time, yet it filled me with a strange but satisfying feeling of familiarity.

I turned back toward Metatron, Michael, and the other two angels to ask them if they could tell me about the unusual tree and the mysterious water that flowed from it, but after scanning the entire room, I found myself completely alone. With my excitement and curiosity levels competing for first place, my attention once again focused on the enormous, perfectly symmetrical arch looming directly in front of me. I eagerly dismounted the white pinnacle and headed toward it. Reaching its threshold, I could now appreciate the scope of its size.

This colossal work of art measured at least thirty feet high and several feet thick. Moving just up to the opening, I could see that garnishing its inner wall, twelve equally-spaced, triangular-shaped objects protruded from the centerline of its surface. Each of the twelve extended from the white stone in a way that made them look like elegant, three-sided, crystal pyramids, growing flawlessly out of the soft white outer skin. I found them to be stunningly beautiful, resembling giant, precious gems. They looked to be about twelve inches long on each side, and though identical in size, each carried its own unique, subtle color. A pulsating glow coming from within each one made it obvious that all the crystals shared a common connection to one another by some type of energy, which added intrigue to their beauty.

Stepping about midway into the archway significantly changed my perspective. Looking up at the crystal pyramids, I discovered, clearly visible above each crystal, a black, ancient-looking symbol like you might see in an ancient pyramid, extending three or four inches beyond the surface. I estimated these symbols to be about six inches square, half the size of their crystal pyramid counterparts. They appeared to be made of a semi-transparent material, like black glass, making them very prominent against the bright white wall of the arch.

Then something occurred to me. The dark color of the symbols made them quite conspicuous against their all-white background, yet I failed to notice them until I stood directly underneath the arch. Stepping back to confirm my suspicions, the strange symbols disappeared and could indeed only be seen when looking directly up at them.

When I stepped back for this deeper look, I discovered something else worth noting about the twelve crystals. Because they followed the rounded contour of the inner wall, all the points of the pyramids (if connected by imaginary lines) would geometrically converge at the same point directly under the center of the arch.

This seemed to be more than just an interesting fact, though, for some reason I felt a strong intuitive impression that this characteristic explained the significance of the crystals themselves. In fact, the feeling was so strong I felt compelled to try to find the exact spot where the focal point of all those imaginary lines would be.

Centering myself beneath the arch, I paused momentarily to admire the beauty of the colors of the crystals and the exquisite intricacy of the dark symbols. I could not help wondering who created it and why. Then, fixing my eyes on one particular crystal, the indigo-colored one, I noticed that my whole body felt warm and intensely alive. I made a conscious effort to remain motionless so as not to lose the sensation.

At that same moment, all the crystals began to grow progressively brighter and started to pulsate in harmony with my heartbeat. The brightness of the combined lights expanded outward, combining with each of the others until the intensity melded into a churning tunnel of pure white light encircling me and sending a soft, tingly feeling rushing through my entire being, with vivid images racing through my mind.

Without a warning or explanation, I found myself recalling in a dream-like fashion every significant memory of my life. Scenes, pictures, and feelings streamed through me at an increasing speed, moving faster and faster until my brain could no longer keep up with what my mind *needed* to gather. The memories teased me with unbelievably vivid, detailed accounts, but many of them seemed totally unfamiliar to me. I felt like a greedy little thief trying to sneak away not only with my own personal memories, but everyone else's memories too. At the same time though, I subconsciously felt entirely removed from any sense of being, as if I dwelled in another place and could only experience myself in a lingering dream.

Immobilized by the surrealism of the moment, I felt like I had stepped into another dimension where time and reality as anyone knew it did not exist. All I know is that I've never felt anything like it before. The intense feelings hyperextended my imagination, and I prayed it would never end. However, as quickly as it began, the experience abruptly stopped.

In that last instant, I felt suspended in total nothingness as a soft, unfamiliar voice somewhere deep within my subconscious whispered, "You are not yet strong enough."

I didn't remember closing my eyes, but when they opened, I found myself still staring up at the arch, noting that everything remained as I first found it. After standing motionless for the longest time, I attempted to adjust my stance in hopes of recapturing the dream-like occurrence, but to no avail.

Before the mind-opening experience of the reflective images began, I had just started examining the unique pattern and artistry of the symbols, and caught a quick glimpse of something glittering on one of them. Since nothing suggested these symbols could be made of *any* type of metallic material, this fact added a new twist of mystery to everything. Thinking this might also be a clue to what I blissfully experienced, I re-established all my attention again on the same ancient-looking symbol.

My heart danced in anticipation, but no matter how hard I looked, the dark-colored design revealed nothing. Determined to unlock its secrets, I tried moving slightly to the right and left and back and forth while never taking my eyes off the symbol. I didn't know where the glittering object or the secret spot went, but it no longer seemed to be there.

Since adjusting my position while concentrating on that particular symbol did not seem to work, I shifted my gaze and looked intently at several of the other symbols, searching for … well, I am not sure what I hoped to discover, but I didn't find it.

I finally gave up the idea of repeating the experience, at least for the moment, and shifted slightly back and forth a few times to examine the inside of the arch from different angles. Then, deciding to try one last time to find that special euphoric location, I returned to what I believed to be the precise spot I needed, underneath the center of the archway, and … nothing!

However, a new feeling started nudging at my brain. Without taking my eyes off the middle of the arch, I felt almost compelled to lie down on the floor so that the twelve crystal pyramids and their accompanying black symbols centered themselves directly above me to the right and left.

I could now easily see all of the symbols and crystals by moving my head slightly from side to side, and I could have picked any one of them, I suppose, yet my first inclination—no, more like my inner need to understand—pushed me again near the center, to the indigo-colored one. I stared at the crystal's accompanying black symbol for several minutes until my body again relaxed. Then I saw it. A second symbol appeared inside the original black symbol, plainly visible from this vantage point.

Somehow, I could now see right through the dark symbol, like looking through colored cellophane. I slowly shifted my gaze to each of the other symbols, with the same gratifying result. I saw a pattern of three gold-colored lines located within each of the clear, black symbols. The lines boldly displayed themselves and apparently had been there all along, like one of those computer-generated pictures that you can see only if you stare at it in just the right way.

I studied each one carefully. They seemed to all be the same length, slightly smaller than the translucent, black symbols that contained them. However, the thickness of the lines or spaces between them differed slightly, giving each a unique pattern, like a short bar code. These golden lines appeared suspended in the symbol somehow. I could clearly see them, but they didn't seem real; it was like looking at a holograph.

I admired the golden lines, dark symbols, and beautiful crystal pyramids for several minutes, wondering what their significance might be, why they had been placed in the arch, what, if anything, their connection might be to the fountain, and, most of all, what any of this might have to do with me. The really weird part is that I kept noticing this strong déjà vu type of feeling that I once knew the answers to all these questions, but I couldn't explain how or why. Besides, I most certainly did not know the answers now.

I could easily have marveled at the intriguing lines, symbols, and crystals much longer, however, it dawned on me that I had not yet gone completely through and examined the other side of the arch. So, I quickly leapt up and hastened through it.

A soft, bright light immediately engulfed me, halting me in my tracks and shielding my vision from anything in view. Then, from some faraway place, I sensed someone calling my name, so I listened closely.

"Jeremiah," a voice said faintly. "Jeremiah, it is time to come back." I heard it clearly this time and recognized it as Angela's voice!

Opening my eyes, I looked around the room.

"Are you back with us?" Angela asked, smiling.

"I think so," I sluggishly replied. I took a deep breath and said, "Wow, it was so real!" I slowly sat up in my chair, with all the grandeur of my experience still rushing through my mind. I adjusted my posture and sighed with a smile. "I've had vivid dreams and very convincing nightmares before, but *that*, by far, was the most incredible and realistic adventure I have ever experienced—even if it was only in my mind."

"Dreams," Angela stated, "are glimpses of reality mixed with non-reality that our minds put together, sometimes in the most obscure ways, to remind us of people, places, or things from our past or sometimes even our future, but quite often in ways our conscious thoughts and memories find hard to interpret.

"Whereas meditation," she continued, addressing all of us, "is a wonderful doorway through our subconscious that can show us the way to serenity and wholeness. It can settle our busy thoughts enough to allow us to develop focused mindfulness and condition our minds to receive universal wisdom and enlightenment."

"Well, I don't know about all that, but I do know I've never experienced anything like it before!"

"We certainly look forward to hearing all about it," Angela said in her usual serene voice. "Make sure you write it down so you don't forget any of the details."

After each of our meditative sessions with Angela, she recommended we first write down the highlights of our meditation in our journals and then share them with the rest of the group. I described for my friends the adventure I just experienced with as much clarity and detail as possible. In turn, the others shared their stories.

Once we all told our stories, we usually socialized over homemade refreshments (Elizabeth had a wonderful talent for making the most scrumptious desserts) and herbal tea or freshly ground coffee (Ed's favorite) before returning to our homes to patiently wait for our next get-together.

Arriving home much closer to daybreak than nightfall, I went to bed with the images of my meditation still rumbling through my mind. I found that I was even more tired than I realized and faded quickly into the world of dreams, but not before a very brief but clear vision of an elderly Asian man standing in front of me, smiling and shaking his head up and down as if to say, "That's right, fall asleep. I am waiting to take you with me."

CHAPTER 3

IN SEARCH OF
ANSWERS

IT SEEMS TO BE A universal human experience to try to find meaning out of the events in our lives. Often, when faced with the mystery of suffering and death, the question "Why?" becomes all-consuming. This pretty much sums up my experience during the last months of my dad's life as he fought a futile battle against bone cancer. Emotionally and spiritually, I felt drained by his suffering and struggled with my own search for comfort and relief. Even though Mom believed deeply in the power of prayer, I totally blamed God for all of Dad's suffering, so praying did not seem much of an option for me. Fortunately, a series of what I believe were destined events led Dad and me to Angela.

Through her, I now understand, and truly believe, we all possess the innate ability to comprehend not only life's most basic and perplexing questions, but also its deepest secrets. All we need to do is find enough faith in ourselves, be sincere in our search for answers, and most of all, be ready to accept the answers once we find them.

At this point in my life, truths such as these became pillars of strength for me, because I carried a lot of personal challenges besides dealing with the rapidly declining health of my father. For his sake, I found myself changing jobs, moving back into my parents' home, and putting my long- and short-term goals on hold indefinitely. As a thirty-nine-year-old single parent of two wonderful pre-teenage boys—I had enjoyed the privilege of raising them by myself since their teething and crawling days—this became a life-changing event for all of us.

Like many of the people in my small town, I could only find work through a temporary employment agency, so I jumped from one part-time job to another. It gave me enough of a paycheck to feed my kids, but without the assurance of a stable income, I experienced a lot of despair and hopelessness in my day-to-day existence.

Only six months earlier, I felt confident and secure in my life. I proudly served as an officer and senior helicopter pilot in the armed forces, living comfortably in a nice split-level home on a lake. I owned a really fun boat as well as a rare vintage motorcycle, and I enjoyed driving around in my classic custom Chevy. Since the military provided me with a good salary and total job security, I never worried about taking care of my children properly and giving them all the things they needed. Of course, being in the military also meant keeping in top physical shape. So, I enjoyed staying active and doing a lot of outdoor adventuring with my kids. In my personal life, I shared some great times with a few close friends and a serious romantic interest who all swore I looked like a younger Tom Hanks. Putting everything else aside though, the primary focus of my life at that time, and now for that matter, always revolved around doing the very best I knew how for my two boys.

So, why did I leave the military when I had everything going for me? The biggest reason, as I've already mentioned, concerned the declining health of my parents. When the doctor told my dad about the cancer, he also recklessly told him he only had, at most, a year to live. Since Dad spent most of his days taking care of Mom, who had spent several years confined to a wheelchair from a degenerative spinal condition, they both required almost full-time care. My siblings all claimed to have busy, complex lives, which prevented them from dropping everything and moving home, so I felt that taking care of our parents fell on my shoulders.

After making the decision to leave the military, I convinced myself that my quality of life and personal freedoms would be greatly improved. Above all, I looked forward to ending the deployments, which meant being away from my kids for weeks or months at a time. Being in the desert proved challenging, but being away from my children was what I found most intolerable.

Moving back to my hometown meant that my boys would be able to go to the same school without the hassle of moving every three years or so, and they would finally have the opportunity to build lasting friendships. As for me, I would be able to attend all their plays, recitals, games, and other school functions. The biggest plus, though, *had* to be the fact that I would be out from under the governments' control of my life ... and that certainly had to be a good thing.

I came up with a simple plan; I would find a place in a nice neighborhood where my kids could make lots of friends, yet still be close enough to my parents so I could quite easily take care of them until Dad recovered. I would build my own healthcare business with the multi-level marketing company a fellow pilot recently sponsored me into. I would join either the national guard or reserves, which would guarantee my military retirement as soon as I reached retirement age. In addition, I confidently thought the woman I had dated on a semi-serious level for the past seven months would give up her mediocre job and come to New York to be with me.

Yes, indeed, everything certainly should work out just fine. Moreover, as part of the Army's post-war drawdown plan, I was promised over thirty thousand dollars of separation pay. So, all in all, my lifelong plan of being rich and famous seemed possible, and, at least for the first year or two, things should go pretty easy.

Even though I joked about it all the time, the truth is, I didn't really long to be rich and famous. We never had any money to speak of growing up, so doing without really didn't bother me. However, with most of my dad's mediocre retirement check going toward his mounting medical bills, there wasn't enough left over to properly upkeep the house and aging car. So, between my final military pay and what I hoped would be a successful new business, I figured I could help out both financially and around the house, making life better for all of us.

I know now, for both my family and me, my real search didn't have anything to do with money, but it did have a lot to do with happiness. The problem for me has always been that deep down I struggled with the belief that there really was such a thing.

In leaving the high stress of military life, I thought all my big worries would be behind me. However, my transition to civilian life and moving back home did not exactly go as planned.

I'll save the bizarre details of my stranger-than-fiction personal side story for another time. In a nutshell, I sold my motorcycle and boat to a "friend" that never paid me, my Chevy blew up, my girlfriend ran off with her ex, the business flopped, I couldn't find any openings in the guard or reserves, and between lots of taxes and unexpected bills, my bank account went from "I can have anything I want" to "Looking down for change in the Wal-Mart parking lot," in less than three months.

I found myself with no job, no vehicle, no girl, and no money. My children and I reluctantly moved back in with my parents, a very stressful ordeal for all concerned, and I took any part-time job I could get my hands on through the temp agency just to break even on the monthly bills.

In spite of things not going as smoothly as I had hoped, the experience of moving back home ultimately turned out to be the most positive thing that has ever happened to me. My boys took advantage of the opportunity to spend quality time getting to know their grandparents, a luxury that military life usually does not allow. I also took advantage of this opportunity to, for the first time, really get to know my parents on a very personal level. In doing so, I learned more about my father during his last year than I'd previously known my whole life.

One of the most significant and fascinating things Dad shared with me involved his grandmother, whom I learned was a Native American medicine woman and the tribal healer from one of the Algonquin tribes. I asked him what it meant to be a medicine woman and why, in all the years, he never mentioned it before.

He said he used to talk about her quite a bit when we were younger and she was still alive. Then he explained that a medicine man or woman is a very important member of the tribe, as is the tribal healer. In some of the smaller clans, some not much bigger than an extended family, the same person took on the roles of both. Such was the case with my great-grandmother. She not only acted as a counselor and comforter, but as a healer of illnesses and wounds, both physical and emotional. One of her most important duties made her responsible for instructing the tribal children about the spiritual teachings and sacred traditions of their people.

"It was your great-grandmother's vocation, responsibility, and passion to pass on to the new generations all the wisdom she acquired through a lifetime of hard living, as well as the collective wisdom of her ancestors and other tribal elders," Dad stated.

"She possessed a great respect for the plants, the animals, the environment, and even the changing of the seasons, which she called the balance of nature, and was very tenacious about us grandchildren having the same values. She achieved this not only through personal experience, but through wonderful stories told to her by her own grandfather, a great medicine man himself, that she loved to re-tell to us as kids."

I told Dad I knew that American Indians believed very passionately in their sacred rituals and ceremonies and in respect for all of nature. I even recalled hearing somewhere that many scholars believe that the Native American traditions and beliefs seem to be more in harmony with nature and the universally accepted concepts of God than any other nation of people.

"In fact, did you know," I asked my father, "that according to one educational program I recall, unlike any other group of people on the planet, there supposedly is no known war ever fought between two Indian nations over religion!"

"No, I did not know that," Dad admitted.

"It's a shame that most of what I know about Native Americans I learned from educational television when there is probably a rich history and source of knowledge right in my own family," I commented.

"I could name a lot of things I wish I had taken the time to teach you kids," Dad said in agreement.

"When you get to be my age and there is so little time left, one of the biggest regrets I have is that I didn't use the time I was given more wisely. I hope when you reach your final days, you don't have the same regret."

The reason Dad wanted to introduce me to my heritage at this point in time directly involved him, his grandmother, and me. Because, as fate would have it, the last time Dad saw her, his grandmother gave him a gift that he now wanted to pass on to me.

He reached into his top dresser drawer, and digging under some socks, he pulled out a small, gray leather pouch with a matching drawstring. Its elegantly seasoned look reflected the wearing of many years.

"This belonged to your great-grandmother. She gave it to me just before she died and asked me to pass it on to one of my own children. I want *you* to have it." When Dad handed me the pouch, I noticed that the leather felt soft, almost velvety.

"It feels too soft to be real leather," I said.

"That's from carrying it around for so many years," Dad said, smiling. "In fact, not only is it real, but according to my grandmother, it came from the hide of an old, gray wolf that used to follow and watch over the tribe wherever they went."

"What's in it?" I asked.

"Open it and find out," Dad instructed.

I opened the pouch and poured some of its contents into my hand. As I spread them out in my palm, he pointed them out to me one at a time. The pouch contained: corn; bean and squash seeds; some clean, white sand; several small pieces of natural salt crystals (most of them about the size of a kernel of corn); a small, slightly off-white seashell; a small, black-tipped, white feather; some flower petals (rose, I think); and some broken-up pieces of tobacco leaves. I shook the pouch a little, and its final treasure dropped out, a tuft of sage tied in the middle with a small piece of hemp and scorched on one end.

"What is the meaning of all this?" I inquired.

"That is exactly the same thing I asked my grandmother when she gave it to me. Do you know what she told me?"

"What?" I asked anxiously.

"She told me I would need to learn it on my own. So that, son, is the same thing I am telling you." He raised his eyebrows and then looked confidently at me and smiled.

"This also belongs in the pouch," Dad remarked as he reached into his pocket and pulled out a clear quartz crystal. Its size closely matched that of a jellybean, but with a crystalline, facetted surface and angled, faceted, dull points on both ends.

"I always carry it with me. It came from the Herkimer area over by Syracuse," he said. "It's good for the soul."

After putting the other items back in the leather pouch, I took the crystal and looked at it in the light. It reflected light from the lamp on the night table like a small prism. I examined it for a minute or so, and then I handed it and the pouch back to Dad.

"Thank you. I didn't know we had any family heirlooms. This is a remarkable gift and a great honor, but I don't need it yet. You do."

"I just want to make sure it goes to you."

I felt very touched to receive such a personal treasure from my dad. "I know where you keep it, and when the time comes, I will make sure it comes to me, okay?"

Dad smiled and nodded his head in agreement.

"And I promise I will always take good care of it the way you have."

"Good enough," Dad said, returning the pouch to its hiding place and pushing the drawer shut.

"Now get out of here so I can get some sleep."

I always saw my dad as a good man in every respect, but I never thought of him as being very spiritual. This conversation changed that perception and marked the beginning of a series of discussions with him about many topics involving spirituality.

Being an avid reader all of his life, Dad knew an astonishing number of facts and ideas on several spiritually related topics— everything from lost books of the Bible to New Age concepts. So, we enjoyed many hours of fascinating talks and debates over the relevance of such things.

During one of our discussions, we discovered that, over the years, both of us recalled several times where spiritual or unexplainable events left an unforgettable mark on our lives. Of course, we were both eager to learn more. This turned out to be a critical discovery and major turning point for me, because a day or two after a discussion about people who could see into the future like Nostradamus and Edgar Casey, there happened to be a Spiritual Awareness Seminar and workshop taking place at the City Convention Center.

Several vendors would be selling a variety of items from fancy candles and meditation tapes to religious artifacts, aromatherapy oils, and multi-colored stones. In addition, some well-known mediums from the area would be giving personal readings. Since neither Dad nor I ever visited a real psychic before, we both thought it would be a fun thing to do.

We didn't arrive at the Convention Center until after lunch, so by the time we got there, the sign-up sheet for a psychic reading filled one full sheet and was halfway down another. I figured it would be at least an hour wait or more, even though the person working the list told everyone twenty or thirty minutes. Anyway, with a room full of interesting vendors and an opportunity to be told our futures, neither of us minded the wait.

Fortunately, they called each person's name as it came up on the list, so there was no need to stand in line; we just needed to be within calling distance. While we waited, we checked out some very unique homemade jewelry and met the organizer of the event, a mystic-looking fellow named Jara. He turned out to be a very cordial host whose heavy Indian accent and high-pitched voice definitely did not match his no-nonsense, business-like appearance.

After asking Dad and me some semi-personal background questions concerning our beliefs in the paranormal and any experiences we might have had, he asked us about what we thought of the event and what particular interest or questions we might have in the area of spiritual or psychic phenomena. Following Dad's example, I didn't say very much. Jara then gave both of us one of his business cards and invited us to sign up for spiritual enhancement classes that he co-taught with his wife each Thursday night. Dad told him we would think about it, and he left us alone.

While my father examined some cool geodes, I made the rounds of the different vendors, and then I peeked around the corner into the adjoining room to see the layout of the readings.

Twelve tables lined the wall, six on each side. In the back, left corner, I spotted a nice-looking, middle-aged woman, with an average build, sitting by herself at one of the tables. She wore stylish, straight, shoulder-length, black hair and light-colored, plastic-framed glasses. Except for the glasses, she reminded me of the actress Kate Jackson, from the old *Charlie's Angels* TV series. As soon as I looked at her, she smiled and motioned for me to come over. I asked the person controlling the list, and he politely said my name should be called within ten to fifteen minutes, and I needed to wait like everyone else. I said okay and went back to the concession stand where Dad was, but then, about a minute later, he retrieved Dad and me and took us to see the same woman who had motioned to me.

With an infectious smile and warm, caring voice, she said that her name was Angela and that she had been waiting for us. The man that led us in introduced her as a very well-known medium and spiritual advisor from the Lilydale Community, south of Buffalo, and, in his opinion, one of the best in the whole country.

Unfortunately, I left there feeling neither her psychic readings for Dad or me lived up to her reputation. She told me my life recently turned from satisfying to chaotic and that I felt like with my future looked bleak and uncertain. I guess that part of her reading seemed pretty accurate, but she then went on to assure me that everything would soon make sense and fall into its proper place. I took that as a generic thing to say, but then she added that she saw me embarking on a series of life-changing journeys unlike any I could ever envision. In addition, in the end, I would be responsible for changing the lives of people all around the world and would gain wealth in ways I could not now imagine. I guessed her psychic abilities weren't good enough to know I that could barely afford to go see a movie, let alone go on any exotic vacations around the world. However, I did occasionally play the instant lottery, so the wealth part did seem like a real possibility.

This same woman told my dad that very soon, he too would be taking an incredible journey. It would be a very well-deserved trip, and loved ones would be waiting for him at the other end. Clearly, Dad's decreasing health did not leave him in any condition to do any traveling, and she never even mentioned the fact that he was dying from cancer. She even went as far as to tell him that the main reason for her being there that day was to meet us, and more importantly, that she looked forward to helping us and would see us again soon. At the time, I thought that to be a very unusual thing to say to a couple of strangers, but I figured she probably said that to everyone, so I didn't dwell on it. At least it surprisingly didn't cost us anything. We expected to each pay twenty dollars for the reading, the advertised price, but in spite of the fact that Angela had never met Dad or me before, she refused to let either of us pay her.

Despite the obvious inaccuracy of the readings, I talked Dad into signing up for the spiritual enhancement classes with me anyway, and that is where we reintroduced ourselves to Angela. She offered to help out because Jara's wife, Carol, a good friend of hers, asked for her help, at least for the first few classes until they thinned out. Angela is one of those people who truly believes in helping others, knowing there is nothing personally in it for her. Of course, when Dad and I saw her again, we only thought of her as the so-called psychic from the convention center, but she came across as such a pleasant person that neither of us minded spending more time talking to her. At the time of her readings, we couldn't have possibly known how spiritually profound her predictions would turn out to be.

We only went to three of the weekly classes. Following the last class we attended, Angela invited us to join her meditation group, which met at her best friend Elizabeth's house. Dad and I took her up on her offer, and that is where she taught us the relaxing benefits of meditation.

After spending a few weeks with Angela and witnessing the sincere and dynamic passion she demonstrated, Dad and I both believed in her genuine concern for his spiritual well-being. Just being in her presence, we could both "feel" her compassion and knew she sincerely meant it when she offered to help us make it through the trying times ahead.

Angela knew very well the physical and emotional turmoil my father would be forced to endure after dealing with a prolonged cancer that claimed her late husband. She wanted to help in any way she could by offering us her wisdom, counseling, and most importantly, her compassion.

One of the first things she taught us, and said often, is that nothing in life happens by chance and that prayer, beseeching help beyond our level of consciousness, is very real and *very* powerful. She believes that everyone, through prayer and meditation, is capable of understanding what they need to know to deal with all the troubles life throws our way. In fact, if not for Angela's extraordinary talent for teaching even non-believers or slow learners such as me, my ability to share my story with such detail and self-confidence would not likely exist.

I guess Angela could also sense that I struggled with Dad's dying as much as he did, so she compassionately spent a lot of time comforting and counseling both of us about it.

Dad had always been a fighter, and the meditation techniques Angela taught him helped him significantly in dealing with depression and pain, but the bone cancer progressed rampantly through his body, and the doctors could not stop it. He never directly talked to me about dying, because it was more than I wanted to deal with. However, through the discussions we shared together with Angela, I could tell that he in no way felt reassured enough about what follows death not to be afraid of it.

As for me, looking through my sadness and anger, I could not understand why God, if one truly existed, could let this happen to such a warm and loving man. Throughout my life, I admired my dad as not only the kindest and smartest man I've ever known, but my best friend and confidant as well. Now he stood at death's door, and neither one of us knew what awaited him on the other side.

CHAPTER 4

THE ORB

ON THE EVENING OF THE summer solstice, several months after Dad's death, our little meditation group gathered together for a much anticipated feast. I continued to meditate with my friends on a regular basis and did my best to juggle taking care of Mom, raising the boys, working, and going to college at night. Spending time with the others—Angela, Nancy, Ed, and Elizabeth—often revived loving memories of my father and brought forth a deep gratitude for the support and love of my friends who helped me through those grief-filled months.

Our hosts, Ed and Elizabeth, both civil engineers that work for the county, had become dear friends. Ed creatively cut out a beautiful, little campfire spot in the wooded area behind their home and made it available for a festive potluck get-together. It gave us an ideal setting for enjoying an old-fashioned cookout and quiet evening outdoors. Since it was also the first day of summer, as well as the longest day of the year, it seemed like a perfect excuse for a relaxing night of marshmallow roasting, socializing, and meditating.

Mother Nature even cooperated. We could not have asked for a more beautiful evening. The crisp night air made it just cool enough for long sleeves, and the moonless sky made the heavens so clear you could see the millions of stars seeded deep within the Milky Way. The best part about being with these friends, though, came from our mutual belief that, despite all the terrible things we hear on the news, people, basically, are good. If we always try to maintain a positive attitude and practice positive thinking toward others, we individually and collectively can make a difference in our own lives, the lives of the people around us, and, ultimately, our world.

After eating more than a healthy portion of Swedish meatballs, homemade garlic and chive potatoes, corn on the cob, and Ed's famous vegetarian shish kabobs (not to mention Elizabeth's chocolate-raspberry cheesecake), I welcomed the opportunity just to sit and relax. Ed provided seating for all of us on well-placed logs around the fire pit, so while I let my dinner settle, I quietly sat and watched the cherry-red glow of the embers reflecting off everyone's faces.

With the addition of Angela's younger sister, Chelou, who occasionally joined us, and Nancy's brother, Joe, and his wife, Liz, home on leave from the Navy, our modest little group consisted of seven this time. I happily found myself in the midst of a great circle of friends. When the last two guests finished eating, they joined the rest of us next to the relaxing warmth of the campfire.

Just sitting still and watching the fire felt so relaxing on a full stomach. You could almost follow the crimson flames as they jetted out from under the logs, scurrying up the sides to reunite again on the top; it was a very soothing experience.

For the benefit of Joe and Liz, who had never meditated before, Angela described the art of meditation and explained how a guided meditation works. She explained that some people who practice meditation believe you should try to relieve your mind of all thoughts while others believe you should concentrate intently on the full awareness of your physical body. Angela's view of meditation is that it presents an opportunity to get in touch with our thoughts and feelings by deepening our relationship with our higher selves. She quite often described meditation as a form of prayer, emphasizing that instead of only talking to God, as most people describe it, one listens to God, as well.

"Meditation offers us the opportunity to seek guidance for any situation or challenge life throws our way," Angela explained. "Most of all, it opens up a quiet avenue to really listen to our hidden thoughts and invites our inner selves to show us what we need to see and do to better our lives."

Ed placed a couple more logs on the fire while Angela encouraged all of us to relax as much as possible. She then began her guided meditation.

"Take slow, deep breaths and try to release all the tensions and stresses that we all tend to keep bottled up inside from the demands of a busy life. Just let yourself go and free your mind, at least temporarily, from the confinement and pressures of your physical world. Let your thoughts expand outward until they reach a balance with your own inner being and connect with the consciousness of your higher self. This is the part of you, part of all of us, that lets you search for deeper meanings and understanding without watching the clock or the kids or the person next to you."

She paused for a few minutes, allowing everyone to think about her words before continuing.

"The notion of a guided meditation is to help you learn how to relax your mind and body by focusing on something you can easily visualize. Then, as your own thoughts take over, your subconscious mind will stop listening to me, and your inner self will take my place and do the rest. And if all you do is get so relaxed that you fall asleep, it's okay. This is *your* time. You will probably find it to be a very tranquil sleep and in all probability what you really needed right now anyway."

Angela said a little prayer in which she asked for divine help in understanding what each of us needed in our lives to heal our physical, emotional, and spiritual pains. She then asked that we receive insight into what direction our lives should take and for the wisdom and courage to overcome obstacles along our way. Following a brief supplication for the cleansing and renewal of our planet, Angela asked angels to protect, guide, and watch over us during the meditation, so "only positive thoughts and energy can enter our circle of friends." Closing with, "Amen; so be it," she paused for a moment and turned on a small portable cassette tape filled with soothing harp music. She said it would help us focus and relax as she started us on our journey.

"Close your eyes and picture yourself in a beautiful garden. All around you are exquisite flowers of uniquely contrasting sizes, shapes, and colors. Your favorite ones can be seen everywhere, along with many exotic plants and flora with stunning features you may have never seen before. They are gently swaying back and forth in the warm breeze. You can touch and feel their softness as you smell their lovely aromas. You see honey bees gathering nectar all around you as well as an assortment of beautifully colored butterflies and dragonflies dancing in harmony with each other." Angela paused so we could savor the beauty of the garden.

I immediately noticed the wonderfully scented air; it smelled so fresh and clean. Each of the flowers, evergreens, and grasses carried its own unique fragrance, yet they blended in a perfect potpourri with one another. The delicate, dark markings and vibrant orange colors of three monarch butterflies captured my imagination as they danced above some vividly purple and highlighter-yellow daffodils with sunny, pastel-orange centers. Angela spoke again.

"In front of you is a well-groomed path of white, marble stones leading to a beautiful archway on the other side of the garden. Go through the archway, and I will rejoin you when you return."

Looking down the pathway, I could not believe my eyes. There, not more than twenty feet in front of me, I saw the same archway as before! I hurried down the path until I stood about five feet from the front of it. A quick examination left no doubt that this arch and the one I experienced previously *had* to be one and the same. However, this time the garden seemed to go all the way around it. If it did, I wondered, what happened to the curious, round room with its colossal, white walls, multicolored, triangular windows, and that flawlessly sculpted, angelic fountain? Reasoning out a logical answer, I concluded that perhaps the archway represented some sort of doorway, and the façade of a garden merely disguised the other side of it.

Yes, of course, I thought. *This lovely garden* looks *like it goes all the way around the archway, but I'll bet when I pass through it, instead of continuing into the garden, I will be stepping once again into that remarkable chamber I visited before.*

Detailed memories of the spotlessly white, round room animated my mind with visions of the angelic, crystal fountain, the blue-highlighted, ancient fruit tree, and the mysterious and complex adornments of the arch. My inflated anticipation quickly transformed into the hope I might not only re-encounter my previous, almost psychedelic experiences but perhaps find some thrilling new ones as well.

I promptly moved to the base of the arch, stopping just long enough to mentally applaud the convincingly realistic view of the white stone path and garden on the other side. Of course, knowing I was clever enough not to be fooled by this obvious mirage, I took a reassuring breath, smiled, sort of closed my eyes, and confidently burst through the magical doorway like a hero entering the stage. Almost immediately, if not sooner, I found my brain slamming the brakes on my enthusiasm as I realized that … nothing happened!

I stood there, patiently waiting and hoping, shifting my eyes and head from left to right just in case there could have been a slight delay or something, then …

"Bummer." I sighed with the breath I had unconsciously been holding. "That's not what I was hoping for."

As I caught up with my fractured certainty, I turned around and once again faced the archway, this time from the identical other side of it. With much lowered expectations, an adrenalin-deflating pause, and a few more steps, I positioned myself directly underneath the center of the arch, looking up at its multicolored crystals. Once again confidently smiling, I was sure Angela *had* guided me to at least a replica of the very same archway, but the rest of "the magic" seemed to be gone.

One of the most fascinating things Angela taught us about allowing our minds to delve into the amazing heightened state of meditation is that, whether we recognized or could understand it at the time or not, there would always be an important thought, message, or learning experience that came out of it.

"Perhaps during this meditation, I am only meant to study the architecture of the arch itself in much more detail," I said to myself in a slightly disappointed tone.

Without taking my eyes off the crystal pyramids, I adjusted my stance slightly to place myself exactly beneath the center of the arch, clearly remembering my previous extraordinary moment of deep inner peace and revelation, not to mention mind-blowing bliss.

As soon as I placed myself beneath the center of the ancient-looking symbols, an emotional commotion of child-like pleasure took hold of me. The entire archway abruptly flooded with an intense white, whirling light. Closing my eyes, I first experienced a feeling of stillness. Then euphoria swept throughout every part of my body. My mind released me from all worries or concerns, and I began floating upward through the warmth of the sensation. I felt no sense of speed but an acute sensation of slowly floating and turning in a clockwise direction.

"Jeremiah," called a familiar voice, almost in a whisper. I heard him clearly and smiled, but at first, I chose not to answer him or open my eyes.

He called again.

"Jeremiah."

"Metatron," I blurted out with excitement as I opened my eyes wide to find my angelic friend standing close in front of me. This time he already appeared in a wingless, almost human form, except for his faint, but still really cool, glowing aura. As before, he radiated an expression of unmistakable love. To my delight, I turned my head to the right and left to see his two companion angels at my sides. They, unlike Metatron, however, chose to display their powerful wings.

41

"Peace be with you," Metatron said. "Your commission is before you."

I only briefly considered asking him what he meant by his unusual statement but ended up saying nothing, because all my other senses were being unexplainably but quite wonderfully stimulated, and at that point I was content with just going along for the ride no matter where they were taking me.

As the four of us ascended into the warmth and security of the now less intense light, other folded-winged angels joined us from all directions. The further up we went, the larger the mass of angels grew. By the time we stopped ascending, I'm sure we left the Earth and all the galaxies and star systems well behind us because, when I looked out, instead of stars, I saw only angels—countless numbers of them, all in white, resembling an endless field of cotton.

Looking back at my angelic friends, I found myself standing in a clearing about the size of a basketball court. On the other side of the clearing stood a gigantic mountain unlike any I have ever seen. The very clean and sculptured appearance took on almost a conceptual Shangri-La look. An elegant, bluish-white glow highlighted its polished, smooth surface, and no rough or uneven edges could be seen anywhere. In fact, after scanning the entire mountain, I realized it consisted of an immeasurable number of individual, smooth rocks, all about the size of a loaf of homemade bread, each one fitting exactly in its place, like a perfect, three-dimensional puzzle.

An astonishing fact at once became clear to me: *every* rock carried an illumination from within that, in unison, created the mountain's soft, bluish-white glow. Between where we stood in the clearing and the base of the mountain, a small, solid, waist-high altar came into view. It appeared to be made of highly polished, white and rose-colored marble, which brilliantly reflected the top of the mountain like a mirror. One of the mountain's illuminated rocks rested in the center of the altar. It softly glowed, like an airy wisp of faint blue smoke.

Metatron stepped forward and moved his head in a beckoning gesture, indicating that his two companions and I should follow. As we approached the altar, four figures emerged from a suddenly present, ethereal, white mist at the base of the mountain. They too headed toward the altar, stopping a short distance in front of us. I looked closely at the four who joined us and immediately recognized three of them.

Jesus, in the middle of the group, led an all-white stallion, at least sixteen hands high, with a beautiful, shiny coat and dramatic presence. He stood quietly behind him. On his left towered the Archangel Michael in his radiant, golden armor, and Moses, staff and all, was positioned about a half step back and to the right of Jesus. On the right of Moses stood another man unfamiliar to me; he carried the classical Hollywood appearance of a biblical-era, average-looking guy. His tunic-style clothing, beige in color, hugged his waist with a corded, black leather sash that complemented his dark, high, leather, strapped sandals. His thick, black hair matched his very heavy beard and eyebrows, and his face mapped the lines of deep experiences. However, his eyes gleamed with an alert, youthful look like those of a child.

At first, no one spoke, so, in the course of the silence, I almost forgot about the millions of other angels that surrounded us. Looking all around me, however, I found they were still there, patiently watching, waiting, without making a sound. The sight of all these heavenly beings stirred emotions in me of an elemental nature as I perceived in their faces expressions of hope and anticipation, like those of my children on Christmas morning. With no idea of the reason they brought me here, I knew no matter what happened, it unquestionably would be something fantastic I would never forget.

The Archangel Michael stepped over to the altar and picked up the rock. Without saying a word, he handed it to Jesus and bowed as a sign of respect. He then stepped back slightly to the rear of the others. Jesus, Moses, and the other man moved closer to us until we stood only a few feet apart from each other. I gazed upon their faces and felt overwhelmed with such a tremendous feeling of love that tears filled my eyes. Jesus passed the rock to Moses and looked at me with a warm smile. Then, as Moses stepped in front of me, he reached out and silently handed me the rock. With a reverent nod, he took a step back in line with the others.

I glanced down at the rock in my hands, realizing it felt completely weightless. The pulsating of the gentle glow within and the delicacy of it spiked my curiosity and sent my mind scrambling for answers. I could feel my heart pounding faster in anticipation. As my heart rate and breathing increased, so did the rock's tempo and intensity. The whole idea of holding this rock that pulsated in perfect time with the rhythm of my own heart seemed a bit scary and yet mysteriously exciting at the same time. I could feel the adrenalin rushing through my body. Simultaneously, the weightless rock began to glow brighter than before, and as it did so, I realized that my perception of the rock began to change.

When the intensity of the glow diminished, the rock-like appearance softened, and the original shape of the stone in my hands revealed itself now as a perfectly round, crystal orb. Its paper-thin shell contained a blue, smoke-like mist that hid its true nature and gave it the illusion of being solid. While I examined it, the mist inside began to clear, revealing a wondrous surprise.

Inside the crystal shell, a distinct, three-dimensional image appeared, its masterful intricacy beyond expression. Like sitting in a balcony, viewing a performance below, the sights and sounds and even smells I began experiencing felt as real as my own presence. I scanned my memory trying to understand why the scene within the crystal and the feelings that accompanied it seemed so familiar, but my mind preoccupied itself with the present, not the past.

Within the globe, I saw a young man at the bedside of another man probably three times his age. The bedroom portrayed a very stately appearance. The young man knelt on one knee, holding something in front of the man in the bed. As the scene became clear, so did the words of the young man. I brought the crystalline rock close to my eyes in a determined effort to see what both men found so intriguing. What I saw astonished me. Their eyes focused on a crystal orb identical to the one in my hands. I strained to see what images their crystal held when, in that instant, I became more than just an observer. The young man's crystal became the same crystal I clutched in my hands. I found myself seeing through his eyes, hearing through his ears, and speaking through his mouth.

The older man spoke. "Make known to me that which was placed in my dreams while I was asleep."

"You, oh, King, have been favored by the God of heaven. The God who knows all mysteries has filled your dreams with what will take place in the future," I said. Then, leaning forward, I held the orb even closer for the king to see, and I spoke again.

"Witness before you the day when all kingdoms will pass except the one which will endure forever." We both focused on the images in the orb. Inside it, I saw a great statue, not one constructed by mortals, but by God.

"Behold, oh, King, the interpretation of your dream." The king listened intently as he examined the scene unfolding before him.

"The statue represents the passing of all the kingdoms throughout all the lands. See how the feet are constructed. First, you see potter's clay built on a solid base of white sand and seashells. The clay is then skillfully mixed with iron. Great historians speak of the iron legs on which these ancient kingdoms first stood. As time passed, people worked together to form alliances with each other and with their own gods so they could grow in strength and numbers. They searched for answers to life's questions and the nature of their own existence. The kingdoms grew stronger and spread throughout the Earth. You can witness this, oh, King, in the powerful workmanship you see in the upper thighs and belly of brass. Through the ages, the knowledge and wisdom of time that passed from mother to child, from king to king, and from father to son can be seen here in the master craftsmanship of the breast and arms of shining silver."

The king looked up at me with widened eyes and silently beckoned me to go on.

"The head of the statue is of the finest gold," I exclaimed. "It represents all that humankind chose to understand of good and evil. In spite of the wisdom and warnings from soothsayers, philosophers, and prophets, however, the head of solid gold has been cast from envy and greed. Humanity pursued great wealth rather than great compassion and understanding. This head can see and hear everything that takes place within its domain but lacks the caring to separate the good from the bad. It has the power and might to control all life but lacks the willingness to understand life. This golden head of the statue represents the very pinnacle of human desires but lacks the compassion or concern for what drives those desires. Therefore, this kingdom is greater than all that came before it, and its wealth is beyond measure, but it carries a darkened heart and an empty soul."

"Its wealth is beyond measure," the king blurted out with a look in his eyes that revealed his desire for ultimate wealth and power. "I will surely be the ruler of this kingdom. Tell me more," he demanded with excitement.

"Do you see, oh, King, that as we looked upon the great and powerful statue of all the empires, a mountain has been steadily growing behind it?"

The king looked intently into the orb.

"This mountain represents the will of the God of righteousness."

As the mountain within the orb continued to grow like an awakened volcano, a boulder left its peak and struck the statue at its foundation, crumbling it to the ground. A great battle beneath darkened skies filled the world with cries of doom and hopelessness. A cold death prevailed over all the Earth; it gripped my soul. I felt totally helpless and lost. The despair overwhelmed me.

Suddenly, my mind cleared, and an all-consuming peace and cleansing warmth filled my entire body. Looking up, I realized I was once again standing in front of Moses holding the orb. He had gently put his hands on mine. I looked thankfully into his compassionate eyes. He lifted his hands and looked back down at the orb. I also shifted my attention to the crystal globe.

In that instant, I found myself alone in a small, dimly lit room. The walls appeared damp and filthy, as did the floor, and a pungent smell filled the air. A graveled, eerie growl focused my every fiber on the darkened corner opposite me. I tried to step back but found nowhere to go. Three malnourished, dirty, tormented beasts stalked toward me. I fell to my knees and began to pray, my eyes shut tightly. My mind screamed while I waited for the inevitable, but … nothing happened. My heart pounded through my chest, and I heard only my own labored breathing. I became lightheaded with the fear of what lurked in front of me, but I *had* to know. I opened my eyes.

My mind froze in disbelief. The lions stopped only a few feet from my trembling body and lay down on their bellies, their mouths closed in silence. Still shaking, I slowly stood up and backed myself against the cold, dirt wall, all the while staring into their eyes with raw uncertainty. The lions stared back but with eyes that did not look like the eyes of wild beasts. The room suddenly filled with a brilliant light, and a powerful-looking angel appeared before me. His wings, partially extended, highlighted his prominent figure, illuminated by a shadowy, sky-blue aura.

"Peace be with you," he said. "No harm shall befall you this night. All creatures are sacred and one-in-being with their creator."

As he said this, a core level of understanding filled me with the realization that all creatures of the Earth play an important part in some sort of divine master plan.

The lions seemed to go into a deep sleep, and from each of them there arose a small, beautiful, multi-winged angel. In a flash, all three disappeared into the light. I looked back at the glowing blue angel, but he too had vanished. As the bright light faded, again darkening the now empty room, I leaned my head back against the damp wall, looked up, and tearfully smiled.

A sudden feeling of total exhaustion came over me. Being too tired to stand, I slid down the wall to the ground, closed my eyes, and fell into a deep sleep. A moment later, I opened my eyes, feeling alert yet very relaxed, as if awakening from a much-needed rest. Moses had placed his hands on my shoulders. I looked up from the orb and into his caring eyes as he reached down and removed the sphere from my grasp. Still peering into my eyes, he said, "Daniel."

CHAPTER 5

THE CAVE

WITH MY HANDS STILL EXTENDED in front of me, Moses stepped back in line with the others and handed the crystal to the bearded man standing alongside Jesus. Accepting it, the man stepped forward and returned it to me once again, placing it carefully in my palms.

"Peace be with you. I am Elijah."

As he looked down at the gift he just returned to me, I too shifted my gaze once again to the crystal sphere. In it, I saw an elderly, disheveled-looking man crouched over a makeshift table. The single smooth stone opening to his right suggested he must have been inside a cave. Strewn before him lay writings on heavy-looking, irregular-shaped, brownish paper or some form of smooth bark in a language unknown to me, yet both the writings and the setting I found myself in filled me with a feeling of familiarity that beckoned memories barely out of reach.

The man sat motionless, with his elbows and forearms resting on the table but still mostly upright, with his head bowed and his chin resting almost on his chest. So, through the dim light of burning oil, I concluded that he was probably asleep, praying, or maybe even in a deep meditation. The flicker of a reflected flame darted off the shiny object clutched in his left hand. I examined it closer and found it to be a crystal orb like the one in my hands.

I wonder what he sees, I thought. In that instant, in a transformation that happened so quickly that I missed it, I found myself now physically in the cave standing about five feet behind the man at the table. Having experienced, only moments earlier, a very realistic and terrifying encounter with hungry lions, I temporarily froze while my mind tried to catch up with my new, unexplainable reality. Through a concerted effort of my mind successfully convincing me that this might only be a *very* realistic dream and a persistent, little voice in my head saying, "It's okay and safe to remember," my curiosity surpassed my fear, and I refocused my skeptical attention on the man at the table.

I moved slowly across the uneven stone floor so as not to wake him. Then, stepping close enough to lean over his shoulder, I looked directly into *his* crystal orb. In it, I saw only the hand of someone writing on the same crude form of paper. However, I could only see about half of the orb because the man's fingers covered the rest. My curiosity beckoned me to see if the writings in his orb matched those scattered on the table.

In the hopes of not being discovered, I stole a quick glance, leaning in just close enough to make sure his eyes were closed. This gave me the extra courage I needed to gently turn his hand enough to look into his orb. What I saw sent a chill through me. With the illumination of only the burning oil flickering in the background, I saw an eerie, distorted, mirror image of my reflection looking back at me as if I had been trapped inside the orb looking for a way out!

Locked in a stare with myself, I couldn't say for sure which side of the crystal reflected reality, but that no longer mattered, as the image that mimicked me grew less and less clear. A fog or mist now unexplainably filled the orb. With my focus keenly fixed on my own disappearing image, I hadn't realized my surroundings were filling up with the same foggy mist until I looked up.

Almost instantly, my vision blurred to nothing, and everything disappeared into white. Taken by surprise, I felt disoriented for a moment and a bit anxious but still in control.

Have I been sent into the now familiar white light? I wondered, searching in every direction, only to find my outlook the same.

"No, this time, it is more than only the light," I said to myself, perplexed. "It has some sort of cloudy substance to it."

The film-like appearance seemed to be very thin, almost transparent, but just dense enough to hide whatever was on the other side of it. Desiring to touch it but not knowing what *it* was, I cautiously extended my hand. It *had* to be only inches in front of me, yet it seemed to be unreachable, like a heavy haze. Nonetheless, its presence filled my entire view.

Suddenly, like a blast from a trumpet, a voice resounded through the room, breaking the silence.

"*Peace be with you,*" the voice said, with the echoing effect of a loud speaker in an empty amphitheater. My lack of any visual reference made it difficult to tell where the voice originated. Nevertheless, I instinctively turned around, twice, which didn't help.

"*I am one who has known you since before your own birth and who stands in review when all shall have come to pass,*" the voice said.

In my mind, I perceived the words to be coming from a man, yet they echoed, in perfect harmony, suggesting that of both a man and a woman, together as one.

"Blessed be the prophet in fulfillment of his commission. His eyes shall be opened so others might see, his testimony known to all the peoples of Earth, even to the end of the age."

I listened, motionless and speechless.

"Write in a book the revelations you witness before you and ponder not the realms in which they dwell. They will be proclaimed in all seven temples yet remain as one before the throne. The power of love and discernment shall guide your hand."

As these words resounded through me, the mist-like veil gathered itself into a fist-size, brilliant ball of silvery light. I instinctively looked straight at it, but it immediately flickered out like a dying Fourth of July sparkler. Then, after only a second or less of total darkness, it exploded back to life in the form of seven swirling spheres of multi-colored light, each spectacularly transforming into a beautiful angel, suspended gracefully before me. With long, flowing, wavy, silvery hair and the purest of complexions, they appeared vividly real yet almost transparent, like spirits.

The seven angels gracefully aligned themselves in a single line facing me. A soft, colorful aura enveloped each one of them, extending several inches beyond the outline of their bodies, and each wore a body-length breastplate sparkling with the brilliance of polished gold. As one angel stood behind the other as if on bleachers, a perfectly proportional step-up in height allowed me to only see the head and shoulders of all but the front angel. This, bleacher effect, along with the radiance of their colorful auras, created the semblance of a golden candelabrum holding seven lighted candles. With all seven aligned, the blending of their auras and brilliance of their breastplates joined to form the expression of a spiritual being whose manifestation mirrored the Son of Man. The aligning of the seven shielded him in a harmonious, golden girdle of heavenly light. I shut my eyes tightly and knelt before him.

As he materialized from an apparitional state into "real life," he moved toward me. Though unfamiliar to me in a physical sense, the spiritual recognition was immediate and complete. With the contrast of his curly, shoulder-length, black hair and golden, olive complexion, his gown exemplified that of the purest white, and wherever he stood, a beam of golden light flowed up through his feet like golden sandals. At the same time, a torrent of pure-white light streamed down upon him in such a way that his whole head gleamed like newly fallen snow.

He spoke to me in a voice of great tranquility that filled the entire room like the echo of a deep well, and in his hand, he held a book wrapped and bound tightly with a linen cloth cover, held closed by only one unbroken blood-red seal in its center and three broken ones on either side of it.

"Do not be troubled, my brother," he said. "Am I not known to you? Fear can mislead only those who know me not. Walk in the way of faith and the light of truth as I have shown you, and the righteousness of absolute love will always prevail."

He helped me stand up straight and affirmed, "Heed the spiritual voice that whispers your name, for all shall be sealed in a fate of their own choosing when the doorway of death releases them to stand before their creator in their own nakedness."

His words resounded through me, bringing strength to my soul and conviction to my spirit. I opened my eyes wide with wonder as he lifted the veil of humanity and allowed my spirit to behold all the wonders of time. Like a book written in a language, yet to be learned, the end of the age revealed itself to me in a way indescribable with words. An understanding of the meaning of life and death and life again reassured my soul that the eternal verdict, foretold and recorded, through the finality of its revelation, awaits us all.

A feeling of completeness raced through my soul. I felt serene as my vision faded, and my eyes felt comfort in their un-commanded closing. When I opened my eyes, my spirit was at peace. I found myself once again at the foot of the mountain, face to face with Elijah. His hands tenderly cupped mine. As Elijah looked deep into my eyes, and I into his, he repositioned his hands and lovingly reclaimed the crystal orb. He addressed, me speaking only one word: "John."

CHAPTER 6

THE PREACHER

HANDING THE ORB TO JESUS, Elijah stepped back, allowing Jesus to take a stance directly in front of me. Radiating compassion, he smiled at me, gently nodding. Then, in a single motion, he closed his eyes and slightly bowed his head. He placed the orb in my hands and stepped back. Humbled beyond expression, I froze motionless, in awe. I lowered my eyes and stared at the orb for what seemed like an eternity and wondered what this all meant, and more importantly, why they chose me. Tears filled my eyes as I looked back up at Jesus. He reassured me with his loving countenance.

Following his lead, I again shifted my attention to the crystalline vessel resting in my palms. At first, the orb appeared to be cloudy with only one point of light occasionally appearing and disappearing. It reminded me of a cloudy night when the moon would pop out briefly, only to vanish again behind a quickly moving cloud. Then the glow within the sphere began to grow brighter. An illuminated flow of energy in its center began spiraling in a counterclockwise direction, like a small tornado. The effect rejuvenated my curiosity in anticipation of what would happen next.

The pulsating, churning torrent of light energy grew faster and faster, brighter and brighter until ... a cathedral!

I thought I saw a cathedral flash by in the eye of the orb's storm. I intently watched, hoping to catch a glimpse of it again. Bringing the orb closer, I felt the power and velocity of the whirling energy. I looked deeper and deeper into it until the storm literally surrounded me. My senses all told me that I must be falling or flying out of control and spinning in every direction, yet, for some reason, my mind perceived it only as an illusion. The sensation left me feeling anxious and with a heightened adrenaline rush but without the feeling of being dizzy or sick.

"Perhaps *I'm* stationary, and everything around me is moving," I rationalized to myself. I couldn't be sure. All I know is that I no longer concerned myself with the cathedral because my immediate focus shifted all my thoughts to where the storm would take me. Moving deeper into the churning eye, an overwhelming feeling of anxious uncertainty started to fill my soul. Then, in an instant, the spinning ceased, and I found myself standing in a large stone hallway. All was still.

I sensed the presence of someone else, so I quickly turned around and found myself face to face with an enormous, wingless angel. I immediately recognized him, by his size and beautiful aura, as my new friend Metatron. He smiled.

"Peace be with you," I said, before he had a chance to speak.

"May love guide you to all that is precious within," he responded with a big grin.

"Um, thank you," I mumbled just to say something.

We both just smiled at each other for an unnaturally long time, until I ended the standoff by looking around at the marvelous architecture, stained-glass windows, and frescoes that covered the walls and ceiling.

"Are we inside the cathedral I saw in the orb?" I inquired of my angel guide.

He only smiled. Turning, he gestured for me to follow him.

"Is this a great holy place?"

Metatron stopped and faced me.

"This place symbolizes the human side of the dual natures you possess. However, it is not the form or origin of this place that is significant. Today, many of the institutions that claim to care for the spiritual well-being of their followers no longer remember their true purpose. Teaching the wisdom of their creator has become secondary to maintaining the institution itself. Generations have nurtured their personal demands for self-fulfillment without remembering their need for spiritual growth. Empty rituals or indifference long ago replaced the fundamental search for divine truth. Without a spiritual path to follow, this will ultimately leave those who long for answers finding only an indecisive pathway of despair.

"This is why you are here!" Metatron concluded with a confident look and upbeat tone as he turned back toward the long stone hallway.

"That is why I am here?" I mumbled to myself as I tried to figure out what Metatron had just explained to me. Unfortunately, the meaning of his words escaped me, but the conviction in his voice touched my adventurous side. I, like Metatron, turned back in the direction we originally started walking, only to find myself now standing directly in front of two very large, dark, deeply carved wooden doors. Metatron looked over his right shoulder at me and then stepped forward. As he did this, the doors opened, and his two companion angels appeared on either side of us.

Together, the four of us entered what seemed to be the main sanctuary of the church through doors located off to the left side, near the front. With a service already in progress, we directed our interest to the one-step-high platform in front of the assembly where a religious leader stood in front of a large congregation.

This distinguished-looking preacher with an average build and very pale complexion stood silently in front of his congregation, scanning the room as if he was searching for something or someone. His medium-long but well-groomed, silvery-white hair and youthful face suggested to me that his age probably fell somewhere between thirty and fifty.

He wore a well-fitting black suit adorned with a multi-shaded, bright green, shawl-like vestment and was standing alongside a dark wooden podium with his left forearm resting on its top. Several other men in business suits, some standing a little farther back on either side of him and others in the aisles, apparently acted as his personal attendants and ushers.

At first glance, it appeared to be an almost normal church service, except for a couple of very peculiar things. First, I noticed all of the people swaying back and forth, chanting in a low tone. They could have been staring at the preacher, but I couldn't say for sure; they did not seem to be actually looking at *anything*. In fact, everyone's face seemed to have more of a blank look on it as if they were totally lost in their own thoughts or in some sort of trance. I was also surprised by the considerable variety in the styles of clothing and adornments worn throughout the room. There seemed to be people there from all over the world, representing probably many different religions and cultures. So of course I had to wonder why they were all together at this particular service.

Metatron turned toward me and peered deeply into my eyes.

"Pay close attention and remember everything you witness here today," he sternly commanded.

Looking toward the pulpit, we then redirected our eyes back on the preacher now addressing the people. He gave us a quick glance, acknowledging that he was aware of our presence, and then he spoke.

"You must teach others what I have taught you. *You* are the lord and master of your own destiny," he loudly proclaimed.

"Only *you* can heal the pains and afflictions of your own body and your own spirit."

He snatched a cordless microphone from the podium and, repositioning himself closer to the congregation, he brought it to his mouth, stating slowly and deliberately, "There is *no* absolute truth." He paused.

"There is *no* right or wrong." He paused again, and I noticed all eyes silently focused keenly on him.

"The only real truth is how *you* feel inside." The preacher paused again, lowering his voice slightly.

"I'll tell you where to find God." He put his left hand with the microphone down to his side and brought his right hand up to his mouth, pressing his index finger against his lips. Then, following a long pause where he looked over the entire congregation, he brought the microphone back up to his lips. Grasping it with both hands, he continued.

"Better yet," he said with his voice much louder now and more demanding, "I'll tell you where you *won't* find God." As he continued, he took on a condescending tone.

"Do you honestly *believe* that God is sitting around in each and every one of your quaint little churches and temples? That he 'joins' you every time you hold a service?" He paused to give people time to think about the question and then continued.

"Are you so foolish and simpleminded that you believe all you need to do is *pray* for something, and it will happen? If that is true, why aren't we all rich and living perfect lives?" He closed his eyes and slowly shook his head. Then continuing in the same tone but almost in a whisper, he opened his eyes and said, "My poor lost sheep, I will show you the *true* way to find God and the road to everlasting happiness in paradise."

The preacher smiled, closed his eyes again, and nodded as he continued.

"I can show you the way because I *know* the way; I've seen paradise with my own eyes and spoke to God face to face." Opening his eyes wide, his voice getting louder and louder, he stated, "I've seen it. I have been to the Promised Land, and it *is* everything you have ever dreamed it could be. But you can only get there if you know how." He paused again briefly and then continued.

"It surely is not by blindly following an old man in Rome, praying while facing a certain direction, or bowing in front of an ancient wall. Nor is paradise attainable by burning incense or kneeling in front of your television or by sending your hard-earned paychecks to some evangelist or charity."

The preacher lowered his voice.

"No, my friends, my brothers and sisters, you have all been very misled. Organized religions have tricked you into doing exactly what *they* want you to do. But you know, don't you? You are not stupid! You can see that they are *only* after your money and the power it brings to them, *not* your salvation. If *any* of those churches really cared about your soul instead of your wallet and their agenda, then why do they ask you to pay, and pay *dearly,* for the right to find God?"

The preacher moved toward the heavy, dark, wooden podium where an old and well-worn-looking Bible rested. On the way, he stopped briefly and asked, "Are you going to *keep* letting them play you for fools and do whatever they ask without holding them accountable for what they are telling you?"

He took a few more steps, passing in front of one of his suited assistants. Then, reaching the podium, he put down the microphone he had been carrying and picked up a smaller portable one that he clipped to his lapel.

Throwing both hands up in the air, he shook his head from side to side while blurting out, "Nobody ever asks for proof!"

Slamming his hand down on the Bible in front of him and continuing with a defiant look on his face, he asked, "Why do you think there are so many different religions?"

He took a strategically longer pause and in a deliberately drawn-out manner asked, "How can you ever know which one is telling you the *truth* if you automatically believe everything they tell you only because *they* say it is so?"

Raising his voice significantly, he continued, "Do you think your *God* wants you to just blindly follow *any* of them, without making them *prove* they are preaching the truth?"

In one quick motion, the preacher picked up the Bible off the podium, forcefully slammed it back down, and demanded, "Or, did God give you the intelligence and ability to *know* what the real truth is by reading it in this book?" Stepping from behind the podium to a stance in front of it and at the same time continuing his diatribe, the preacher asked, "Have any of you *ever* been given proof that *your* religion is true and speaks for God?"

As he said this, the preacher pulled out a pistol from inside his vest and without any hesitation aimed point-blank at the chest of the suited man standing slightly behind him and fired. The man dropped to the floor, his jacket and shirt soaked in blood. The congregation screamed in shock and disbelief. The preacher dropped the pistol, went over, and slowly knelt down next to the wounded man. As he lifted his head off the floor, his mortally wounded assistant looked into the eyes of the man who shot him, and he died. The whole room fell into total silence.

The preacher stood up, his sleeves and hands bloodstained. Without emotion, he coldly stared over the heads of the motionless, silent assembly.

Then softly and deliberately, he asked, "Where is the *proof?*"

Walking back over to the podium, with a hollow look, he snatched up the Bible, and holding it above his head, he angrily shouted, "Did not Jesus himself say that *we,* the *true* disciples, would be able to do greater miracles than he if we *truly* believed?" He paused for several, deep, sighing breaths as he scanned the still silent congregation.

"If this is so," he continued as he indignantly walked back around to the front of the podium, still carrying the Bible in his left hand, "if I am *truly* sent from God ..." He again dramatically paused as he took two quick steps and stopped next to his murdered assistant. "If I have *truly* been sent from *God,*" he repeated, "then according to scriptures, shouldn't I be able to raise poor Stephen here?"

Dropping to his knees next to the motionless man on the floor, the preacher grasped the Bible with both hands, held it up high in an offering gesture, and looking upward, slowly and dramatically shouted, "By the power given to me by *God,*" he paused and thrust the Bible toward the dead man on the floor with his outstretched arms, "I *command* you to rise to your feet, good and faithful servant, for you are not yet finished with God's work here on Earth."

All eyes focused on the blood-covered man lying lifeless on the floor. Nobody moved or made a sound. The preacher again bellowed, "*Heed* the word of God and rise to your feet—*now.*"

The man, Stephen, who we all saw murdered, suddenly sat up and sprang to his feet. He turned toward the preacher with a quite convincing stunned and confused look. It persuaded me this was not a staged event. Then he faced the startled congregation, and pulling off his jacket and tearing open his shirt, he revealed the very bloody and swollen bullet wound to his chest. Stepping down into the middle aisle, holding his shirt open and still looking quite shocked, he walked slowly toward the rear of the church allowing anyone who wished the opportunity to see and touch his clothes and wound.

"*Never* believe without demanding proof," the preacher concluded as he stood back up and faced the congregation.

Still in a state of disbelief, I looked at Metatron. Neither of us said a word. The preacher repositioned himself back behind the podium, still holding the Bible in his hands.

"And what gives you the right to demand proof?" he asked. Again, he raised the holy book up over his head briefly and then brought it back down to chest level.

"*This* does!" he shouted, pushing the Bible out at arm's length.

Then in a quieter voice, the preacher asked, "Have you all forgotten the fact that God's greatest gift to humankind is free will? What good is *this*?" The preacher threw the Bible down on the floor.

"If you don't *use* … your … free … will?" He gestured at the scriptures now lying on the floor in front of him.

"Isn't that what it tells you to do in that book?"

He walked to the edge of the platform and opened his arms in a welcoming manner, stating, "That, my brothers and sisters, is precisely the reason why *God* gave us feelings and intuition. We were given this gift to have the ability to choose for ourselves what *feels* right or wrong."

He brought both of his hands to his chest over his heart and in a deliberate voice continued saying, "Can't you *feel* in your very soul that I am speaking the truth? Haven't I given you *proof* that God has sent me to show you the way to paradise?" While he said this, the preacher nodded his head up and down. As I glanced out over the congregation, I noticed that practically all the people mimicked him by nodding their heads in confirmation.

"Yes, my dear friends, I was chosen and personally directed by God to lead *you,* the chosen people, to the Promised Land."

Then, with a look of genuine sincerity, the preacher asked, "Do you *want* me to fail because *you* are too selfish to think of anyone but yourself? Do you *want* to be left behind, to spend the rest of eternity watching and feeling your flesh burning and melting from your own body in the fires of *hell?*" he asked with a grimacing look on his face.

Then closing his eyes and tipping his head upward, he nodded and, with a big smile, opened his eyes wide and asked, "Or do you want to be with the rest of us living perfect lives of ecstasy in the glorious mansions of heaven?"

The crowd went wild, screaming affirmations. He waited until they calmed down and continued. "It's so simple," he said, still smiling. "All you need to do is surrender your minds and souls to God to prove yourself worthy to be one of the chosen.

"It's so simple," he slowly repeated in a whisper.

Walking to the front of the platform nearest the congregation, the preacher then slowly looked around the room, searching for someone. He stopped when he came to a young woman in a wheelchair near the front. Stepping quickly off the platform, he took a couple of steps into the aisle and bellowed at her like a crazed man, asking, "Do you have enough faith? Can you *prove* to us that you are worthy to join our flock?"

The woman burst into tears and slid out of her chair and onto the floor. Then crawling to him, she grabbed at the preacher's pant legs, saying, "Yes, Master, I will do anything you ask of me." He grabbed her by both arms and jerked her to her feet, shaking her violently.

"Then *walk*. I command it," he shouted.

The poor woman clung to his shirt as he backed away from her and made her follow: first one step, then two, then three. He grabbed her wrists and harshly pulled her hands free from his clothing, leaving her standing on her own.

"Now go stand over there," he said, pointing to the right of the platform. "You have been sitting long enough." The whole congregation went crazy with emotion.

Then, ignoring the "healed" woman, he pointed to a young couple with three children. "And what about you, and you?" he roared as he pointed first to the man and then to his wife.

"Yes, Lord," shouted the woman as she sprang to her feet, pulling her husband and children up with her.

"We do believe. Take my whole family, Lord. Take us with you to the Promised Land."

Another person joined in, and then several others, until everyone in the room stood up, crying and screaming words of praise to the preacher while begging him to take them as one of the chosen ones.

He turned around and headed back to the platform. As he stepped back onto it, he turned his head, and without stopping, he looked directly at us with a devious smirk.

I looked into his eyes and found myself captivated by them. I'd never seen eyes like that before. They gleamed with the fury of their deep, penetrating, reddish-purple color, and I could see no discernible pupils. His entrancing glare felt almost hypnotic, even from across the room. He only stared straight into my eyes long enough to make a direct contact, but it was enough to make me feel vulnerable and within his control. As he reached the podium, he picked up the Bible from the floor and readdressed the congregation.

Gripping the holy scriptures firmly with both hands, he held the book silently above his head with his eyes tightly shut and waited until, once again, the church fell deathly silent. Then, dramatically bringing the Bible back down to chest level, he slowly opened his eyes. Speaking barely above a whisper, and with a cry in his voice, the preacher promised, "No matter what sacrifices I am asked to make, I will make them for you."

He stopped talking abruptly as he shut his eyes again ... and waited. The tomb-like silence was chilling. When he re-opened his eyes, they were filled with tears, and his voice trembled as he finished the sentence. "Because that is what God sent me here to do."

Again, he paused. I looked out across the congregation, and I saw most of the people now weeping aloud.

The preacher regained his composure and the volume in his voice. Firmly and very deliberately, he stated, "*God* has sent *me* to stand for the *truth* and the *light*. I asked God to show me the way to paradise, and he told me, *I … am … the … way.*"

The preacher stepped to the side of the podium, glancing over at us with a sadistic grin, and his hideous eyes opened wide. Then refocusing on the people assembled there, he asked, "Who will join me?"

In a gathering motion with both arms, he beckoned the people to come to him while asking in a quiet, resolute tone, "Who is ready to surrender your soul to the Lord?"

Masses of people flocked to the front, knocking over chairs and anyone who got in their way, including the woman who the preacher "healed." Throwing themselves on the floor at the preacher's feet and hoping to touch any part of him, they cried out words of praise and worship, pledging their lives to him.

Metatron looked at me with saddened eyes.

"Not only the people, but even their leaders, like lost sheep, search desperately for answers, any answers," he said slowly, looking over the congregation. Then looking back at me, he stated, "They believe in him because their souls are empty and yearning to be filled. They long for answers and have forgotten where to find them. Their spirits hunger for truth, yet when they see it and hear it, they can no longer distinguish it from the lies. He tells them what they want to hear, so they let *him* fill those voids."

Metatron sighed, and with great concern he concluded, "People search throughout their lives for the fulfillment of their most fundamental of human and spiritual needs. However, they keep looking outside themselves to others, to the society they have created. They look for answers from someone else who is looking for answers, and the cycle repeats itself until the questions themselves are accepted as the answers."

Metatron and I turned and headed toward the doorway with the other two angels following close behind. As we passed through the doors, they closed behind us, and his two companion angels disappeared, presumably staying inside.

We headed down the great marble-stoned hall toward another set of double doors at the far end. As we walked, I continued seeing the face of the preacher in my mind. I thought deeply about what we just witnessed.

"Did you see his eyes?" I asked Metatron as I stopped to face him.

"How did he make you feel?" Metatron asked back, acknowledging my question.

"His actions scared me, but I felt drawn to listen to him. His words seemed confusing but easy to accept, creating questions in my mind that left me feeling bewildered and unsure of my own beliefs."

"Yes, Jeremiah," Metatron said, affirming my thoughts. He put his hands on my shoulders like a father guiding his son.

"He is Abaddon, son of perdition and the master of deception," he declared in a stern, focused voice.

"He thrives on the emptiness of a temporal existence without hope, all the while knowing that the dual nature of humanity cries out for inner peace and divine guidance. Too many people have turned away from divine strength and spiritual nourishment. They no longer acknowledge the inner voice they listened to as children, the voice that encouraged them along the right path. If people would only open their hearts and their spiritual eyes, they would see that the light of truth is still there and will always show them the way. Instead, they keep their hearts and their eyes closed and cry out, looking somewhere outside of themselves for direction." He paused, waiting to make sure I understood the urgency of his words, and then he continued.

"They cry out for love, they cry out for understanding, they cry out for meaning, and they search from every nation, every people, and every belief. They search for answers, Jeremiah, answers that will quench the need for truth, answers that will make them feel whole again. The sad reality is they do not have to go anywhere or do anything special to find them. All people everywhere are capable of unconditional love, and that is where you will find the true secret to life. It is already within and around us all, yet most people have hardened their hearts so they no longer recognize it."

With the deepest conviction, Metatron stated, "Embracing this gift of love is but a simple prayer away and as reachable as a thought."

We took a few more steps when Metatron stopped again and stated, "The one we saw as the preacher knows that this is his last but strongest hour. The time is at hand. It is, therefore, the most vulnerable time for all of humanity. We are on the very threshold of an all-out spiritual war. You must be vigilant in your mission and steadfast in your dedication."

What does he mean I must be vigilant in my mission and steadfast in my dedication? What mission? What dedication? I thought quietly to myself.

Once again, I found myself having a hard time comprehending the full meaning of his words, but the urgency in his voice left me more determined than ever to search for an understanding.

As Metatron turned back toward the direction we were walking, I also turned and found that we were now standing directly in front a new set of large wooden doors. His two companion angels had reappeared and stepped forward, one on each side, to open the huge beautifully carved, gold trimmed, white oak entrance.

CHAPTER 7

HALL OF ANGELS

METATRON AND I STEPPED THROUGH the doorway. I looked over my shoulder at Metatron's two companion angels. They displayed welcoming, polite smiles as they slowly closed the huge doors behind us and remained outside. Turning back to the front, my entire state of mind immediately shifted away from the preacher and focused on the splendor of the place we were now standing.

The domed, perfectly round room was as big as an arena and exemplified beauty beyond expression. The walls and ceiling adorned themselves with enormous, curved stained-glass windows depicting three-dimensional scenes of people, places, and dreams from cultures throughout their worlds and throughout history. From landscapes to seascapes in multilayered crystalline frescos, from King Solomon's First Temple to the Earth's isotonic lines and magnetic fields, to signs of the zodiac and celestial maps of the universe, incredible glass murals portrayed everything from ancient architecture and symbols to futuristic insights.

A highly polished, white marble floor gave the whole room a mirrored, elegant luster. Except for the plush, five-foot-wide, royal-blue carpet, edged with a golden-threaded crisscross pattern, the room appeared to be empty. The stylish carpeting led us from the doors we had just entered down seven shallow, extended stairs that looked like giant, overlapping rings, guiding us toward the room's center.

I followed Metatron down the carpeted path, toward the circular core of the room. There, under a brightly illuminated, gold-enhanced, glass-domed ceiling, we found ourselves now standing at the bottom of a four-tiered, perfectly round platform. Because the entire platform and stairs adorned themselves in the same regal blue carpet, a marvelous optical illusion rendered them completely unnoticeable until we stood directly in front of them. We climbed the first three tiered steps to the top, with Metatron leading the way.

Centered on the platform where we now stood, about twenty feet in front of us, I unexpectedly discovered three more tiered steps made of a sparkling clean, crystal-clear glass. In the center of the top, round, glass platform, which measured about fifteen feet in diameter, stood an effortlessly beautiful, clear, crystal pedestal. In spite of its breathtaking elegance and delicate look of vulnerability, the pedestal projected a clear and unwavering impression of impervious strength.

Spotlighting it in total vividness from the glass dome above, a brilliant beam of golden light, without warning, abruptly dropped onto the pedestal. I looked up to see where the light was coming from, but the intensity reminded me of looking directly at the sun, much too bright for my eyes.

When I looked back down at the pedestal, it now displayed a very large, pure white, illuminated book. From where we stood, this surreal-looking text appeared to have at least three times the dimensions of a regular, full-size, hardcover book in length and width, and measured a good twelve to fifteen inches thick. It reminded me of one of those giant wedding albums, only considerably thicker and without the frilly things.

The beam of light continued to fall like an extremely fine, dry mist onto the book. However, to my astonishment, it did not stop there. It continued, in a cascade of pure energy, pouring over the book like an airbrushed waterfall. It drifted past us, down both sets of stairs and out across the floor in every direction, filling the entire room with a dazzling display of colorless radiance. Smiling, I looked back at Metatron, who smiled back at me, and then back out across the room only to discover that the curious light filling it carried a flickering effect to it.

In that silent instant, the entire room had filled up with thousands and thousands of beautiful, kneeling angels, each holding a single white candle that glowed brighter than any I had ever seen.

I guess they somehow materialized out of the radiant light, I thought to myself in an astonishing way. I could not possibly imagine what sort of miraculous wonders I would have the privilege of experiencing in this magical place. The whole room emanated a rejuvenating energy that was so much more than just a display of awesome beauty. Between the light from the candles and the beam of light flowing over the book, the entire room glowed with an inspiring feeling of hope that both physically and spiritually reawakened a childlike peacefulness within my soul.

Looking back toward the crystal pedestal, I found myself facing the Archangel Michael. Towering well above everything else, he majestically stood guard in front of the book, temporarily shielding it from our view. He looked at us, smiling, and raised his extremely large, deep red and silver, emerald-jeweled, golden-glowing sword in a saluting gesture. Then, returning his sword to his left side, it vanished into his robe. He motioned for us to join him.

Barely in control of my excitement, I gave Metatron a confirming glance to get his approval and stepped ahead of him toward Michael. I promptly climbed the three remaining steps that led to the crystal pedestal and stopped when I reached the top platform. Michael had stepped toward us and now stood only a couple of feet in front of me.

"Peace be with you," Michael said in a slow, relaxing tone.

I smiled at him, overjoyed by the privilege of joining him in this storybook place and said, "Thank you."

Smiling back, he stated, "Your return is celebrated throughout the realms."

"This place is incredible," I replied.

Michael stepped forward and tenderly embraced me with his arm around my shoulders. He then guided me to within three feet of the front of the pedestal where the illuminated book rested.

"This chamber has been called the Hall of Angels. We come here to meditate and to wait," Michael said earnestly.

Wait for what? I thought.

Michael leaned closer and whispered, "We wait for you."

I looked directly into his big, sapphire-blue eyes as he leaned back upright smiling. When I looked back at Metatron, now positioned a couple of steps behind me, and out over the thousands of silent, kneeling angels, I felt like I needed to say something. But since both Metatron and Michael displayed very big smiles, I hoped that meant Michael had said it as a joke. My level of heightened embarrassment remained, in spite of that possibility.

Metatron took a step closer and stopped, greeting Michael with a smiling nod of respect. Michael returned the gesture as he stepped back and firmly centered himself directly behind the book. Metatron also repositioned himself closer to me on my right side.

Michael looked intently at me and stated in a serious tone, "Without guidance, all the flock will perish."

Reflecting back on the mixed emotions I felt with the preacher, the potential impact of Michael's words filled me with a deep understanding and mutual concern for the sincerity of his statement.

I examined both of these gentle, illuminated giants and saw in their faces such an unfaltering portrayal of confidence and hope that it supercharged my resolve to undertake whatever they asked me to do.

Looking down at the museum-quality, crystal pedestal and oversized book, I realized that the stream of light pouring over the pedestal had stopped, allowing us to witness a new phenomenon.

The large, white book I previously assumed to be resting on the crystal pedestal instead remained suspended about an inch from the surface. It seemed to be surrounded by a cushion of almost invisible blue energy that completely shielded it, like a flat bubble. This energy layer, which looked like a clean, blue flame, created an aura around not only the book, but in a paper-thin version, over the crystal pedestal, as well. I viewed it as some sort of force field or maybe even a sacred seal. A shudder of unknown expectations rolled through me.

Michael raised his hand and motioned for us to step up closer to the pedestal. We all looked at one another, and then the two angels smiled at each other, and Michael made a nodding gesture toward the book. I profoundly desired to touch it, but I hesitated even asking to do so.

"Jeremiah, you may touch the pedestal and experience for yourself completeness unlike any you have ever known."

I looked at this wonderfully large, smiling archangel and then at my own slightly extended hand and stopped. I wanted to make sure I understood him clearly, so I waited until he again nodded toward the book before continuing. I extended my hand the rest of the way and very gently brought my fingertips near the corner of the crystalline surface, all the while having serious thoughts about the blue energy field protecting it.

I'm not sure if I actually touched the pedestal itself, but the most exquisite feeling I had ever felt reverberated through my whole body. I experienced hot and cold and numbing and electrifying and scared and euphoric and deep asleep and wide-awake sensations all at the same time. Unfortunately, it only lasted for a couple of seconds before abruptly subsiding. My hand was closed and against my chest, though I don't recall pulling it back, but the residual effects left my mind totally energized and my body and brain feeling like I just drank fifty cups of espresso and received a full body massage.

I don't know if my experience with the pedestal is what made the blue force field go away, but for whatever reason, it seemed to be gone, allowing the book now to sit firmly on the crystalline surface. To my surprise, I also noticed that not only had the mysterious blue shield disappeared, but so did the entire base of the podium! The huge, white book now decisively rested on the top of the pedestal, but the top of the pedestal wasn't resting on anything. I bent over and looked carefully to confirm to myself that the base was gone. I also wanted to let my angelic companions know too. However, when I told them, they only smiled, so I just accepted it as strange and pretty cool, but obviously not significant.

With a huge smile I hoped would never go away and newfound confidence, I looked at Michael for assurance that I also had permission to touch and open the book. His demeanor never changed, so I wasn't sure what he wanted me to do. The stunning book rested only inches from my fingers. It presented itself as so white, so radiant, and so ... perfect.

All kinds of terrible thoughts rushed through my mind. For instance, what if my hands weren't clean enough, and I left my oily fingerprints on it or smudged it, or even worse, what if I accidentally tore a page? I decided to definitely wait until I received unmistakable permission to open the book before touching it. While I waited, I rubbed my hands several times across my jeans just in case.

With the protective shield removed and the cover of the book now vividly displayed, I realized a raised symbol, like a coat of arms, adorned the book's cover. As soon as I saw it, I felt an immediate and almost intimate familiarity with it; I just could not recall why or how. I wanted to study the ornate artistry more closely, but before I could get more than a quick look, the book slowly opened itself, hiding its secret from my view. I looked back up at Michael, and he smiled.

"You only need a child's heart and a quiet mind to learn its secrets," he said.

He looked again at the book and contently at me and then courteously nodded.

Taking that to mean he did *not* want me to touch the book, I had to make sure I didn't absentmindedly touch it without thinking, so I put my hands in the front pockets of my jeans, just in case. When I refocused my mind back on the book, I surprisingly found the page to be blank, but only briefly. Then, as if someone flipped on a switch, a kaleidoscope of vivid images started flooding the pages, as well as my mind. As one page after another turned, I suddenly found myself mentally tumbling through an avalanche of bright, vivid colors, symbols, shapes, and sounds that literally came alive as masterful scenes. Moreover, although each one lasted only long enough to give me a quick glimpse, I could see it all as though viewing it from both inside and outside of my mind. Pictures of familiar and unfamiliar people, places, and things passed through my consciousness at the speed of thoughts.

From somewhere hidden deep within the undiscovered treasuries of my own consciousness, a voice revealed to me that the time to remember would soon be at hand. Even though the images reached deep inside, stimulating all my emotions, the voice summoned me to go much deeper, to retrieve something much more profound.

Then, as the living images and pages slowed down, and the three-dimensional cinemas of the past joined those of the present, I found myself once again looking at a blank page. Many pages remained unrevealed, but the book rested quietly and motionless, as did my mind. I waited patiently without taking my eyes off the book, but it remained still. I looked back up at Michael.

"Why is the page blank?" I asked my angelic host as I gave a quick look back down at the book and then again up at Michael.

"As you have perceived, Jeremiah, the rest is yet to be written. Your commission is clearly before you. Hasten to the task at hand, so time and procrastination do not claim the final prize."

I studied his powerful expression, but after failing to understand the full meaning of his words, I turned to Metatron for some sort of assurance. However, right then, out of the corner of my eye, I noticed the book growing significantly brighter. I tried to look directly at it, but it became so bright that it temporarily blinded me. When my vision returned enough to once again see my surroundings, I found myself again standing face to face in front of Jesus at the foot of the beautiful, sculptured mountain with the amazing blue, fiery stones.

So much had happened, filling my brain with so many memories and undiscovered sensations, that my whole sense of time got lost along the way. I had to stop and mentally recall where it all started.

"At least I made it back," I remarked to myself without giving it much thought.

But back where? And from where? My mind kept poking my brain and telling me to get back in the moment and realize I was standing face to face with Jesus.

He smiled like he had been patiently waiting for me to mentally catch up. Then, leaning forward close enough that I could literally feel the presence of his aura, he reached into my hands, reclaiming the orb as he whispered, "Jeremiah."

Jesus, still smiling, stepped back in line with Elijah and Moses, handing the crystal orb to the Archangel Michael. Michael bowed in a sign of respect and then stepped over to the pink marble altar and gently placed the once again rock-looking orb back on top of it. He rejoined the others just as they began to disappear into the returning ethereal, white mist.

Soon, everything around me vanished into white except for the glowing rock, resting on the reflective marble surface. Metatron stepped forward, reminding me he was still there. So, I turned to him and asked, "Why have I been shown all these things?"

"To understand the truths of time," he stated, "you must consider all the possibilities of where it has been and contemplate all the implications of where it could take you in order to consciously *be* in its presence."

I wholeheartedly wanted to understand Metatron, but his words were so confusing. I closed my eyes and tried to come up with some reasonable meaning behind his statement. What I finally decided was that he was trying to tell me I needed to know and understand the past so I could apply it in the present to make the right decisions in the future. Knowing Metatron could read my thoughts, I opened my eyes to ask his thoughts about my analysis of his words, only to find myself all alone.

As if a cloud had swallowed me up, a thick fog was suddenly all around me. The only thing I could make out clearly was the glowing rock, resting on the marble altar. I strained to keep it in sight as long as possible, when, out of my peripheral vision, for just a ghost of a second, I caught a glimpse of a small-statured, elderly Asian man standing very close to me. I no more than looked at him, and he was gone. I quickly turned all the way around to see if I could spot him. Not only was he not there, but when I should have once again been facing the altar, I saw instead a smoky, glowing log come quickly into focus.

When the smoke cleared, I found myself once again with my meditation group in Ed and Elizabeth's backyard, staring at the bright red embers of the fire. I was sitting comfortably on my log seat, feeling quite warm from the soothing heat of the fire. Words could not begin to express how I felt at that moment. All of my senses successfully convinced me that everything I just saw, heard, and felt were as real as the crimson flames dancing before me, but the reality of my own physical awareness told me that this could not possibly be so.

For several moments, I sat there gathering my thoughts. Then, I recorded in my journal everything I could recall. When my turn came to share my meditation with my friends, I attempted to convey, with as much detail as possible, everything I had just experienced.

After reliving the story through my own spoken words, I felt exhausted but peaceful. I left my friends speechless from my graphic account and clarity. Angela explained that receiving such a powerful message and calling meant more than any of us could understand at that time. She believed this meditation contained more than just a message for me—that we should look at it as a revelation and a gift to our whole group and perhaps for others outside the group, as well.

"Therefore," she insisted, "we all need to listen deeply and carefully for spiritual guidance."

After about a half hour or so of socializing with my friends, I headed home thinking about what Angela had said about "a calling." I also thought a lot about the Archangel Michael's comment concerning my commission being before me and wondered what implications, if any, this might have on any of our lives ... especially mine. We usually stayed longer after our meditations, but we all seemed noticeably tired and ready for sleep. At least, I know I felt that way.

Pulling into the driveway, I parked alongside the house where I always do and reached over into the backseat to grab my notebook. In doing so, I bumped the rearview mirror, so after making sure all my loose papers were still secure in the notebook, I reached up to adjust the mirror and found myself staring straight into the deep, penetrating, reddish-purple eyes of the preacher.

I didn't even look back! I sprang out of the car and ran to the side door, unlocking it, opening it, closing it, and relocking it all at the same time. I flew up the three stairs going into the kitchen and immediately turned on all the lights. I had enough adrenalin pulsating through me to run a marathon, and I couldn't get the image of those eyes out of my head.

I don't know when I finally fell asleep on the couch, but the TV and all the lights were still on. At that time, I could not have imagined the extraordinary events yet to come.

CHAPTER 8

JOSHUA

THE NEXT TIME OUR MEDITATION group gathered, Angela asked me if I received any new information or revelations. When I told her no, she paused, looked at me like a patient mother, and then just smiled. Angela meditated on a regular basis at home, as did the others. Shortly after I joined the group, she encouraged me to meditate on my own and to ask for divine guidance every night before I went to bed. She reminded me I probably said my prayers every night as a child and assured me that same child-like faith would help me understand and cope with the difficulties of life. Every time I tried meditating by myself, however, I always just fell asleep. Therefore, in spite of her polite but constant reminding, I only meditated when we met as a group.

Due to the revealing and unparalleled nature of my last meditation, Angela told the group she believed that I, like Daniel or John in the Bible, was chosen to be a messenger or prophet. She explained to all of us that, "A prophet is a messenger selected to bring a particular message to all people and, contrary to popular belief and Hollywood fantasy, prophecy encompasses much more than just predicting the future.

"Rather," she explained, "a prophet, from a timeless perspective, describes reality as he or she sees it and cordially invites others to consider that reality from a deeper, more virtuous point of view." Angela also emphasized that the use of prophets to reach large numbers of people throughout history stretches beyond the boundaries of cultures or empires, and because their influence on society transcends our concept of time, there are prophets among the people today the same as in ancient times.

"Therefore," she reminded me, "you must be very conscientious about writing down every detail of the visions and insights you receive not only in your meditations, but in your dreams and in your daily thoughts as well."

When I tried to tell her that I really didn't think I could be a prophet, "because I'm just an ordinary guy," she replied, "So were Daniel and John." Lacking a smart response, I simply remained silent and smiled.

Angela brought a small, student-size tape recorder with her this time and asked if anyone objected to recording our meditations so that none of us would forget any of the details. No one objected, but since there were only four of us in our little group, it seemed quite obvious she brought it for me. I felt a little embarrassed by it all, but I didn't say anything. With my meditations becoming much more complex and intense, recording it actually sounded like a smart idea. Anyway, the excitement and anticipation of where I might go next, and what I might see, left me eager to begin.

As soon as we all acknowledged our readiness to start, Angela opened with a short prayer of thanks and protection, and began playing a new background cassette filled with the sounds of waves gently rolling onto a beach; this is where we began our journey. With the rhythmic sounds of the seashore in the background, everyone breathed deeply, closed their eyes, and waited for the guiding words of our friend and teacher.

"Listen to the waves as they break soothingly on the shore," Angela softly began. "Look out over the water and feel the refreshing moisture in the light breeze as it fans across your face. The soft, white sand feels warm and massaging on the soles of your feet as you casually walk along the water's edge. Seagulls are playfully gliding over the frothy whitecaps, and beautiful, multicolored stones and seashells are rolling back and forth along the shoreline. The bright midday sun is caressing your entire body with the comforting warmth of its embracing rays."

Angela paused for a few moments while the vision she portrayed manifested itself in our minds. Then, she continued, "As you look out over the water, focus your thoughts on the way the sunlight reflects off the waves as they crest, briefly sparkling like diamonds then disappearing, only to reappear again in the next surge." Again, she paused for what seemed like quite a long time. I felt very relaxed standing barefoot on the seashore, mesmerized by the rhythmic, watery ballet of Mother Nature.

"Shifting your thoughts toward the sun," she continued, "you can see that a beautiful beam of white light is rushing down around you from the heavens. It makes you feel very safe and warm because you know the light has been sent not only to calm, but also to protect you. As you close your eyes and feel the caressing rays penetrate your entire body, you notice that you are now as light as a snowflake and floating peacefully within the safety of the beam." Angela stopped talking, and I became acutely aware of not only my now weightless body, but the emotionally uplifting effect of the cool ocean mist, as well.

Like a seagull, I felt myself hovering, carefree, as the warm light energy scooped up my thoughts and carried them away with the rest of my reality. With my eyes closed, I faced directly toward the sun, still capturing the restful warmth and reddish glow through my eyelids. I assumed, as in previous meditations, I would be ascending upward. However, the only sense of movement I could distinguish came from a slow turning motion in a counterclockwise direction. As if in a dream, I could only guess at the actual passage of time, but I know I made several slow revolutions before the brightness of the light subsided. When I opened my eyes, I discovered my angelic friend, Metatron, standing in front of me.

"Peace be with you," he said, in his usual calming way.

"And with you, my friend," I responded with excitement, ready for another adventure to begin.

"Where are we going this time?" I asked.

"We are already here," he said with a big smile. Taking a step back, Metatron gestured forward with an outstretched arm.

We're already here? It didn't seem like I actually went anywhere, I thought to myself.

Anxious to begin my new adventure, I hurriedly moved in front of Metatron. I saw white ... nothing else, just bright white, like standing in front of a giant fluorescent light bulb. With all references gone, I could not distinguish anything, not the place where we stood, or even the place I just stepped away from. I looked all around me, noticing that now even Metatron could no longer be seen.

Though I knew, with a fair amount of certainty, that my eyes were still open, I couldn't see *anything*, and that is a very frightening sensation. I quickly brought my hands up to my face to actually feel my eyes, or at least that is what I intended to do. Instead, I discovered that I not only lost my sense of sight, but my sense of feeling too, as if I no longer physically existed. In spite of this alarming fact, I didn't panic. I felt sure that, as with my previous encounters with Metatron, I would be safe, and there was no urgency to be afraid.

Although I could physically no longer see my angelic guide, I could still sense his presence. So, in a nervously calm manner, I called out, "Why am I not able to see or feel anything?"

"Peace be with you, Jeremiah. You have nothing to fear. Your eyes, as well as your body, are only instruments and of no service to you here, my brother," came his immediate but perplexing response. Then another newly familiar voice spoke to me.

"*What do you search for, my child?*" the voice asked.

I distinctly remembered this cordial but very powerful voice from my last meditation. Like before, it echoed in from every direction and seemed to be both a man and a woman speaking in perfect harmony. This time, however, I perceived it as originating from inside my head, as well as all around me.

"What do I search for?" I repeated aloud. "Do you mean here and now, in this place?" I waited for a response, but it never came, so I continued, "My guiding angel, Metatron, brought me here and has not yet told me where I am, so it would be difficult for me to answer that question right now. I mean, I wasn't really searching for anything."

A deep silence followed. I waited a little longer and then asked, "Metatron, are you still here?" Again, I received no response, so I figured Metatron left me in the care of the new echoing voice.

"What do I search for?" I whispered to myself again. I thought about several possible answers, but I came to the conclusion that the question was too vague and needed more clarification, so I asked, "Are you asking me what I am searching for in life?" Again, the voice did not answer, but the more I thought about it, the more I rationalized that since an angel brought me here, I *must* be on the right track, so I continued, "Well, I guess I am searching for the same things as everyone else: health, happiness, love, friendship, and a successful life for my children and for myself." To me, this seemed like a reasonable answer, but again, I received no response, so I delved more personally and deeply into the question.

During the months leading up to Dad's death, I thought a lot about why we are here and what difference, if any, our existence makes. So, awash with sad memories of Dad's unrelenting suffering in his final days, I continued in a more somber tone.

"I would really like to understand the whole meaning of life and of God, the reason there is so much pain and suffering and death and disease in the world, and especially how, through it all, people still manage to keep their faith." Receiving no immediate response, I continued, "Is there really a heaven and hell, God and Satan? Is there a reason why bad things happen to good people and why bad people seem to get all the breaks? We are born, we live, we struggle, and we die, but what is it all for? These are the types of questions I would like some meaningful answers to."

I tried to imagine what impact these answers could have on my way of thinking and wondered if life, in general, would actually be easier or more complicated if I started looking at everyday situations and problems from a more religious or spiritual point of view. The whole concept didn't actually sound all that farfetched.

I have never been able to understand the amazing, countless testimonials of people from all occupations and lifestyles who have suffered through unspeakable tragedies and, through it all, never wavered in their faith. Even the stories I witnessed or knew of on a personal level, from my brothers and sisters in arms, defied logic. Thousands of soldiers and marines, most in the prime of their lives, deployed to fight for a cause no one could understand or explain, only to return home maimed or disfigured, destined to live with the agony of that nightmare for the rest of their lives. These young men and women have their entire existence turned upside down. They spend months or years living with chronic physical and emotional pain, suffering day in and day out. In many cases, they have lost everything they held dearest in their previously very healthy and active lives. Yet, with all of their plans and dreams shattered, they not only manage to keep their faith, but also continue to profess that their God is a kind and loving God that will always take care of them. Through it all, their beliefs and their faith, instead of being destroyed, only grew stronger! How is that even possible?

It took me a few moments to shake those horrible images of my combat comrades from my thoughts and force myself back to my present place. Sometimes I need painful mental triggers like this to remind myself how lucky I am to have returned from numerous deployments without any major physical injuries.

At least now, I knew what the voice was really asking me. With that in mind, I was ready to continue.

"I know what you are trying to get me to say. With all the different beliefs, religious convictions, and ways of thinking that exist, you want me to focus my real search on figuring out which faith is the right one. Am I right?" The voice did not argue the point, so I knew I was on the right track.

"You're trying to persuade me to figure out which religion is the 'true' one, and that way, I can filter the rest of life's answers through that point of view. That's it, isn't it?" I thought about the ideas they were suggesting for quite a while. These weren't new thoughts, just ones I hadn't had in a long time. Then it dawned on me what they were *really* saying.

"Okay, *now* I see where you are going with this. You think I am too superficial! Even though you didn't come right out and say it in those exact words, you are clearly implying that I don't give enough thought to things before I do or say something. Well, you're wrong; that is simply not true! If anything, I think about things too much. Then, I have so many options that I don't know which way to go. That's really why I never seem to reach any of my goals or dreams. So why do you think I need to further complicate everything by throwing religion into it?"

They apparently did not want to elaborate their viewpoint, so I continued.

"I do agree with you that understanding a deeper purpose behind why I say and do the things I do *is* probably as important as actually doing it, but I don't see how faith or religion really fits into the non-religious real-life problems I've been dealing with." I think I made a good point, but I have to admit, they did also!

So, to keep our discussion on friendly terms, I acknowledged, "I'm not denying the fact that during many scary or critical times in my life I have tried prayer, lots of prayer! I've been to different churches, Bible study, etc., searching for a deeper meaning of religion and faith to find answers. However, I personally have never heard God speak to me the way many others say they have. And the miracles I prayed for throughout my life never happen.

"So now, you want me to try again to 'find the faith' and believe that this time it will be different? Okay! I'm game. No, seriously, I will try again. I can't tell you how many times I have wished I could have the unshakable kind of faith I have seen in others. Nevertheless, till now, just wanting it hasn't worked. There must to be more to it. I just need to figure out the secret."

I thought deeply about everything we had been discussing. Then I whispered to myself, "I guess this is what I've been searching for."

"Then, grasp your soul and seek enlightenment there. For it shall come to pass, that when all you have sown has been harvested, and the final reward known, the mysteries that lay beyond the veil will be made known to you where your own virtue dwells."

Nothing followed but echoing silence. I kept hoping there would be some sort of explanation, more on my level, to go along with that statement because, at this point, I had no idea what those words meant, but the voice remained quiet. Finally, the silence became too uncomfortable, so I decided to try a more inquisitive approach.

"Is that why I'm here?" I asked. "Am I going to be given the answers to some deep spiritual questions about life and how it all works?"

I waited, but no one answered.

"How can I grasp my own soul? I'm not even sure what a soul is or if I really have one!" Without a physical body for even my own reference, I quite intentionally, even if just in my thoughts, *screamed* out these words in the hope that someone would hear me and end the tormenting quietness. Yet, no one answered.

Since the voice seemed to be probing me to pose just the right question, and obviously wasn't going to continue our conversation until I did, I asked, "If God is real, and heaven is real, and souls are real, then how can I prove it to myself?"

A new, softer, male voice suddenly broke through the barrier of stillness. It also seemed to be coming from every direction.

"Reality, by its own existence, carries the burden of limitations. Release the one that binds you and return to the state where your *real* consciousness dwells."

While my mind attempted to figure out the puzzling words behind these voices, I hesitated to make any kind of rational response. Besides, a logical understanding of this philosophical puzzle wasn't getting me anywhere, so I decided to try a different strategy.

"I'm not exactly sure what you want me to do," I stated humbly.

"You bind yourself with your own restrictions. Within the light, there are no limits, only those you choose to keep," the new voice said. My thoughts again raced ahead of me while my brain tried to figure out the meaning of these words. The voice spoke again.

"Center on the light and embrace your true natures."

Center on the light, I thought. "Okay, I can focus on a white light. I've done it before in many meditations," I said to myself. Then I realized that I could not possibly focus on anything because I could not see. I tried squinting, I think, but that clearly didn't help.

"How can I center on the light when I have no sight?" I asked. I got no answer, so I tried to see something other than the bright light that surrounded me, but I saw nothing else, only the light.

"How can I center on the light when there is no center?" I questioned, with obvious impatience building in my voice. I waited and waited, but only silence could be heard, and it was clearly getting louder and more intense!

The light is everywhere, I finally bellowed out in my mind.

"Good!" the new voice proclaimed calmly. "Continue."

The quick reply first caught me off guard and then it made me smile and relax, so I decided to go on with this new mind game.

"The light has no center, so by centering on the light, do you want me to try to visualize it in my mind or try to remember it from before, or think of how it feels, or what?"

Once again, my question went unanswered, and the rudeness of it all was pushing the limit of my patience. I knew in order to find the answer, I needed to figure out exactly what the man, angel, or whoever, kept trying to lure me into saying or doing.

"Okay, you want me to center on the light and embrace my true nature. Is that right?" I asked. Again, no reply. I started to feel like the only one in the class that didn't get the joke. I aimlessly scanned through any memories I could recall of all the spiritual things Angela tried to teach us, hoping to stumble onto some workable idea. Then, something she said did come to mind.

She once told us, "Every living thing carries within it a part of its divine origin, which is the source of its very being—its soul. This sanctified source *is* the true nature within all of us. It is our inner light and the source of divine love that keeps our spirit charged as we live our lives. It reminds us who we really are!"

That's it! Inner light, I excitedly whispered to myself in my thoughts.

"You *are* talking about inner light, aren't you?" I mentally stood up and shouted! No response.

"That must be the answer," I whispered to myself. However, now that I found the key to the puzzle ... knowing it did not seem to help. I knew I needed to focus on my own inner light. The tricky part would be trying to focus on anything without any sort of visual references.

"Okay, I can do this," I said after thinking about it for a couple of minutes. "All I need to do is center on the light," I told myself again. That didn't sound too difficult and, in fact, would be fairly easy in total darkness. However, since my entire existence consisted of bright white light, I found it extremely difficult to imagine another bright light in the center of it. I tried to concentrate, but I only saw the total illumination that surrounded me.

My next brilliant idea involved imagining a beam of deep blue light shooting up through the middle, which I would then change to white light. However, without anything to reference, an actual middle did not exist, and the whole idea didn't work anyway. No matter how hard I tried to concentrate, the intense brightness covered everything. Then the new voice broke the silence.

"Why do you grasp for what you already hold? Does not all that you are manifest itself from within?"

I already figured that part out, I thought back to him with confidence. "You are talking about the whole inner light thing that Angela taught us about, right?" I hoped he would at least confirm that part of it.

"I just haven't thought of a way to focus on a light within the light, even if it is only in my mind."

"Is it then a thought that keeps you from your goal?" he asked.

I started thinking about ways to answer his question when he spoke again.

"Can something you perceive to be unreal also be real? If the veil between them could be lifted, what then would define reality?" The question sounded very profound and complex, leaving me clueless as to what the voice expected me to say or, for that matter, what it had to do with focusing on the light. I decided to classify his question as rhetorical, therefore not needing a response. However, I knew Metatron brought me here for a reason, and I needed to figure out what that reason could be.

"Okay, I really want to understand, but now you've lost me," I said in a surrendering manner. I had actually felt lost since I arrived, but I hoped a little self-victimization might make him feel sorry for me and respond with a simple answer. Instead, I got no response at all.

I waited until I again grew impatient and then asked, "Who are you?"

"Of what use is a name, unaccompanied by memories?" came the immediate reply. Since I found his voice to be unfamiliar, and I could not see to whom it belonged, what he said did logically make sense.

"Well," I retorted, "if you are going to guide me in my search for answers, I need to at least know who you are."

"Very well," he answered back softly. Again, only silence followed.

I waited at least a full minute before impatiently re-asking my question, "So, who are you?"

"Who would you like me to be?" he asked back.

It appeared that he did not want to reveal his name, so I said, "Okay, if you don't want to tell me your name, then, since my son's name is Joshua, can I call you Joshua?"

"If you wish," he replied. I felt better. At least I could now call out a name for this person I couldn't see.

Neither one of us said anything for a long time. It's amazing how silence seems much more amplified when added to the absence of any other sensory inputs. I finally couldn't take it anymore, so I interrupted the audio void with what I thought was a simple question. "Where are we?"

"You are where you have always been," Joshua responded.

I replayed his curious answer in my mind, and then I asked, "Will I be able to see you?"

"Are your own abilities better judged by another than by yourself?" Joshua replied.

I thought about his question and a few possible silly comebacks, and then I mentally smiled, again enjoying his quick response and witty nature. After several more fruitless attempts at trying to put it all together, I asked him, "Are you an angel or archangel like Metatron and Michael?"

He answered, "The consciousness is but one, yet the frequencies are many. I am here to teach you; therefore, I am a teacher, and you … have much to learn."

"Yeah, I guess I do," I mumbled softly.

"Well," I said in an effort to make a good first impression on my new teacher, "I want to learn all that I can."

"Do you believe there is a limit to learning?" he asked.

"No, I guess not," I acknowledged after thinking about it and realizing we are constantly learning new things every day. "And that being the case, I want to learn everything I need to know to find peace and happiness in my life."

"Then it will be so," he responded.

I waited for Joshua to continue, but he didn't say anything else, so I finally spoke out.

"Joshua, are you still here?"

"I am here," he replied.

Again, I waited for what seemed like a long time and then said, "Is there something that you want me to do?"

"All that you do is of your own choosing."

Again, no clarification, only more silence, so I asked, "What are you here to teach me?"

"What do you seek?"

What do I seek? I mumbled in my mind. "Good question."

I quietly repeated the question in my head a couple more times, but for some reason, only trivial things leaked out of my brain. So I cleared my head and tried for a more profound thought that would really impress my new teacher. Then ... I got it!

"I seek knowledge and wisdom," I paused and thought harder, "that I can share with others," *wait, there's more*, "that will help them better their lives and find true happiness," I concluded, awed with my own words.

"And from where do you seek such things?" Joshua asked in the same tone, apparently *not* impressed.

I couldn't think of anything overly clever to say, but since I was still trying to impress him, I responded enthusiastically, "From a great teacher, like you."

I hoped my compliment would make some sort of impression on him, but he said nothing, so after a brief pause, I humbly asked, "Is there a lot that you can teach me?"

"All things carry their own awareness, their own vibration," Joshua answered immediately. "Before the dawn of humankind, every tone of creation chimed in perfect harmony. If you wish to acquire understanding, you must first seek direction and harmony from within."

"How do I do that?" I responded enthusiastically.

"Center on the light," Joshua firmly stated.

"Center on the light," I mumbled to myself. "So, we are back to that!" Regrouping my thoughts, I tried to explain to Joshua the difficulty in trying to see the center of the light.

"I tried to center on the light, but I—"

Joshua interrupted me. "Do you try to *see* the air that you breathe, or simply accept it, knowing it is always with you? In this way, you must seek the light and realize you are one with it." He paused long enough for me to go over in my mind what he told me and then continued, "Divine consciousness exists within every human being. You must search for it within yourself until you find it."

"Can you help me find it?" I asked, assuming the answer would be no.

"I will help you to understand *faith* and the power of *love*. You must first come to know and appreciate your own self if you wish to understand others and the world around you," he said. "In your dreams, I will guide you. The path you follow must be your own."

"I don't understand. How can I focus on faith or love? They are intangible things and—"

Joshua interrupted me again, saying, "Center on the light!"

"Yeah right, center on the light," I mumbled. I was trying to figure out the best way to ask Joshua for more specific guidance when I felt something tugging on my mind. I couldn't quite identify it at first.

"Tonight we will begin!" Joshua said as his voice grew more distant.

As this new feeling persisted, I realized the sensation of, once again, turning in a slow clockwise direction. It seemed very dream-like at first, and then there could be no mistaking it.

In the distance, I heard a familiar noise. It took a little while for my foggy brain to figure out exactly what and where the sound came from, but after listening closely, the uniqueness of it made it easily recognizable as the rattling of paper. *Someone must be turning pages in a notebook,* I thought. I focused my senses in the direction of the sound and slowly opened my eyes. I guess I moved enough to cause Angela and the others to look up from their notebooks.

"Are you back?" Angela asked. "We've been waiting for you."

I wanted my friends to share their meditations first, because I was hoping to spend a little extra time on the things Joshua tried to teach me. Based on all their combined years of experience with meditation, I figured they could probably give me some powerful insights. When I asked for their feedback, however, I learned that only Angela had personally experienced a similar meditation.

"You have been given a very wise teacher," Angela said enthusiastically. "So, pay very close attention to everything he tells you and do not leave *anything* out when you write it down."

She said that Joshua's profound thoughts and questions would open my mind up to a greater understanding of my own abilities and limitations, and that it now would be up to me to learn all I could from him. All my friends expressed their excitement and support.

When I asked Angela if she would explain to me about "centering on the light," she said I needed to realize it on my own to understand its full meaning but to continue to build on the part I had already figured out.

I took the back way home through the country. It meant driving a bit longer, but I preferred it to going through the city. During the drive home, I tried to recall all the interesting questions my new teacher, Joshua, had asked me and kept thinking about centering on the light and being one with the light, a concept I was sure I had heard somewhere before, but my brain was too tired to try to remember when. I hoped I wouldn't forget any of his questions even though Angela taught us not to worry about forgetting something important from a meditation or dream.

"Everything in our lives happens for a reason, and that includes our dreams and meditations," she often told us. "So any message or meaning you need to understand in your life will be repeated or shown to you again or in another way until you get the point of the message."

This very unusual meditation gave me a lot to think about, but not tonight. After an emotionally stimulating evening and a long day of running around catching up on errands, I realized that though my mind still felt charged, my body did not. The comfort of the plush bucket seat and the soothing stream of warm air blowing in my face from the heater tugged at my eyelids and softened my attentiveness.

I felt myself dozing off but convinced my half-asleep brain I was awake enough to continue driving. That's about when I drifted across to the other side of the road and only through sheer luck kept from driving straight over the bank. I barely regained control in time, but it was enough to scare me awake!

I switched the heater from blowing on me to blowing on the windshield. However, since it only works about half the time (a loose ground wire, I think), I cupped my hand over the dash vents with the back of my fingertips up against the glass to confirm it was actually working.

Just then, a shooting star shot across my view in the dark evening air, and it was one of those awesome, rare ones that actually displayed a long, fiery tail. It was so cool. I was able to watch it the full length of my windshield before it disappeared over the trees on the right side of the road. And, as an extra bonus, for a split second, it unexplainably even appeared to just stop! Of course, I knew that wasn't possible, so it clearly must have been my imagination or a direct result of my sleepiness. In either case, I have always enjoyed seeing shooting stars, and to this day, I'll admit I still childishly make a wish on them.

The windshield felt cold, but the warm air felt good on my hand. The blower was currently working just fine, so I rolled down the window for the added stimulus of fresh air and turned on the radio. I always left it set on the oldies station. I cranked it up and started singing along with The Byrds.

It was quite common to see several deer alongside the road at this time of the night, so I needed to stay focused and alert. The last thing I needed on my nonexistent budget was to end up in a ditch in the middle of nowhere. Singing to the oldies always helps. Besides, I reminded myself, in less than fifteen minutes I would be snuggling up to an oversized pillow and a fleece blanket I brought back from overseas.

"To everything, turn! Turn! Turn! There is a season! Turn! Turn! Turn! ..."

All of a sudden, from out of nowhere, a small, elderly man appeared in the middle of the road, right in front of my car. I swerved to the right and slammed on the brakes, launching me into a skid on the loose gravel. The intensity of the situation shoved his familiarity aside, leaving me with only the reactions of the muscles in my arms and legs to cope with the urgency of the moment. The road curved to the left, but the car continued on its unwavering path. Fate rested on a dusty layer of gravel! The car went off the road into a deep ditch, kissing the backside of an unflinching oak. It stalled as it slammed to a stop.

Through a light shower of fresh leaves and small branches, I caught a glimpse of two sets of headlights careening around the curve toward me. Realizing my own headlights snuffed out with the engine, the probability of the oncoming vehicles seeing me seemed highly unlikely. As they sped by, I could see that the trucks, full of rowdy, yelling teenagers going well over the speed limit, covered both sides of the road. Flying gravel pelted the side of my car, and I heard a rock strike the windshield, hard.

I guess I hit my head on the steering wheel in spite of the fact that I always wear my seatbelt. I couldn't be sure; it all happened so quickly. I felt very sleepy and remembered thinking what probably would have happened if I *hadn't* gone off the road. The darkness made it hard to see if the windshield cracked from the rock, and while I cannot imagine why I would be concerned about the condition of the windshield at that point in time, I felt a deep urgency to touch it and find out.

My mind fixated intently on my hand. I carefully watched it slowly rise from my lap and extend out in front of me in what seemed like a surreal motion. With as much a mental push as a physical one, I think I touched the windshield, but I'm not sure. I remember leaning forward to do so, but I found it so hard to focus that even the thought of it seemed to slip from my grasp. I closed my eyes. Consciousness faded.

CHAPTER 9

TABERNACLE OF SOULS

66 "COME!" A MAN SAID, EXTENDING his hand to mine and helping me up over a ledge. At first, his face appeared blurry, but when I could see it clearly, I immediately recognized him as the elderly Asian man I twice saw in my meditations and in the road just before … I stopped for a moment, straining to remember what happened, but the memory faded away as quickly as a dream. I looked over my shoulder and saw a circle of bright light behind me. It looked, though somewhat out of focus, as if I had just emerged from inside an intensely lit cave or tunnel. A moment later, it disappeared.

As soon as I felt safe and secure on the ledge, the man let go of my hand. Then, clasping his own hands behind his back, he looked deep into my eyes and said, "Now, we begin."

I immediately recognized his voice as being that of my new and, up until now, unseen teacher, Joshua, from my meditation. He only stood about five feet tall and sounded much younger than his outward appearance suggested, but somehow I almost expected that. His pencil-thick, Fu Manchu mustache that draped the sides of the all-white, scraggly beard growing from the center of his chin matched up perfectly with his almost non-existent eyebrows, clean-shaven head, and utterly intense, dark brown eyes. Yet, underneath his age-identifying white hair lay a soft, clear, baby face that suggested a twenty-year-old wearing white facial hair as a disguise. Even though all his fashionably limited facial hair appeared cottontail white, it skillfully emerged, with just enough of a silvery tint, to personify in him an authoritative, masterful look. His white, pajama-like outfit and black slippered feet also helped solidify, at least in my mind, his role as a teacher.

In many ways, he reminded me of the mysterious but very wise old "Chinaman" from a *Kung Fu* television series I watched every week with my dad in my younger days. Since Dad never seemed to allow himself much time to sit around and watch TV, that particular show turned out to be one of the few I can recall that we watched together, making it my favorite and pretty much the highlight of our TV viewing while the series lasted.

The ledge Joshua just helped me onto looked, and felt like, the top of a very high mountain, but when I looked back over the edge, I saw nothing! The light blue, cloudless sky above seemed to continue all around and below us, as if we were standing on a floating island in the sky. I can't explain why such a sight didn't send shivers up my spine or at least make me apprehensive about where I was and how I got here, but it just didn't. In fact, to the contrary, I felt completely calm and at peace, recalling stories from my youth that described heavenly beings as "coming down from the clouds ..." I wondered if maybe this could be heaven.

I slowly studied my new surroundings and found it to be breathtaking. I was now standing on the side of a very picturesque, vibrant, bright green pasture that hugged a rising hillside around me in a horseshoe-shaped semi-circle, limiting my view from anything beyond the gently rising hillcrest in front of me. The grass was thick, short, well manicured, and weed-less, from what I could tell. It also appeared to be exceptionally green, almost like the color had somehow been enhanced. It swathed all the way up over the top of the knoll. The beautiful, blue sky and green landscape melded together along an effortlessly cresting horizon and a soft, very clean-looking, white stone path waiting to lead us away from the ledge, through the meadowland and over the hill in front of us.

"Come," Joshua said again, quickly walking away from me and breaking the tranquility of my observations.

"Where are we?" I shouted, rushing to catch up with him.

Joshua stopped abruptly and looked at me.

"Of what nature is your question?" he asked in a slow, deliberate, philosophical manner. Then, before I could say anything, he turned around and again walked quickly away. I stopped to think for only a second or two, and, in that short time, Joshua had already moved far enough ahead that he started to crest the top of the hill, forcing me to run just to catch up with him. As soon as I reached him, he again unexpectedly stopped, almost causing me to plow into him. Unaffected by our near collision, he looked straight into my eyes and serenely stated, "Behold the Holy City and the temple that is *The Tabernacle of Souls.*" As he said this, Joshua, without taking his eyes off mine, smiled and raised his hand in the direction he wanted me to look.

As my gaze traveled down his arm to where his extended fingers pointed, I witnessed before me the most incredible palace I had ever rested my now widely opened eyes on. It towered high into the sky and surrounded itself with beautiful, multicolored gardens that flowed majestically from its base in every direction.

From our vantage point at the crest of the ridgeline, the geometric flow of the architecture and rich landscaping gave it a fairytale appearance.

I wanted to express my feelings to Joshua, but to my bewilderment, when I looked back toward him, I found that not only had he continued walking on without me, but he also seemed to be quite unconcerned about leaving me behind.

"Hurry!" Joshua commanded, without slowing down or even looking back. "You have much to learn."

I caught up with my speedy guide once more when he again abruptly stopped, looked over his shoulder at me, and smiled. We had arrived at a point where the white stone path guiding us, which until now measured only wide enough for a single person, opened up into a pristine, golden-brick walk. As I took a moment to admire the extravagance of the meticulously clean, golden bricks, I noticed that the path also progressively widened out as it continued up to and around a large fence that seemed to encircle the palace and its surrounding courtyard. A beautiful, exotic assortment of enchanting orchids painted both sides of the golden walkway with a mixture of knee-high, dark, shiny-leafed shrubbery, and deep red and fiery-orange grasses that intermingled with clusters of vivid, lavender, bell-shaped flowers and stalks of lacey white and orange-striped bouquets.

The variety and color schemes stretched well beyond any garden I had ever seen. A full palette of maroon, fuchsia, magenta, turquoise, and chocolate-colored roses peppered throughout the gardens that were so perfect you couldn't help but to be taken aback not only by their beauty, but by their comforting fragrances, as well. There were even flowers that looked like baby-blue starfish.

If this is heaven, I thought to myself as I slowly turned around in a full circle so I wouldn't miss a thing, *it certainly is everything I ever dreamed it could be. However, if it is not heaven, then where are we? Where are we going? And why are we in such a hurry?* My thoughts finally started catching up with my situation. So many questions stirred through my mind. I did not know where to begin.

Filled with excitement and wonder, I hoped to take advantage of our pause to question Joshua about, well, everything! However, my situation left my mind whirling with intrigue and uncertainty. I turned to face Joshua, only to find that he had, as before, simply walked away and left me behind.

Realizing that Joshua allowed no time for long delays, or even short ones for that matter, once again set my body in motion to catch up to my impatient companion.

"Joshua."

Maybe he didn't hear me.

"Joshua," I said, louder this time.

He stopped, gave me a cordial glance in silence, and then pointed to the now fully exposed, white palace looming directly before us. It looked ever more glorious as we drew closer. The grand pillars, scrolled borders, and sculptured, trumpet-blowing, golden, rooftop angels rivaled the breathtaking architectural wonders of ancient Greece and Rome and the magnificent structures of ancient Persia. Yet the smooth, polished edges and surfaces suggested a modern, very futuristic design.

Arriving at the white and silver wrought-iron fence that apparently encircled the mansion and its courts, we found ourselves blocked by a quite narrow, straight gate. It appeared to be the only entrance into the courtyard in front of the palace. We moved to within about ten feet of it and stopped.

It *had* to be the main gate going into the courtyard, but why was it so small and simple looking? *If this is heaven, then wouldn't that make this the Pearly Gates so many have written about?* I was expecting to see an enormous and heavy-looking golden gate with elaborate scrollwork and decorative adornments. However, this was just a straight, almost single-person opening. It was unassuming with a top, center, and bottom rail holding up spear-like, round, vertical bars that matched the fence. They didn't even look very strong, and the vertical bars were far enough apart for any child to pass easily through them. In fact, it looked like anyone could get in with very little effort if they really wanted to. Joshua smiled at me and stepped closer. As he did, the gate silently opened inward, allowing us passage.

Following the golden walkway into the palace courtyard, we passed a well-orchestrated array of meticulously manicured, fiery orange, flowering bushes. Each bush displayed such a delicate wisp of very tiny, multicolored flowers that it required careful examination to keep from being tricked into believing they were anything more than just tiny, colorful highlights. I would have stayed to enjoy them more fully, but Joshua, once again, didn't slow down enough to allow it.

With the palace itself now only perhaps two hundred feet directly in front of us, I found it most curious that, after a few more hurried steps, our path suddenly ended in a circle of smooth, flat rocks, also spotlessly white, within which other rocks crossed from one side of the circle to the other, giving it the resemblance of a large, stagecoach-style wagon wheel.

The rocks were *not* all evenly spaced and differed quite a bit in size and shape, which I found very surprising since the rest of the landscaping seemed so symmetrically choreographed and perfectly arranged. I smiled to myself, thinking some rookie probably got yelled at for not being more careful. Joshua, in the meantime, had stopped in the center of the stone circle, so I joined him at his right side.

The rock circle we found ourselves in placed us directly in front of the veranda that extended the entire length of the white stone manor. Four massive, evenly spaced pillars supported its roof and seemed to be made of the same polished white stone as the mansion. Between each of the four pillars, on the wall facing us, a huge, imbedded, three-sided, pyramid-shaped crystal presented itself about chest high from the ground. With the flat side on the bottom and their tips pointing outward, all three appeared equal in size, but each one glowed with a beautifully different color.

My excitement overwhelmed my patience, and I darted ahead, calling out over my shoulder, "Come on, let's get a closer look." Not waiting for Joshua's response, I enthusiastically ran toward the building, stopping close to but still outside the veranda.

From this closer vantage point, I could clearly make out the distinct colors of the giant crystals at the base of the palace. The first one actually had an effervescent, diamond clearness throughout, but contained many changing colors blended within its facets. If I had to describe it, I guess I would say it was jasper. The second crystal was the most beautiful ruby red and sparkled like a red diamond under a jeweler's lights. It reminded me of the ruby-red slippers Dorothy wore in *The Wizard of Oz*. The third crystal didn't have a jeweled, diamond-like depth the other two had, but its meticulously unified red-tinted, high-gloss, opaque orange was quite stunning nonetheless.

I also discovered that the massive pillars that *looked* like plain cylindrical columns from a distance actually consisted of intricately carved figures of lacy-gowned female angels with long, flowing hair flying upward in a turning motion, their hands holding up the massive roof of the veranda. The entire veranda and palace delicately glowed with its own almost invisible, silvery-blue aura.

In addition to the uniqueness of the building and its pillars, the ground all around it and extending out several feet into the gardens also exhibited features different from anything my imagination could have possibly anticipated. Everywhere I looked, I noticed the ground appeared to be a silver-tinted, glass-like substance, perfectly level, with no seams visible anywhere. Looking straight down between my feet, I also observed that it carried a distinct, but almost hidden, gold tone to it, resembling a very fine, gold metal-flake. Beneath this "glass" floor, I could see flickers of rapidly changing red and orange flashes, like little darting tongues of fire. It mesmerized me! Crouching like an excited kitten, I slowly got down on my hands and knees to get as close a look as possible. I attempted to figure out what could possibly be moving around so quickly yet gracefully, barely beneath the surface, but it moved much too fast to see it clearly.

I leaned back on my knees and looked high above my trifling nature at the towering palace before me. Three statues of trumpet-blowing angels stood majestically over each corner of the roof. Their polished, life-like faces and white, flowing hair and gowns of stone were highlighted by their long-stemmed, shimmering, golden trumpets. They leaned forward as if to emphasize their calling, and the silence of their instruments could be heard above all the courtyards. Between the corners could be seen only a single, unbroken fascia of smooth, polished stone.

As I slowly moved my head and eyes from the three angels on the left to the three on the right and then back again, I could have sworn the ones looking down on me followed my every move. I watched them carefully, but they never moved while I was looking at them. Finally pulling myself away from their scrutiny, I followed my eyes down to one of the middle pillars as the elaborate architecture lured me from the life-like faces to the three progressively stacked ringed bases.

Now standing and once again facing it, I walked up to one of the middle pillars and continued to take in the unstoppable wave of sensations and possibilities my senses poured into my imagination. After several minutes of admiring its architectural splendor, I redirected my attention back to the palace wall itself, which stood about twenty feet beyond the pillars.

For my own gratification, I first confirmed my hunch that the large, pyramid-shaped crystals imbedded into the wall resembled the smaller ones I had examined in the archway. Then, continuing my inspection, I eagerly searched for the accompanying black symbols, but I found none. However, since I had learned from my earlier experience under the arch that the symbols only appeared when looking directly at them, I moved from in front of the pillar and centered myself instead in front of one of the crystals. Sure enough, as I expected with great anticipation, the black symbol appeared. Of course, I ran to the centering point between the other columns and confirmed the two other crystals displayed their accompanying symbols, as well.

Being proportionally bigger with this newly enlarged size, I could see the very ornate intricacy of the symbols. Without a doubt, they were meticulously crafted out of the same mysterious glassy material as the ones in the arch. However, instead of being black, as I originally believed, they may have been a very, very dark green. Also, instead of being a solid substance like a rock, I found the inner characteristics of these fascinating symbols seemed to be made of very delicate-looking, multidimensional, layered, fine strands of dark, glassy material. It honeycombed in various woven layers in the same manner as a very delicate, spiral-shaped spider web, and all interconnected with differentiating, symmetrical, geometric patterns. Each part joined to the next in an uninterrupted finale of the entire symbol as one complete, multidimensional masterpiece!

"Wow, Joshua," I mentally and physically stated in an awestruck manner, "this is the most remarkable thing I've ever seen."

I couldn't say how long I stared in amazement over these wonderfully elaborate creations, but when my mind was full, I stepped back once again to take in the big picture, and in doing so, I shifted my perception back to the overall crystal pyramid itself.

"Joshua, these are exactly like the crystal pyramids and symbols I saw in the archway," I said while still semi-consciously visualizing the elaborate details of the symbols. Joshua did not answer.

Of course, being very excited about my new discovery, I anxiously wanted to hear the explanation behind them.

"What do the symbols mean?" I asked. Still met by silence, I turned around and realized I was once again having a high-spirited conversation with Joshua that only involved me. I looked back toward the circle of stones and spotted my mysterious friend, sitting on the ground with his back toward me, his hands in front of him.

"Joshua," I called out. He did not move.

"It's fantastic," I continued in a loud voice. "Can we go inside?"

Joshua did not answer, nor did he change his position, so I ran back to where he sat and asked, "What are you doing?"

"Sit!" he commanded, without looking up at me. "We will meditate."

"Meditate?" I said in disbelief.

Joshua remained motionless, with his eyes closed. His arms rested in his lap, with his left hand cupping his right, and his legs crossed in a very uncomfortable-looking yoga position.

I very stubbornly stood over him, watching and waiting and waiting and watching. He took slow, deep breaths and let out a low-pitched, barely audible, humming sound each time he exhaled. With a surrendering sigh, I finally sat down in the circle across from him. I struggled to put myself in the same body position, but it felt too awkward. Instead, I sat cross-legged in an "Indian style" position.

"Clear your thoughts; think of nothing," he said in a low, monotone voice.

I followed Joshua's commands, and after taking several slow, deep breaths, I too reached a relaxed meditative state. I soon found myself echoing the sounds of my teacher, and I could feel each tone vibrating through my entire body. I made no attempt to picture anything in my mind, focusing rather on the sounds I heard from Joshua and those coming from my own deep breathing.

The vibrations increased. Each successive tone seemed to grow clearer in my mind and deeper into my core. It moved through me from my solar plexus outward in every direction, stimulating my muscles with a pulsating wave of unstoppable energy. I could feel my whole body, inside and out, buzzing with every breath. It had the same effect as that prickly feeling you get when your hand or foot "goes to sleep," only in a good way. The buzzing intensified until it evenly covered every conceivable part of me, as if my very molecules were being rearranged. I tried to open my eyes, but I could not.

It's challenging to try to describe the actual feeling because it felt painfully stimulating, like a deep-tissue massage. And, to make it even more interesting, even though I was firmly sitting on solid ground, I felt my entire being slowly turning in a counterclockwise direction; it was a very weird feeling indeed.

CHAPTER 10

THE TABLET

I DISTINCTLY DID NOT REMEMBER getting up or opening my eyes. So, when I suddenly found myself standing, still in the circle, face to face with Joshua, my brain had to catch up to the new reality I was facing. Before I could say anything to Joshua, a faint, white mist quickly rolled in around us, masking the ground like dry ice on a theatrical stage.

Joshua looked into my eyes, smiled, then turned and walked quickly away.

"Come!" he said, without looking back.

Ahead, a brilliant light was visible through the foggy mist. It was very similar to the white light I had experienced on numerous occasions. This time, however, it seemed brighter, or to be more precise—it was much whiter! It flowed upward and outward in dancing waves like the Northern Lights.

Between where we stood and where the light seemed to be coming from, a very large, faintly glowing structure slowly came into view. At first, I thought it was a four- or five-story building. However, its hazed shadow masked any perceivable details. Joshua was leading us directly toward it. The ground was completely obscured by the mist but apparently was solid and safe to traverse without actually seeing what we were walking on.

As we drew nearer, and the mist began to clear, the now easily observable structure revealed itself in all its glory. Probably the best way to describe it is a rectangular monolith resembling a large, thick, stone tablet. My best guess would put it at least forty feet tall and almost as wide. From where we stood, still a good fifty feet away, it looked like a giant, solid white rock, one that could have come from the face of a mountain. It was covered with well-defined parallel lines and some sort of complex etchings.

The closer we got, the more it became obvious that this huge structure and the white stone palace were made of the same smooth material as well as the surface we were walking on. The lines I saw from a distance segmented it both up and down and side to side, giving it a checkered-board appearance, evenly dividing it into twelve perfect squares, three wide and four high. All of the squares adorned themselves with imbedded, highly polished, intricately designed, dark symbols. The splendor of its magnitude and the contrast between the dark color of the symbols and the dazzling whiteness of the monolith gave it an exquisitely sophisticated and futuristic appearance.

Because there were twelve symbols in the colossal archway and twelve symbols on the tablet, I reached a logical conclusion that they probably matched each other. These symbols, however, being significantly larger, afforded me the opportunity to appreciate both the uniqueness of each one and their similarities as well, especially since I could now view all the symbols at the same time and on such a large scale.

Since the closest ones stood at eye level, I tried to relax my mind enough to see if these symbols, as the others, hid golden lines behind them. To my dismay, I found that either they did not or my excited state would not allow my mind to relax enough to see them.

The bright light coming from somewhere behind the tablet spilled over the top left side of the massive structure in finger-like streams, grabbing ahold of it like giant fingers of energy.

Perhaps it is being held by the hands of God, I thought.

"Perhaps," Joshua responded in a very quiet but sincere tone, without ever taking his eyes off the tablet.

Joshua's remark shocked me, not only because of the magnitude of such a statement, but also because I never said it out loud. I only thought it, so the fact that he responded at all took me by surprise. This chance of actually seeing God, however, prompted me to attempt a closer examination of the light source behind the stone monument. Unfortunately, it chose that very instant to intensify enough to make it a little too bright to look at. I tried squinting, but looking directly into the light, even through almost closed eyes, became painful enough to force me to close my eyes tightly and turn away. I glanced over at Joshua and noticed him staring at the top right-hand corner of the tablet, so I also focused my attention back on where he seemed to be looking.

"What do you see?" I asked.

"What do *you* see?" Joshua asked back as he shifted his gaze to me.

"Are you talking about the square in the upper right-hand corner?"

"Of course," Joshua responded in a tone suggesting it should have been obvious. I thoroughly examined the symbol.

"I see a sort of stick person, sitting on a broken chair, holding pieces of something, with another, larger stick person standing behind him, also holding something." The look Joshua gave me told me that I had better look again.

"You must see it from within," Joshua directed, as he brought his fingers to his chest to emphasize the notion and then refocused his interest back on the symbol.

"Yeah, right, from within," I repeated, tapping my fingers on my chest. My chest felt solid and muscular, much more so than it should have. I looked down at my arms and hands and found to my pleasant surprise, not the arms and hands of an out-of-shape forty-three-year-old, but rather, ones of a much younger man. I quickly looked over the rest of my body and found that I looked the way I did back in my Marine Corps days in my late teens and early twenties. At that time in my life, I unquestionably reached what turned out to be the best physical shape I have ever been in, and probably my most mentally alert, as well. I flexed my biceps in both arms and felt the size and firmness of them—it felt great!

"What's happening?" I questioned Joshua, pleasantly surprised about my new physical appearance.

"Creation!" he answered with a soft firmness while never taking his eyes off the massive tablet.

His response quickly brought my consciousness back to the symbol in the upper square. For the moment, I shifted my thoughts away from my new physique and focused on the symbol, with quite a few earnest diversions to the other symbols for comparison. A strange kind of déjà vu feeling convinced me that if I tried really hard, I would be able to not only understand the symbol Joshua wanted me to focus on, but its relationship to the others, as well. However, in spite of the fact that something about it seemed very familiar, I could not successfully recall what or why. I looked over at Joshua for guidance.

"Relax," he instructed without looking at me. Then he remained silent.

After taking a few deep breaths and relaxing my head, neck, and shoulders, I briefly closed my eyes to calm my mind. Then, opening my eyes and intently concentrating back on the upper right-hand symbol, I decided to try a method of meditative communication I witnessed Angela and some of the others using more than a few times over the years. She called it a "soul-to-soul" connection. I couldn't tell you how or why it works; I can only say that I've witnessed it, and it's for real.

Angela told us, "Anyone who honestly believes and sincerely desires to 'see' the true nature of anyone or anything through their spiritual eyes would indeed be able to see beyond the external surface and into the very soul of that person or thing."

The way it works is actually quite simple, and yet, it is in this simplicity that achieving a satisfying result becomes so difficult. All you need to do is focus your mind on a particular subject—an object, a person, a tree, or just about anything. Then, while keeping your concentration singularly and unwaveringly focused on only that subject, completely move your mind aside so it's not blocking your natural intuitiveness, and you will "see" and feel its soul. The final step is accepting what you see and learn from them or it without questioning where the knowledge comes from.

I witnessed Angela successfully doing this on both people and animals in a very short time with astonishing results. As for me, though, I had only kind of gotten it to work once, with her help, when she first taught the group. She had us all concentrate on "feeling" a very old oak tree. She wanted us to try to envision what the tree had "seen" and "experienced" over its long lifespan. Anyway, I figured it was worth a try and that being here with Joshua would also help. Just the fact that he told me to relax *actually* made me feel relaxed, and, deep down, I emotionally felt a strong desire of wanting to please him.

Even with that thought though, it took a number of re-starts and I don't know how many non-responsive minutes, but, surprisingly, the symbol started to move! It vibrated back and forth as if someone grabbed and briskly shook it. Then the entire symbol, working its way outward from the inside of the square, seemed to separate into hundreds of tiny pieces and spread out over the entire surface. When it settled, I found myself looking at rows and rows, only centimeters apart, of ancient-looking figures in a tight, counterclockwise, spiral pattern. Some of the figures seemed complete, and some partially fragmented.

At first, I thought I was looking at symbols mixed in with numerous crude figures of people or animals, or a combination of the two, or perhaps hieroglyphics superimposed on top of each other. However, after looking more intently, I realized that the entire square now contained hundreds and hundreds of intricate, geometric, three-dimensional shapes. It obviously depicted some form of ancient writing or code of some kind; however, it seemed much more complex than anything I recalled ever hearing or reading about. A quick glance at the other squares revealed they remained unchanged.

"Do you know what this means?" I asked Joshua.

"Do you wish to tell me the meaning of these writings?" he replied, in a light, inquisitive way.

"No," I said slowly. "I am asking if *you* would tell me their meaning."

"Do you not recall that which you once taught to others?" he asked.

Somewhat surprised, I quickly looked back up at the square and then back at Joshua, who tapped his chest with his fingers and looked at me with an expression that implied, "Well?"

Determined to unravel the mystery, I took a deep breath and slowly exhaled as I studied the figures carefully. I kept trying to let my mind stay completely focused and relaxed so I could concentrate, but relaxing proved to be quite difficult, given my excitement level. Finally, after several minutes and several stern self-reminders to stay focused, the square once again revealed its spiral design!

I had just begun examining the symbols, noting that some were darker or heavier than others when the whole spiral pattern started moving inward toward the center in a slow, clockwise flow. The centering spot in the square began to glow like a charcoal briquette going from red to white hot. Beginning in the now fiery spot in the middle of the square, each symbol, in succession, started disappearing into the center like a cake mix blending in a strawberry swirl. As they disappeared, each one also began throwing off tiny sparks, comparable to someone flicking a lighter that was out of fluid, and when it sparked, it made a quick but audibly noticeable sound.

The drain-like movement of the symbols continued to pull the contents of the square into and through the central point, and as their speed steadily increased, so did the sounds they emitted, until only a constant stream of a modulating musical tone could be heard. If asked to try to recreate the sounds, I would, ironically, choose to use the harp to do it. Of course, realizing this threw all kinds of notions and questions into my head. Here I was, in the realm of angels, witnessing an ancient script made up of complex musical characters, and they just happened to be harp tones! Well, I guess considering everything else, it was quite appropriate. After all, I have always heard most legends and tales of old are usually based on some degree of truth.

Within no time, the symbols in the middle were moving too fast to discern what they individually looked like, and the outer symbols, farthest from the center, made short, quick gyrations, suggesting they had to be in a precise alignment before entering the "drain." There was too much going on to keep up with everything, so I decided to concentrate all my attention on just the sounds. The notes seemed to be completely random but followed each other so quickly that they seemed to merge into one continuous tone that resonated in what sounded and "felt" like an inconsistent but rhythmic wave pattern. I closed my eyes and tried to maintain a relaxed state. I was hoping to pull some answers from deep within myself or, for that matter, anywhere else I could find them. Unfortunately, the meaning of everything I was seeing, hearing, and feeling remained an unsolved mystery. After a few moments, I opened my eyes and just stared at the sparkling musical show.

From a common-sense point of view, I was very aware of the fact that the number of symbols that first appeared in the square should have run out in a matter of seconds. But instead, they just kept flowing from somewhere. For all I knew, they could have filled the entire monolith, and I was only looking through a tiny window into what lay on the other side of it.

I'm not sure how long I fixated on the flowing rhythm of the symbols, but somewhere between forcibly relaxed and super excited, my brain went into a dreamlike trance. As I stared at the sparking epicenter, my mind became a viewing screen suddenly flooded with quick, explosive flashes of an ancient recollection. At first, I could make out only bits and pieces. Then, like re-reading a favorite novel I haven't read in a long time, it chronically started coming back to me. I briefly closed my eyes for a quick memory check and in an unexplainable mental transition, I wondrously, though unintentionally, found myself witnessing this symphonic phenomenon from the center of the square with the spiraling symbols "draining" beneath my feet and the others encircling me like a 3D IMAX extravaganza. I turned my head from side to side but quickly realized I only needed to look straight ahead to see the twirling symbols meld into picturesque ancient scenes.

"Yes!" I exclaimed, as much for my gratification as Joshua's. "I *do* know …" My mind did not allow me to say anything else for several minutes as I quietly watched in amazement while the ancient, symbolic script revealed itself to me on a multidimensional plane.

With my inner and outer thoughts now flooded with newly acquired memories, I confidently exclaimed to Joshua, "This is the language used in classes I attended long ago." While I spoke, the memories kept coming, so I once again stopped talking and watched as the panorama unfolded in my head. The scenes of small groups of students all wearing simple, comfortable-looking clothing, like hospital scrubs, filled every corner of my mind. Each young adult displayed vibrant, multicolored auras and appeared quite at home and at ease in their beautiful, futuristic, geometric surroundings.

I could recall the magnificent gardens and picturesque cliffs overlooking the deep blue sea, the intricate, silent-running, non-metallic machines, and the stylish domes where the masters of science plumbed the secrets of the universe. Most of all, I could clearly remember the incredible, flowing, seamless architecture of the cities and the harmonious day-to-day life of all the citizens there.

"Could this beautiful Eden-like land have been the ancient city of Atlantis? Or perhaps, this is one of her secretive Minoan colonies on the island of Crete or off the coast of India?" I wondered to myself aloud. I opened my eyes and gazed with excitement at the stone document before me and then at Joshua for a possible confirmation of my assessment, but he gave me none.

I continued, "This language originated in a place only spoken of in legends. Brought to our people by 'The Travelers' during their initial visits, it quickly became the universal language accepted by all levels of society."

I looked at Joshua, who smiled at me while nodding his head, prompting me to go on. Again closing my eyes, the memories took me farther and farther back through time. Eons of long-forgotten civilizations flashed through my mind, perpetuating a slide show of historical transparency that spanned many lifetimes. And, without any logical explanation whatsoever, it all made sense to me. The first things I saw were beautiful gardens and landscapes within futuristic, interlinked, pristine dome structures filled with very happy-looking young adults. Then, as we went further back, I started seeing bigger dwellings and noticed that angels roamed freely amongst the people. As time digressed, there were fewer and fewer people, mostly older looking, and very few dwellings, and then only angels and no dwellings, at least not on our dimensional plane of existence. Then the memories I had unconsciously been waiting and hoping for, the ones that launched all the rest, eased into my mind.

"I remember," I said to Joshua, almost in a whisper.

"What do you remember?" he whispered back with encouragement.

"I remember a time before the separation," I exclaimed as I opened my eyes wide with child-like excitement.

Joshua smiled and nodded a confirmation.

"These ancient writings ..."

I re-stabilized my thought patterns on the scripted tablet determined to see if I could find them. There they were! Right in front of me, as if written into the very fabric of heaven itself and as clear as the day they first appeared—the writings that preceded all others.

"These writings ... they contain the directives," I said, still staring at the tablet. Then, understanding the sanctity of this moment, I slowly turned back toward Joshua. Speaking to him only with my mind and barely above a whisper, I sang an ancient tune in a dialect long ago forgotten.

[Sa ap ko aka kin Na Ngwa unsey du tei ya si du kria Diat mo Mya sen kyo]

"These are the directives given to all at the very dawn of creation."

[tuk si trient qwa tu]

"You have done well," he answered in the same ancient tone and dialect.

Returning to our native tongue, Joshua continued, "Tell me about the other symbols."

The other symbols? They look like the same symbols I saw between the pillars on the wall of the palace and in the archway of the round chamber, I thought.

"What do you remember of the temple?" Joshua inquired.

I closed my eyes and pictured the white chamber in my mind the way I remembered it while Joshua simultaneously explained, "Since ancient times, the archway and chamber of which you speak have been known by many names. To some, it was known as the Home of Sky People or the Great Temple of Life. Others referred to it as the Cave of Dreams or Bridge to the Gods. For countless generations, the temple chamber you visited has been highly revered as a great holy place, accessible only to high priests, oracles, and powerful medicine men and women. Many cultures hold it in the highest esteem, thinking it to be the sacred chamber where the Creator sits on a golden throne and rules the universe."

"That's awesome!" I declared, opening my eyes wide with enthusiasm. "I could tell without you even saying anything that it was a very holy place, but I didn't know it was—"

"A way station?" Joshua said, cutting me off.

"What?" I responded with surprise. "What do you mean a way station?"

"Simply that, Jeremiah. It is merely a relocation point, a portal, a threshold to the numerous dimensions within the kingdoms. Many see it in their meditations or in their dreams as they travel in spirit or inspired thought."

As Joshua said this, I closed my eyes, hoping again to picture the temple as I remembered it from my meditation so I could recapture all the intricate details. It quickly dawned on me, however, that Joshua had stopped talking. When I opened my eyes, I found myself actually standing once again in the temple, facing the archway with its colorful crystal pyramids and hidden ancient symbols. I quickly turned around to see if the imposing crystal fountain of angels was still there—it was. I looked at Joshua and smiled.

"This place is awesome. Thank you for bringing me here again," I said with immense gratitude. Joshua looked at me as if he had no idea why I thanked him. I started to ask him about the fountain, but without saying a word, he walked past me and stopped at the centering point directly underneath the archway. Quickly rejoining him, I tried to slide in really close so we could both enjoy the fantastic, euphoric, centering spot's effect. Unfortunately, nothing happened.

Joshua looked annoyingly into my eyes, and intentionally brushing across my face with his arm, he pointed up at the arch and said, "Tell me about these symbols."

I hesitantly took a step back out of Joshua's personal space, and even though I no longer stood directly under the archway's center, all twelve black symbols were clearly visible.

"Well, I discovered," I said proudly, "that hidden behind each one of them is a set of three golden lines—"

"What of the symbols?" Joshua interrupted, apparently not impressed with my great discovery.

Silently searching from one to the next, I stopped at the symbol from the tablet that transformed itself into the ancient writing.

"That one," I remarked, pointing to the symbol above the indigo-colored crystal, "that one is the symbol that turned into the ancient writings containing the directives."

"And the others?" he asked, apparently still unimpressed.

I again looked carefully at each one, hoping to trigger lost memories of the secrets they held, but no such inspired memories came forth.

"Am I supposed to know the meaning of each of these symbols as well?"

"If I said this was so," Joshua responded, "would it bring forth the understanding you seek?"

I took that to mean no, so I humbly asked, "Will you teach me the meaning of the symbols?"

Joshua slowly scanned the archway with his eyes, as well as with his outstretched hand, saying, "Together they signify the oneness of the Creator, both in being and in purpose, throughout the realms. Separately, each symbol holds the key to the essence of its existence, revealed to all who are open to its meaning."

"So each of the symbols hides a mysterious, deep secret about God?" I excitedly interrupted.

"No secret," Joshua snapped, "a simple truth present in each of the twelve, *always* present! They act as a reminder of our true natures, as well as a direct link to the source of all knowledge. Together they guide us toward the enlightenment that returns us to the wholeness of being."

Joshua's words, though mindfully confusing, contained an unrecognizable familiarity that I could no more shrug off than explain. Together we stood in silence for a few minutes and mutually admired the incredible architecture. He then continued.

"As we are one, so too are the others. We are in total completeness with the whole of creation, as we are with each other, no matter how separate our paths might be. This, Jeremiah, is the door through which the crossing begins and through which all will pass at their journey's end."

"A door?" I asked. "A door to where?"

"Through this archway, this crossroad, *all* of the realms are manifested before the one consciousness, sanctified by the very thought that gave birth to their creation," Joshua explained.

I listened closely to what he said, but the meaning behind the words only partially made sense to me, so I asked, "Why did you say *all* the realms? Are there other realms in addition to those of heaven and Earth?"

Joshua paused and peered deep into my eyes. Then with a sincere voice, he asked, "Just as there are the heavens and the Earth, is there not light and dark, good and evil? What of these realms? Have you never marveled at the expanse and untold mysteries hidden within the realms of the seas and the skies?" Joshua paused again, giving me only a brief moment to ponder his questions. He then continued, "Tell me, Jeremiah, where do you say thoughts and dreams belong if not in a realm of their own? What of the many seen and unseen energies, as well as the forces that act with or against them? Are they not part of this same reality?

"What about *time* itself? A realm meant to both intensify and humble the Creator's benevolence! It was sanctified through sacred love, not only as one of the seven divine gifts, but as an inexhaustible tool for personal growth and spiritual development. Yet humanity has lost control of it, turned it upon itself, and relinquished its authority and power to a consciousness that is no longer recognized. That divine endowment, conceived by grace, has callously been consumed by misunderstanding, ignorance, and fear."

After he had finished speaking, Joshua continued looking directly into my eyes with a serious tone. Then he smiled, looked back up at the archway, and said, "Yet, when we pass through this archway, the synergy of all the realms becomes one again in perfect harmony with both creation and creator."

I still did not understand what Joshua tried to explain to me, but I trusted him and figured that it would become clearer as I started to put all the pieces together. I could not help but wonder what all this might mean in *my* life. After a brief time of silence, Joshua continued, again pointing to the arch.

"As you can see, there are twelve realms in this dimension, as there are in the others."

Since there were twelve crystal pyramids in the arch, I assumed that signified the twelve realms he spoke of.

"Within each realm, there are gathered twelve tribes, or groups, which the Creator chose, to represent that realm. Do you understand?"

"I think so."

"Explain it to me," Joshua commanded.

"You said that our dimension and the other dimensions all contain twelve realms each, and within each realm there are twelve groups or tribes. Is that right?"

"What, then, is not clear to you?" Joshua asked.

"Well, I think I understand most of it. You said that there are twelve realms and twelve groups or tribes in each realm, so I am assuming that because there are twelve crystal pyramids and twelve symbols to go with them, that there must also be twelve dimensions. Am I right?"

"The greatest teachers of ancient wisdom could not begin to comprehend the enormity or complexity of the Creator. But, for your understanding, within the human races, there are one thousand dimensions," Joshua said.

One thousand dimensions? I whispered in my mind. I figured scientists might someday discover a couple more that existed beyond our current understanding, but ... one thousand stretched far beyond anything I could wrap my mind around. Thinking in regards to my current situation, I asked, "Do the other dimensions also have heavenly beings like angels?"

"Representatives, one from each of the tribes, of every realm and every dimension, serve as teachers, messengers, and guides. So, in all, there are 144,000 chosen to be permanently sealed in the light, along with the twenty-four elders, chosen to show others the way, bringing them into their own fulfillment."

One hundred and forty-four thousand, I thought. I knew I'd heard this somewhere before but couldn't remember exactly where.

"Is the archway also a doorway to the realms of other dimensions?" I asked.

"For the understanding you require, it could be perceived as such. However, only in this dimension does it appear in the form in which you see it. The crystals are timeless, and their facets are many and varied, as are the realities that dwell within and beyond their manifestation."

As Joshua said this, he continued to look up at the inner wall of the arch, making accompanying hand gestures. So, I figured I would take advantage of the fact that he wasn't looking at me and nonchalantly side-stepped closer to the massive wall. Half watching Joshua, so as not to get caught, and half watching my hand, I reached out to cautiously feel the side with my fingertips.

I'm not sure whether I actually touched the inner wall of the arch or just got very close, but I suddenly received a jolting shock that shot multiple times up and down my entire body, like the stunned sensation you get from accidentally grabbing an electric fence. When I could finally recover my hand, I quickly retreated back alongside Joshua. He never stopped talking, so I am pretty sure he didn't notice my absence.

"So you see, Jeremiah," Joshua said, turning to me, "the twelve realms are part of the universal consciousness, and, therefore, their spiritual nature is the same in all dimensions, though many perceptions, such as time, exist in other dimensions in ways that the human races could not yet begin to comprehend."

Still a little rattled and with my heart noticeably pounding faster than normal, I just looked at him smiling and nodded in agreement.

Joshua put his hands on my shoulders and said, "Jeremiah, all of this must be shown to you that you might share it with others. You have been commissioned to bring the remembrance of understanding back to all of humanity so their intuitive awareness might also be reawakened. This will lead them back to the spiritual pathway that will rekindle in them the light of divine love."

For a brief moment, I felt excited about being part of all this, but that feeling quickly changed to one of escalating anxiety. Did Joshua just say he expected me to explain all of this to others when I felt more bewildered now than ever?

"Peace be with you, Jeremiah," he said softly. "No one *ever* goes through life alone, not ever! An angelic presence accompanies you and each of us through every part of our journey. This presence is a manifestation of the Creator's commitment to all of humanity. It is a promise that will *never* be broken. However, we have also been given the special gift of free will. Therefore, if you ever think that you are alone and need guidance and love, you need only to ask, and it will be given to you. But, because your free will is always respected, you *must* ask."

I looked attentively into Joshua's eyes as he spoke, and his reassuring words *did* make me feel much more at ease. I knew that I could not do this on my own, and he just reassured me that I would never have to. Joshua turned slightly, and I noticed that we now were standing once again at the base of the great tablet.

Together we stood silently examining the sacred symbols. I attempted to again relax my mind enough to examine one of the other symbols, but after what Joshua just told me, I had so many questions and thoughts shooting through my head that relaxing was out of the question. Besides, the nerve endings in my arm and hand were still buzzing from touching the archway wall.

I looked over at Joshua as he vigilantly stated, "This monument is here only as a reminder to all of us that eternity is only a measure of time, and time merely a glimpse at creation."

What Joshua said next, still in a soft voice, is probably one of the most profound statements I have ever experienced!

"Creation begins and ends with a single divine thought. Therefore, each single thought of the Creator surpasses even the creation of eternity itself. By its very nature, it is capable of an eternity of eternities. So you see, Jeremiah, the creation of creation itself is timeless!"

He paused long enough for me to grasp or at least try to follow the scope of his words. Then he assured me, "You must be patient and know that if you search within the light, through love, you can only find truth! As you find truth, and you will find it, it will release you from the limits you place upon your own understanding of life and of love, and it will change your level of consciousness throughout the rest of your journeys."

As Joshua finished speaking, a bright light behind the colossal tablet seemed to intensify, capturing our attention. It grew brighter and brighter until the intensity forced me to shut my eyes and turn away. When I opened them a few moments later, the tablet could no longer be seen. Instead, in its place, I found myself facing endless rows of angels, all dressed in bright white, with beautiful, multicolored auras enhancing each of them. I looked at Joshua, still standing alongside me, and then at myself, only to find that we too produced auras of our own and emulated the same radiant, angelic appearance as the others. My aura was a faint but noticeable light purplish-bluish color, whereas Joshua's was mostly just white with distinct golden green overtones.

"Joshua," I said, "what does this all mean?"

"Just as a baby must learn to crawl before it can walk, you are about to take your first step beyond the veil and into a deeper understanding of divine love."

I looked at Joshua's radiant face and then glanced out at all the other angels surrounding us. The area suddenly filled with a concentrated golden light coming from behind me. It lit up all the faces of the multitude of angels facing it like a beautiful sunrise. Following Joshua's lead, I turned and looked up. Because of its intensity, I couldn't look directly into the light, but as the strength of the illumination slowly subsided, we could all see what was materializing within it and heading straight toward us.

CHAPTER 11

A NEW BEGINNING

T HE SCENE UNFOLDING BEFORE OUR eyes brought a rapture to my imagination. A stunningly beautiful, perfectly proportioned angel with full, flowing, waist-length, shiny, golden-red hair slowly descended in our midst. Her sheer, ultra-white robe furled like gossamer dancing in the breeze, and she displayed an aurora of shimmering rainbow colors all around her. As she gently floated down, like a far-off song forcing you to listen harder, her long, fiery hair lightly captured her movement in a living snapshot of perfection. In her hands, she carried what appeared to be a large, perfectly shaped diamond about the size of a soccer ball. It radiated a field of energy similar to one of those static electricity globes found in science labs.

We spread out into a wider circle, allowing her plenty of room to descend into the center of our angelic gathering. Just as her bare feet softly touched the smooth stone floor, a beam of glistening, white light from above, and indigo light from below, merged into the waves of vivid colors flowing all around her, grasping the giant gem in their rays, holding it suspended in front of her. As she relinquished her diamond to the care of the light beams, and the dazzling light show subsided, she raised her arms and directed her eyes upward, then stood motionless and silent in a prayer-like moment.

Lowering her arms with her palms facing outward, she looked in our general direction and with a wide smile declared, "I am Ariana. I come bearing witness to the magnitude of the Creator. That which you held precious long ago shall be rekindled in your hearts. Henceforth, you will remember and make it known to all whose awareness will be awakened."

She turned her head slightly to the left, looked directly at Joshua and me, and stated, "Nevermore shall those who seek enlightenment be dispirited by shrouded wisdom. The time is at hand when the unspoken knowledge of the ages, through perseverance and grace, shall once again be understood, and, in harmony with the others, it will verify the way."

The meaning and importance of her words evaded my comprehension, but the sincerity of her tone compelled me to stay focused. I stared at her for what felt like several glorious minutes, taken aback by the completeness of her whole persona, and then a sudden microburst of golden light shifted my eyes and thoughts to the colossal gem.

The diamond, now suspended about chest high in the beams of light, turned slowly, first in one direction and then in the other. Then, never leaving its position in the light's grasp, it began tumbling end over end. It gyrated faster and faster, displaying a total spectrum of dazzling colors. As we gazed upon the gigantic gem, the brilliant colors encompassing it all merged into a delicate aura of jasper. Ariana, with her arms still extended, stepped back, closed her eyes, lowered her head, and bowed on one knee. All eyes focused intently on the diamond.

As the spinning motion of the gem continued to gain momentum, it simultaneously expanded in size, as if it was an inflating balloon. When the transformation, which only took three or four seconds, was complete, we found ourselves looking into a large, clear, crystal orb that measured about ten feet in diameter. The amazing transformation turned the giant diamond into a perfectly round, spherical shape with the added extraordinary feature of a capturing apex of streaming ice-blue electrical energy on the top and bottom, resembling an enormous, delicate Christmas ornament. A softly glowing jasper mist filled the sphere.

In the center of the giant crystal, three parallel lines of gold appeared, clearly visible from my vantage point about fifteen feet away. I immediately recognized them as being just like the horizontal golden lines I discovered behind the ancient symbols of the archway.

I leaned in and whispered to Joshua, without taking my eyes off the sphere, "I've seen this golden symbol before. These are the three golden lines I spoke of when I tried to tell you what I found hidden behind the ancient dark symbols in the archway." Excited about this revelation, I briefly glanced over at my companion to get his reaction. Joshua made no comment or movement. He remained focused intently on the diamond sphere. So, I also re-established my center of attention there and silently watched.

A wave of energy passed through each golden line in a pulsating, seemingly random order. As the current passed through each member of this golden trio, that line would very briefly be altered in either thickness or brilliance or both. It would then return to its original state as the energy moved on to one of the other lines. At any given time, at least one of the golden lines displayed the surge of power, and each surge only lasted as long as a camera's flash. The choreography of it captivated me.

Considering the angelic audience, the three lines of gold obviously signified something of great importance, so I looked to Joshua for some inspirational wisdom.

"What do the golden lines mean?"

Joshua turned and faced me, but he did so in slow motion. I looked directly at him as well as behind him and toward his left and right, realizing that my movements too were in slow motion. When I re-engaged my gaze so that I made direct contact with Joshua's eyes, time for us abruptly returned to normal. Everyone else, including Ariana, however, seemed to be frozen in time. Even the sphere, though it continued to turn, did so very slowly. As if nothing had happened, Joshua, without even acknowledging the entire altered time thing, asked, "Do they not tell you of their meaning?"

I really wanted to say *something*, but Joshua acted so impervious to our surroundings that instead I silently scanned the room, looking over at Ariana and then slowly at the scores of other angels, then back at Ariana. They were all frozen in motionless harmony with the situation. Looking back again at Ariana, standing there motionless like a flawless, living mannequin goddess, made me realize I could slowly examine her from head to toe without her even knowing ... Then Joshua pinched my elbow in a way that shot what felt like a biting electrical charge up and down my arm. I grabbed my throbbing arm and looked at him. He was giving me that "stern dad" sort of look. I just gave him a "What?" look back, shrugged slightly, and shifted my mind back to the crystal sphere.

I studied the golden lines intently, utterly fascinated by the way they seemed to be floating within the jasper mist. I asked Joshua if I could get a closer look and received an approving nod of permission.

As the crystal turned in a clockwise direction, I slowly circled it in the opposite direction, noting that my view of the golden lines sheltered within never changed. Then it dawned on me. If my view of the lines stayed the same as I circled the crystal … I stopped and stared at the lines, finally realizing that what at first glance clearly looked like golden lines were actually perfectly round, golden rings. I also noticed, for the first time, that each one of the rings carried an engraving of a small, etched, black symbol on its outer surface. As I continued to walk around the sphere, I found another one of the symbols each quarter of the way around.

"Hence," I rationalized to myself, "if there are four different symbols on each of the three rings, then all twelve symbols are probably represented here. But, so what?"

I stopped and studied the rings as they were slowly turning counterclockwise, noting four significant facts.

First, the symbols on each ring mimicked the ones found in the arch and on the great tablet (to the best of my recollection). Second, all of the embedded black (or very dark green) symbols changed positions each time the ring came back around. Third, no two rings displayed the same symbol at the same time. Therefore, I think it is safe to assume that only one copy of each symbol revealed itself at any given time. Lastly, at least one of the rings at all times turned noticeably faster than the other two, but it was one of the remaining two that simultaneously and continuously glowed brighter.

I was quite pleased with the depth of my detective work, but it didn't bring me any closer to having the slightest idea what any of it meant. Looking over at Joshua, I smiled, ready to share with him everything that I had discovered. He smiled back and stepped up to join me directly in front of the sphere. In that same instant, before I could speak, the crystal sphere returned to its original speed, as did the three rings of gold. In doing so, the small, dark symbols on their surface could no longer be seen.

Then, suddenly, the ring's golden energy broke free of its cycle and expanded to first encompass all three rings and then everything within the jasper mist. Not stopping there, as if the crystal shell no longer mattered, this golden wave of unleashed energy continued to expand beyond the confines of the diamond as flowing, jasper-colored, clear smoke. It quickly left the confines of its crystal prison and pushed out in every direction.

Like a wave from a heat lamp, the released energy flashed through Joshua and me like a hot shower on a cold winter morning and then continued 360 degrees across the entire area and out of sight. The unexplainably weird and electrifying effect of the pulse passing through me at once made me feel invincible, as if I were made of stone, and even though at that moment I couldn't move any part of my body, my mind told me I could do anything my mind could imagine. At the same time, I felt emotionally drawn to the sphere the way water is sucked up by tissue. Consequently, as soon as I could move again, I took a step closer to it.

The compulsion to embrace the sphere and become part of its energy came from a deep spiritual longing to reunite with a passionate drive that felt like it once defined me. I raised my arms and wanted to just slam my body against the crystal shell, but I restrained myself and only reached out with both hands to at least touch it and feel where all that exuberant power came from. The urge was so strong that I didn't even hesitate; I reached out full force to complete my encounter.

I don't know if my fingers ever actually touched the divine crystal because I was suddenly swept back by a warm, almost hot wave of a full-impact force emanating several inches out from the sphere. Not only had it forcefully thrown my hands back, but also now my entire body was paralyzed, leaving me unable to move, speak, or do anything! Next, the sphere's energy effortlessly slid me back to the place I started from alongside Joshua, as a much milder version of the weird, electrifying effect gratified my deep desire for more. For a little while longer, I still couldn't move, nor did I want to, but the euphoric sensations rather quickly wore off.

The golden rings are as beautiful as they are powerful, I mentally commented in an overly deliberate and unnecessarily loud manner. I continued to remain motionless and keenly focused on them.

After staring at the pulsating rings and, unexplainably, thinking intensely about totally non-related things, like fishing with my dad when I was very young, I nonchalantly realized I could once again move. I turned, facing Joshua, and emotionally stated in a noticeable whisper, "I feel like they want to be part of me."

Joshua looked at me for a few moments, as if he were seriously debating whether to tell me something or not. Then he asked, "Do you not remember the rings?" He looked at me again like he was scanning my mind, and then he changed his demeanor back to his "normal" self and stated, "These rings are of divine energy. Early civilizations called them *Animus Dei,* meaning life or spirit of God. For countless generations, the rings commanded the respect of all societies. They were acknowledged and revered throughout the realms. They taught us to share in the communion of divine love as they spoke directly to our dual natures. As a gift from the Creator, the wisdom conveyed by the rings unites all the realms, joined in the sanctity and transparency of pure, divine love.

"Each golden ring represents an endless series of exact frequencies and vibrations, which, when combined with the others, tells the full story of the unbroken cycle of creation."

"So, the golden lines I saw in the archway, accompanying each of the twelve ancient symbols, actually tell a divine story?" I asked.

"All beings, in every realm, except those in the lower dimensions, know and understand the purpose of their being. Self-discovery and the immortality of shared thoughts allow each of us to see beyond the veil of solitude within our self-created prison of reality. This is where the limitless treasures of divine truth await discovery."

Joshua gently grasped both of my shoulders, looked deep into my eyes, and avowed, "Our true nature and the Creator's true nature are but one."

The depth of Joshua's statement implanted itself beyond my immediate understanding, but somewhere deep within me, it felt like he just put into words something I had always known.

Joshua took his hands from my shoulders and turned, facing the giant crystal. I followed his example and also turned and faced it. We silently watched the revolving globe for a moment or two, and then he sensitively remarked through his thoughts,

"Deception and complacency, without the safeguard of guided free will, obscure the clarity of true knowledge. The Creator knew that a balanced understanding of the duality of life would be lost in the absence of divine guidance. So, each of the realms was given a visual record of their own creation as a gift from their God."

"By visual record, do you mean a history book or movie covering all of humankind since the beginning of time?" I asked.

"Not only humankind, Jeremiah, all of creation. You must open yourself to greater realities. The wisdom and knowledge that can be taken in through your physical senses are only a preview of the comprehensive natures you possess. Divine perception originates directly within the soul, the center of all knowledge within every created being that links us to the very source of life." He paused and looked at me as if he expected a response. Of course, I couldn't think of anything even semi-thoughtful to say, so I just blankly stared back at him until he continued.

"Having received this visual record, each realm could understand its place within the magnitude of creation. With each window to the consciousness of the universe, all seekers of truth could see and understand the relationship of the Creator to the created, the universe to the cosmos, God to God, the divine order to every dimension within its creation, the relationship of creation to itself, and the significance of each dimension within the realms, especially time."

While realizing that I obviously missed the philosophical meaning and depth of whatever Joshua just said, I did catch the part about the Creator giving everyone "a visual record of their own creation," so I asked, "Joshua, what happened to that gift you said the Creator gave everyone? If all of creation received this gift, then doesn't that mean us humans received it as well?"

Joshua again grabbed me firmly by my shoulders, looked me straight in the eye, and stated, "The Creator's own personal account of creation and all that encompasses this realm of humanity is preserved for all eternity and manifested before us." As Joshua finished the sentence, he looked purposefully at the giant crystal. When I attempted to also shift my gaze to the jasper-filled globe, however, I found myself standing on a mountain peak overlooking a magnificent, snow-covered vista.

"Where are we?" I asked after looking out as far as I could over both shoulders and catching up with my thoughts.

"We are in that place where dreams are made," Joshua responded. With his right arm still embracing my shoulders, he made a sweeping motion with his left arm, his hand fully extended, and stated, "For countless ages, a collective perception of the divine filled every facet of the heavens and the dominions of the Earth. Through all of creation, the real meaning of that truth and the manifestation of it remained sanctified within the light through a gift of sacred crystals given to each realm. Eternally embedded within each of these crystals is the full story of creation."

Joshua looked at me and smiled.

"This gift was given to all the realms, within their respective dimensions, to ensure their knowledge of divine love was not lost. The sacred crystals helped the children stay focused and centered on their spiritual well-being and the true meaning of life. When the inhabitants of the Earth realms multiplied and diversified throughout their domains, more crystal artifacts, twelve in all, were manifested—one for each tribe, in every realm.

"Each of these sacred crystals was specifically designed to be understood and cherished by those who would be enlightened through them," Joshua exclaimed.

"They bring inner peace and balance to all the races through a deep understanding of their place in the order of creation. Through the gift of the sacred crystals, humans could witness the totality of their own existence, share the thought that gave form to the Earth, the sky, the plants, and animals, and breathe in that first breath of humanity itself in the same spiritual state that their ancestors did." As Joshua told the story of the sacred crystals, his words filled me with a powerful sense of belonging.

"So, the Creator gave each of the realms their own sacred crystals as a divine gift," I said, excited about what I now at least partially understood.

"Go on," Joshua said with an approving look.

"And these sacred crystals actually tell us not only the whole story of creation, but the reason for life itself?" I asked.

"Your capacity for understanding is improving," Joshua affirmed.

He continued.

"For the benefit of those of the physical dimensions, each one of the sacred crystals embodied a particular symbolic shape, a likeness that would be recognized by those to whom it belonged. The Creator entrusted it to the wisest of each tribe to be guarded and treasured until the end of the age."

As Joshua said this, I remembered a story my dad told me years ago about some archeologist finding a perfectly shaped, clear, crystal skull that was thousands of years old. It was so anatomically precise that it could not even be duplicated with modern-day lasers. The thought of it suddenly popped into my mind as if it was some sort of enhanced memory. I closed my eyes and could see a perfectly shaped, crystal skull clearly illuminated on a marble stand with a dark, crushed velvet material behind it. As Joshua continued, I realized that the crystal skull I had heard about probably *was* one of the original sacred crystals, and I wondered what ever happened to it.

Joshua continued.

"Do you now recall the sacred crystals, Jeremiah?"

I nodded, keeping my eyes closed.

"These gifts, given to all the children throughout the Earthly realms, were treasured as the most sacred of gifts to be cherished for all eternity."

As Joshua said this, more three-dimensional images and enhanced visions flooded my mind and my senses. Ancient scenes flashed in and out of my view. I saw not only the flawless, crystal skulls of the human species, but other ones belonging to our spiritual cousins of the other realms as well. Some of them were made of clear crystal, and others with very distinctive colors, predominantly clear shades of greens, reds, and gold.

"Yes, Joshua, I see them!"

"The sacred crystals not only carried the knowledge of the Creator, but an understanding of the other realms, as well."

I opened my eyes and asked with excitement, "Do all of the realms still have their twelve sacred crystals?"

"The twelve crystals of each realm, just as this, the first crystal, which Ariana brought before us and which binds the sanctuary of the heavenly realm with all those that followed, are of divine origin, the essence of which is as eternal as the thought that created them."

I looked intently into Joshua's eyes and allowed his beliefs to fill me with a clear understanding of the memory and promise of the sacred crystals.

"I remember, Joshua," I whispered while staying keenly locked in his gaze. "I remember how the beams of heavenly light would release the energies of the crystals and charge our souls so that we *knew* a direct union with the Creator."

"Good! You do remember," Joshua said, breaking my deep concentration. "Do you recall the teachings of the crystals that spoke of the divine plan for creations yet to come?"

So many memories and thoughts started cascading through my mind. I think maybe Joshua was allowing me to tap into his memories, but they were going too fast to keep up with them.

Joshua continued.

"All the realms cherished their sacred crystals, knowing they were of divine origin. These great treasures, known to all through sacred writings, songs, and storytellers, brought praise and glory to both creation and the Creator. One of the tribes went so far as to house it in a beautiful golden ark."

"The Ark of the Covenant?" I asked.

"Do you remember the golden ark?" Joshua asked.

"Only from movies," I mumbled. "Whatever happened to that sacred crystal and to the ark?"

"Through a direct proclamation from the Creator, the powerful Earth-angels could neither touch nor interfere with the use of the crystals. They did, however, possess their own free will to influence people who could."

My eyes lit up as Joshua's story became more intriguing.

"After the separation, religious leaders started to grow more and more powerful. They began monitoring and restricting those who sought to understand life through these divine gifts. Before long, access to the sacred crystals, which had been given to *everyone*, was severely limited, by those same religious leaders, to only themselves and those they deemed worthy, which usually involved a considerable amount of valuables, such as gold or land. This forced some to resort to secret gatherings where they could still teach all the wonders of science and creation they devoutly learned through the wisdom of the crystals."

"Such as the Druids?" I asked.

"Many societies since the beginning of time have understood that a divine plan holds together the entire fabric of the universe, Jeremiah."

Joshua paused and then softly affirmed, "This divine plan as well as direct interventions by the Creator, many of which still go unrecognized or misunderstood, have profoundly influenced civilizations throughout the ages.

"The powerful religious leaders understood and feared the consequences of revealing the truth of creation and knowledge of the Creator to the people, knowing that doing so would undermine the very foundation of their control and power. To prevent this, they stopped allowing anyone access to the crystals. They knew these divine gifts could not be destroyed, so they did everything in their power to hide them from the people. To accomplish this, they removed all written accounts of them from sacred texts. That is how and why all of these sacred artifacts 'mysteriously' disappeared in such a short time. Even stories about them were labeled heresy and forbidden to be spoken of in public under penalty of a very painful death."

"So is that why no one has ever found the golden ark?" I asked.

A slight movement out of the corner of my eye prompted me to glance over my right shoulder. Once again, I found myself inexplicably placed among the gathering of angels, still alongside Joshua, looking directly at the spinning diamond orb. I straightened my stance to again face Ariana, standing next to the crystal, about twenty feet in front of us. Ariana looked at me and smiled. Her smile stirred me deeply. I smiled back in a young boyish way and wanted to say something, but ...

A bright, warm light fell upon us, and I could no longer speak. Following Ariana's example, we all reverently knelt in exaltation to our creator whose spirit manifested its presence in our midst. As the warm, penetrating light permeated my entire body, I closed my eyes and listened. A resilient, loving voice echoed throughout the room. I knew it *had* to be the voice of God.

"That which has come to pass, concerning the creation and destruction of the flesh, has brought forth a new horizon of enlightenment and truth. The end of the age again is at hand; the gathering hastens its arrival. Be vigilant in your devotion to faith, uncompromising in your fidelity, and generous with your love. In this manner, I will fulfill the promise I have made to you."

The subsiding of the light cued me to open my eyes, and in doing so, I witnessed a spectacular phenomenon happening inside the giant crystal. Tongues of fire rained down inside the orb, setting it aglow like Roman candles on a moonless night sky, pushing waves of peaceful energy in every direction. I could feel it revitalizing my very soul. Looking around, I knew that it had the same profound effect on all present. We were undeniably experiencing an intimate encounter with the divine.

Again, we heard the voice.

"As I am, so then are you, my beloved children. I have established my covenant with you and with all my children before you. This bond shall never be broken. Through my love, all sovereignty of judgment rests."

With these words still resounding through the multitude, we transcended time to the end of another era where the voice of the Creator was also clearly heard.

"I have grown impatient with humankind. I have seen their loathsome and wicked ways. Among themselves, they seek counsel, and unto the spirit of perdition, they find comfort. No longer do they ask for divine blessings or desire guidance in their lives; they would cast aside their very inheritance for the momentary pleasure of self. The immoral beings they have become reflect shame even onto the unclean spirits. The day is at hand when the corrupt carnal nature of humanity shall perish. That which is of the flesh will return to the domain from which it began life. When all the Earth is once again cleansed and a new beginning is at hand, the Spirit of God shall be known to all the dominions of this world and shall go forth in harmony with the whole of creation."

When the Creator finished speaking, I felt thoroughly energized yet completely relaxed. The rain of fire instantaneously ceased inside the crystal sphere, and in its place, once again, the three golden rings of divine energy appeared, suspended in the jasper mist.

Ariana stood motionless as she lovingly gazed into the sphere. The golden rings dissipated into a series of beautiful scenes of an ancient yet seemingly futuristic culture. Quickly moving from one scene to another, like a 3D movie on fast-forward, the panorama in front of us depicted the beginning and end of a divine journey.

"In the great temple of light," Ariana began narrating, "all the divine children of Earth, that is, all life within the Earthly realms, gathered in the circle of energy and love."

Through the enhanced images of the sphere, I witnessed multitudes of spirit beings joyfully descending onto a giant version of the wagon-wheel-shaped circle of stones Joshua and I had discovered at the end of the golden walkway.

Ariana continued, "In this state, the essence of the Creator would descend from heaven on a stream of the purest light and teach all who would seek enlightenment about the miracles of life and all the wonders of the kingdoms.

"Angels, who no longer resided in heaven but now lived upon the Earth, became elders and teachers of the humans. Thus, the Creator allowed them to partake freely of the Tree of Knowledge, which enabled them to evolve through wisdom and teach with prudence and understanding.

"As time passed, some of the more powerful Earth angels were not satisfied that the Creator so loved and trusted them that they alone had been blessed with unlimited, direct fellowship with their creator and infinite wisdom. Because free will permitted them to live and act in the same manner as the Earth beings they were sent to teach, they let their 'new' world influence their thoughts and cloud their judgments. With a growing desire manipulating their yearning for continuously wanting more, they began teaching not from divine wisdom but from their own interpretations and experiences. Thinking they already possessed as much knowledge as their creator, they grew tired of their Earthly restrictions and eventually abandoned the divine plan altogether. The strong prevailed, and the weak became enslaved and forced to build huge stone structures to honor the reign of the Earth angels and their chosen servants.

"They even began to experiment and manipulate the very foundations from which life emerges, and many of them slept with the daughters of mortals and created children by them. Without divine guidance, the Earth angels began to construe and teach the mysteries of the heavens and of life in a way that generated confusion and disharmony among all of the children of Earth.

"A self-proclaimed supreme leader, once highly favored by the Creator, emerged from among these Earth angels, slowly gaining the confidence of all those that followed him. His deep, reddish-purple eyes were captivating and his cunning words inviting. He brought unity and false security back to the Earth children by teaching them to focus entirely on themselves and trust in his interpretation of the divine plan instead of focusing on the spiritual strength of truth and love.

"Because of his commanding presence and persuasiveness, his followers, who also possessed exceptional intelligence and knowledge of the natural laws, scientific technologies, and unseen mysteries of creation, came to believe that they too had been created equal to their creator. The Earth angels convinced the human races that *they* alone understood and could influence the ultimate purpose and destiny of humanity. Their new powerful leader persuaded many of them to center their lives on uncompromising personal fulfillment through self-righteousness, as well as emotional and physical superiority. Therefore, the arrogant and the pretentious prevailed over the humble and meek. They lost sight of the very foundation of the divine teachings based on the light and love within their own souls.

"With his ability to move freely, both on and within the Earth realms, this powerful Earth angel planned to become the sovereign ruler of all the human races. Once he fully enslaved the Earth children within their own concept of what they believed to be their divine right, he planned to rule with unchallenged power over all their worlds until the end of his time.

"The much wiser ancient ones, the dolphins, told the Creator of the deceiver's plans, hoping that the Creator would stop him and save their spiritual brothers and sisters from a path of certain destruction. After being reminded of one of the Creator's greatest gifts, that of free will, however, they realized all would unfold as it was destined to be.

"Through visions, thoughts, and dreams, the Creator sent warnings that once darkness and greed clouded their minds and shadowed their souls, their own self-consumption would radiate throughout the reality they created. In its place, a new era of uncertainty and separation from the light would come forth. However, none would listen, so, by their own choosing, the misled children of the Earth brought on their own condemnation and annihilation.

"The Creator, frustrated and angry, was about to annihilate all creatures of the flesh when the ancient ones once again interceded on behalf of their brothers and sisters, begging for mercy on at least the innocent. They pleaded with the Creator, insisting that, because of the cunning words of the master of lies, and the gift given to him of superior intelligence, the less gifted children of the Earth were easily deceived into thinking themselves equal in essence to their creator.

"'Because they are only mortals and so easily fooled,' the dolphins pleaded, 'would it not be prudent for you, oh gracious creator of might and mercy, to only punish those who chose to accept a life of treachery and lies, keeping in mind they are mere mortals, possessing not the power nor the wisdom bestowed upon the angels. The one who leads the Earth angels is a spirit and not subjected to their weaknesses. It is he that misled your children. They, having the privilege of free will, should be subject to the consequences of their own making, but, being just and compassionate, should not all those who remained faithful be spared by your mercy?'

"The Creator listened earnestly to the request of the dolphins and permitted them to travel to all the ends of the Earth in search of any whose innocence should spare them. They searched and searched, but the master of deceit, with his army of Earth angels, had already found a way to unite the whole world as one. By giving them leaders of their own choosing, he could let the people condemn themselves, by perpetuating and justifying their own lies while preaching and proclaiming words of hope and invoking the name of their 'God.' As long as people were gullible enough to believe everything their civil and quasi-spiritual leaders told them, the Earth angels needed only to wait. Eventually, through the death of their wisest elders, peer pressure, and the powerful sway of public opinion, enough doubt and deception permeated the land until unfaltering faith and complete trust in the truth of the Creator completely vanished, first from everyday life and then even from *true* interpretations of their own holy scriptures.

"The dolphins searched the entire planet in pursuit of any innocent souls, but their search came up empty. In the end, they could only return to the Creator with heavy hearts, saddened by the realization that not one would be saved. However, in admiration for the love and devotion displayed by these wise creatures, the Creator told the dolphins that their selfless determination would not be in vain.

"On that day, the Creator made a covenant with the ancient ones. A promise that one family representing every living creature of the flesh that belonged in the Earth realm, including the human races, would be spared destruction. However, there would be a non-negotiable set of conditions.

"Following the first fall from grace, the Creator rightfully took away the gifts of human immortality and ultimate wisdom. Since those early times, many generations passed, and humans once again turned their back on their creator and the divine opportunity given to them to experience direct spiritual enlightenment. Beginning with this new age, the children of the Earth would no longer speak one language. The human tribes would no longer communicate freely with the other animals, or even with each other.

"To ensure this, the Creator, who originally gave all creatures the ability to remember and understand the wisdom of the ages, reduced their mental capacity down almost to the level of mere survival. In addition, since time governs the depth of knowledge, understanding, and wisdom that a lifetime of learning reveals, the life cycle of all creatures, including the humans, would be only one year for every seven they previously enjoyed.

"The ancient ones again beseeched the Creator. 'All-powerful and loving Creator,' they pleaded, 'if your children are no longer born with the light and understanding of your infinite wisdom as well as awareness of the realms, will they still comprehend the divine essence of life?'

"The Creator replied, '*My beloved ones, the knowledge and understanding of the natural worlds, as well as the mysteries intrinsic to all the realms, is derived from love itself. To search elsewhere would fall short of the spirit of creation.*

"'*Yet, if I again empowered each soul with this information freely, it would once again be taken for granted or be as unrealized as the passing of inspirations through dreams.*

"'*Therefore, I will not reveal or endow this understanding on any of my children. Neither will I keep it hidden from them. They must discover it on their own, for it will always be in their possession. They will carry it with them throughout eternity, a gift that will never be taken away.*

"'*Remember that understanding the fullness of love carries with it a great responsibility. When love and truth join with faith, righteousness and peace will ultimately prevail. When my children realize and accept this truth, life filled with enjoyment and peace, which comes through wisdom, will be theirs. Bear in mind, awareness brings forth its own vindication, thus it will be cherished or feared accordingly.*

"'*Peace, healing and strength in body and soul will be freely given to all that seek it through love. To obtain it, they need only ask, but to recognize it, they must be pure in heart. As before their separation, all my children will have the capacity to know the design and tenacious nature of their creator. However, they must first bring their natures to a level of enlightenment worthy of such knowledge.*'

"The ancient ones seemed very pleased with the Creator's plan but concerned that no mention had been made of the destruction of darkness and the domain of the Earth angels.

"'But, what of the evil one who claims dominion over all the realms of Earth?' the dolphins asked.

"'These creatures of flesh are no match for him. His reign will be unopposed and his harvest unending. Should he and the other Earth angels not then be destroyed by you, so your children may live in harmony and peace?'

"'*The covenant I made with all my angels shall never be broken,*' the Creator proclaimed.

"'*The time will come when they too will transform all that is now within their understanding, but first, much is to be learned of the character and knowledge of faith, humility, reconciliation, and free will. To this end, all my angels will play their part, that humans may be judged through the measure of their own wisdom and through their capacity to love and understand themselves and their bonds with one another.*'

"The ancient ones proved themselves true messengers of love and peace, as well as devoted and faithful emissaries. For their valiant efforts, the Creator bestowed upon them a special gift.

"'*For your wise intervention, on behalf of your brothers and sisters, you alone shall be spared and retain your wisdom throughout the ages.*'

"'*As for the rest of my children of the Earth, it is true that, as beings of flesh, they are no match for my Earth angels. Therefore, I proclaim that, until the end of the age, all creatures of the Earth will suffer the ills and weaknesses of their mortal existence. However, within them, my spirit shall be always present. From this day forward, as my children go forth into any realm, including the realms of humanity, an angel from heaven will always be watching over each of them.*

"'*I further decree that Abaddon, the teacher of fear and confusion, as well as his followers, will no longer be permitted to live and roam freely and unrestricted in or among mortals.*

He must reach out, in the spirit, from his own place but not of his own initiative. Where he is not invited, he will find no resting place.

"'*As my guardian angels go forth on their missions, they will be forever enlightened and encouraged by my love and understanding, through directives, which I will make known to all. Take comfort in these words, for they bring strength to the spirit when there is weakness in the flesh.*'

"The dolphins were happy with the covenant the Creator had given them, but saddened that not all of their spiritual brothers and sisters would remain on the Earth. The Creator had agreed to replenish the earth only with those creatures that were originally of the Earth.

"Therefore, the magical unicorns and beautiful winged horses, the mermaids and giants and enchanted little people—all the "travelers" that had made Earth their home—were sent back to where they had come from and asked to remain there until the Creator was convinced that humans could live in harmony with the rest of creation. Only then would they be permitted to return to the Earth realms and once again make them their home.

"When that which the Creator set forth came to pass and the end drew near for all creatures of the flesh, the ancient ones, with heavy hearts, could only watch and weep as a continuous rain covered the entire planet with water.

"Through the torrential storms, all that could be seen was a single ark, under the personal protection of the Creator, and the great evil dragon with his deep, reddish-purple eyes circling above it, waiting to begin again."

CHAPTER 12

UNCONDITIONAL LOVE

As the scene we just witnessed slowly faded back into the jasper mist, Joshua and I gave each other a look of understanding. I still felt saddened by the magnitude of what transpired, but grateful that the courageous dolphins were such wise and loving creatures. When I looked back, the sphere could no longer be seen. In its place, Ariana once again held the remarkable, sparkling diamond.

The brilliance of that extraordinary gem perfectly complemented the radiance of Ariana's long, fiery, golden-red hair. Her beauty and the ever-changing splendor of her aura put my mind in a fantasizing spin. She shifted her gaze directly toward me, and I could feel my heart racing. She was so beautiful, so perfect; just looking at her made my palms sweaty, and I felt myself smiling uncontrollably. All I could think about was getting closer to her and being able to share my feelings with her.

I closed my eyes and imagined her warmth. When I looked back at her, she smiled the most loving smile, and I knew she could hear my tender thoughts. With the gentleness of a soft breeze, she moved in very close to me and took my hands in hers. I looked over at Joshua, and he smiled and nodded his approval. Hand in hand, with our eyes and thoughts locked in a heartwarming bond, we drifted upward as Joshua and the others faded from view. We ascended through the clouds toward her angelic domain without either of us saying a word.

She took me to a place of celestial solitude where I knew our most intimate thoughts would be ours alone, and our hearts could beat as one. Then she moved into my inner space, and our bodies touched as our fingers smoothly locked in a loving embrace. I gently placed my hand on her back and immediately felt the pulsating heat of her aura as I delicately pulled her closer. She held me in her arms with an angel's touch and laid her head on my shoulder. Her skin was as soft as a newborn baby, and her eyes sparkled like diamonds. The clouds magically vanished, revealing a picturesque clearing on a tropical island, with a magnificent waterfall reflecting the brilliance of a full moon. A Hawaiian-style sonata soothingly whispered through the swaying palms, inviting us to dance slowly in step with the steel guitars and Pahu drums. A faint crashing of the plunging waterfall added nature's rhythm to the harmony. She felt so soft and warm. Nothing else mattered.

When Ariana twirled, the sheer covering of her chiffon gown lifted to bare her perfectly toned legs. Her equally illuminating, low-cut top would have exposed the perfection of the rest of her heavenly form had it not been for her long, golden-red hair that flowed across her bosom like two delicate leaves hiding the beauty of a flower. I drew her in close, and as my cheek ever so lightly brushed along hers, I whispered softly in her ear, "I've been waiting to talk to you."

"Be silent! Pay attention!" Joshua said, as he painfully poked me in the ribs, sending a brisk pain all the way up to my face and down to my feet, abruptly ending my daydream and forcing me to open my eyes.

Ariana was still standing in the same place in front of us, and she began to speak.

"Embrace that which has been given to you by our creator. Throughout your journey, it will bring forth comfort, strength, understanding, and perseverance. As a foundation for the testimony you are destined to discover, let it empower, guide, and protect you as you continue on your chosen path."

When Ariana stopped talking, she released her hold on the massive gem, closed her eyes, and raised her hands in a prayerful gesture. The mysterious diamond slowly floated up to a point in front of her, about three feet above her head, and then it began revolving slowly in a clockwise direction. As the turning motion increased, it not only picked up speed, but sound, as well.

From where I stood, it sounded like blowing wind, the echoing sound that you hear on a cool fall evening when a brisk breeze is pushed along by an impending storm charging through the treetops. Apparently, it created only the sound because I felt no actual wind.

The great diamond spun faster and faster, once again morphing its shape into something spectacular. This time, it evolved into a ball of spectacular energy, revealing ultra-vivid red, yellow, and orange waves. It blazed like a flaming marble. Then, all at once, it stopped turning, fell silent, expanded upward and outward, and exploded without making a sound into hundreds of individual droplets of fiery energy, which gently descended on and energized each one of us.

At the climax of this phenomenon, my eyes stayed keenly focused on Ariana. When the fiery tongue touched her aura, it ignited her entire silhouette like a Fourth of July sparkler. Then it traced the curves of her body as it slowly transcended from her head to her feet and disappeared, but her aura remained supercharged. Since the same thing simultaneously happened to all of us, I know she felt it as a warm, tingly gust of immeasurable happiness.

The sparkling energy sensation, as breathtaking as it looked and felt, could not match the feelings that tickled all my emotions every moment I studied the incredible beauty of Ariana. I stared at her for several distinct heartbeats, wondering whether I would ever get the chance to get closer to her. I am not sure if I believed in love at first sight before I saw her, but now ... if only ...

She opened her beautiful, dark eyes wide, looked straight at me, and smiled. Not just any smile; she displayed the most infectious, inviting, perfect smile I'd ever seen. With a boyish embarrassment, I smiled back with all the passion I could muster. All of a sudden, in an unanticipated paradigm shift, she rapidly floated directly toward me. My mind slapped me speechless, and I couldn't move. Stopping only inches away, she looked deeply into my eyes with a loving but parenting sort of no-nonsense, intense look. Her almost black eyes were as excitingly alive as the big, innocent eyes of a puppy.

We continued to share deep eye contact for a short but very satisfying moment. Then, just before my brain could catch up with my emotions, an amazing transformation took place. Ariana's eyes, her face, and then everything around us dissolved into a new but familiar reality.

I found myself staring into the excited, loving eyes of my young mother as she smiled and rocked me gently back and forth. She gazed down upon me with so much love in her eyes that her entire countenance beamed with joy. I felt so safe and secure. I returned her love in the facial, wiggling, giggling, "I am so happy to be alive and here with you" way that only a baby can, when again, the scene changed.

My mom's eyes transformed into the older eyes and caring face of my Grandma Busia as I, in my little Catholic schoolboy uniform, reached the vestibule of the church and ran smiling into her arms. She hugged and kissed me and told me how very happy and proud she was of me receiving my First Communion. Holding my young face in her hands, she looked fervently into my eyes. Beneath her glasses, her tears of joy followed the creases of her well-aged face, and I felt the all-encompassing intensity of her love.

As her glasses faded away and the outline of her face shifted, I experienced myself being thrown into the air caught up in the overabundance of excitement and wild animal yelps of my dad. He gave me a huge twirling hug and said how much he loved me and how proud he was of my first Little League homerun. He reminded me I could do anything I put my mind to and showed off the biggest smile I had ever seen. I kept staring into his eyes. They sparkled and smiled, and I felt so much love. I couldn't have asked for a more caring and loving father.

The joyful vision of my dad faded away, replaced by quite a different but very pleasurable vision, this one affecting my entire being. I felt the super-intense, trembling fear and unimaginable wave of excitement that joined forces at my lips when Pam, the girl of my dreams, the only girl I could ever love forever and ever, kissed me for the first time in the basement of her parents' house.

With my passionate gaze still locked into her young eyes, my body still tingled as my surroundings evolved one more time from my first love to my greatest love, that of my two boys. At only five and seven years old, they together fixed and brought me breakfast in bed for my birthday. I felt so moved and loved them so much that it seemed like my heart would burst, and I wept for joy over how much I have been blessed. I closed my eyes and held them tight, hoping and praying that they knew how very much I loved them.

When I opened my eyes, I found myself again looking into the flawless, celestial face of Ariana.

"There are many ways to express, appreciate, and cherish that which we find beautiful and desirable. But true love is seen not *with* your eyes, but through them, with your heart." She said this with a heartbreaking smile as she floated back to within an arm's length away.

"You have experienced true love throughout your life, Jeremiah, and it will be with you always. Keep it close to your heart, remember it often, and help others to do the same in their lives. With love in their hearts, they too will remember, and through that remembrance, they will be able to restore the power of love given to them at birth, when pure love became life, through pure light."

As she said this, Ariana's multicolored aura lit up in an electrifying display, and her whole being personified the pure love of the divine one. The perfect blending of ever-changing rainbow colors highlighted the outline of her unblemished complexion in a supernatural way that looked so incredible I just wanted to touch her. Neither one of us spoke, but she continued to look deep into my eyes. I hoped she could read my mind and my intentions as Joshua and the other angels could. When she smiled and moved closer, I felt confident it would be okay.

I nervously brought my slightly trembling fingers slowly up toward her face and could feel the heat and energy of her aura reflecting off my own. Still gazing very intensely into her warm, dark eyes, I believe my fingertips touched her cheek, though I am not sure we actually touched. In that instant, an inexpressible surge of unconditional love and joy filled my entire being, and at that same instant, she vanished in a wisp of golden mist. I closed my eyes and felt renewed in a metaphysical, spiritual, and emotional union more complete than any words could ever express.

Ariana's moving gift lifted me from the void of spiritual darkness into the light and warmth of a new beginning. Totally unrestricted, totally myself, I felt embraced and held, cherished as most precious, loved with an intensity and a passion that became at once immediate and eternal, and reminded in the deepest sense what it feels like to know true, unconditional love, bathed in the assurance that true love is not bound by time, not now, not ever.

When the feeling subsided enough so I could open my eyes, I found myself moving in slow motion. I turned to the right, once again conscious of Joshua's presence alongside of me. I realized in an almost out-of-body presence that he seemed to be calling my name.

As time snapped back to normal, so did our appearance. We no longer physically looked like angels, and there were no longer any other angels standing behind or alongside of us. We once again stood only in the company of each other.

It took me a very full moment before adjusting to my present reality where I could once again speak. I summoned my attentiveness and asked, in a still recovering whisper, "Where did she go? Where are the others?" I felt like I just unwittingly awoke from an eternal daydream and clearly missed everything going on all around me.

"What others do you speak of?" Joshua asked in a serious query.

Somewhat surprised by his answer and not too sure at this point which reality, if any, could be considered real, I merely looked at him standing there with his usual straightforward, no-nonsense expression. Then I chuckled, shook my head, and said, "Never mind."

When I looked back in the direction where Ariana originally came from, I saw only a concentrated pinpoint of light. It came from a spot about thirty feet to our left front but only lasted a microsecond before spontaneously expanding, shooting outward into thousands of beams like a disco ball full of lasers.

I quickly looked over at Joshua for an explanation, only to find him wide-eyed and staring in the direction of the light source. His peaceful countenance turned into a growing smile that compelled me to trade the light show for a unique opportunity to capture the assurance I felt in the face of this little giant of a man. His eyes smiling in a very fulfilling manner and the brilliant flashing illuminating his face heightened the sense of joy I suddenly felt pulling me into an understanding; I really did not understand, but I knew that it was okay.

At that moment, like a dark cloud snatching up the sun, a shadow slid down the face of Joshua and continued, uninterrupted, crawling toward his feet. I quickly turned my head to see what was happening and followed the motion with my body, just in time to catch it face on.

CHAPTER 13

THE SACRED BOOK

ANIFESTING ITSELF BEFORE US, IN midair, slowly
descending on a beam of golden light until reaching a
height about chest high and firmly resting on nothing, I found
myself once again experiencing, in full optical ecstasy, the large,
pure white, surreal book I was introduced to while I visited the
cathedral in meditation. It centered itself above an unexplainably
illuminated, three-tiered, sparkling clean, clear glass or crystal,
round platform. Our deliberate angelic positioning left us
standing about five feet from the base of the platform.

Everything seemed the same as when I visited this chamber
before, except for the obvious absence of the previously centered
and sadly missed, flawless, crystal pedestal. Joshua and I both
glanced at each other and smiled. I looked above us at the
timeless stained-glass masterpieces and the prominent, gold-
embossed, glass-domed ceiling, confirming my welcomed return
to the Hall of Angels. When I looked back down at the large,
radiant, white book, it, without any rational explanation, once
again now rested on its clear, crystal pedestal, surrounded by its
protective, bluish-white halo of light energy.

Triggering my previous memory of this heavenly expressive
place, I gazed out across the room and discovered it once again

filled with thousands upon thousands of beautiful kneeling angels, each holding a single, exceptionally bright, white candle glowing passively, like a moonlit pond. My soul applauded in unison with my thoughts.

Looking back toward the crystal pedestal and book, I found myself facing the Archangel Michael gallantly standing guard behind them. He looked at us briefly and rendered a salute with drawn sword and a heartwarming smile. Then, bringing his sword back to his side where it abruptly faded away, he motioned for us to join him on the platform.

This place—this amazing place, and the book—and all the angels … it made me feel so important, so honored. I glanced at Joshua with exhilaration and ceremoniously proceeded up the three steps toward the Archangel Michael, stopping about five feet in front of the book.

"Peace be with you, Jeremiah," Michael said energetically.

"Peace be with you, too," I responded, delighted to again be in the presence of this mighty archangel and this divine book. For some reason, just being here filled me with such a strong sense of belonging that I felt like all those kneeling angels were my friends and family. I closed my eyes, and an intimate flow of nostalgia coated every one of my deepest feelings. I felt Joshua standing behind me and opened my eyes as Michael addressed us.

"As you have witnessed, that which is, is that which shall be, when the remnants of time are forever swept away by the winds of truth, which will endure forever."

I smiled and nodded in humble confusion as I stepped a little closer to the diamond-like pedestal and book.

"Is he now ready to fulfill his destiny?" Michael asked Joshua.

"We will see," Joshua responded without looking at me.

I didn't know what to think of their comments. But, with this remarkable Archangel standing directly in front of me, Joshua standing next to me, and that incredible, radiant book and crystal pedestal only inches from my grasp, I was feeling more blessed than anyone could hope for in a thousand lifetimes. I was ready to take on any task they had in mind.

With another quick glance into the large arena-style room, I smiled contently at the multitudes of kneeling, white-gowned angels silently watching in anticipation. When I realized that they were all smiling back at me, the most incredible sense of awe shivered through me. When I looked up at Michael, he gestured with his eyes and open palms toward the distinguished book, so I took a couple of short steps, leaving me within arm's reach of the pedestal, and shifted my concentration back toward the book.

As Michael slowly lowered his hands, the thin, transparent, fiery blue energy that created a seal around the book and pedestal faded away, revealing a now clearly visible, dark, three-dimensional, raised symbol adorning its cover. Fearing the symbol might vanish as quickly as it appeared, I took a half-step closer, and hurried to examine it more closely while the book was still closed. It was then that I realized the elaborate design portrayed a three-dimensional copy of the same symbol that transfigured itself on the colossal tablet. It looked to be about the size of my fist and seemed to be intricately hand carved from a very dark-colored, solid green stone.

I tried to study the symbol long enough to firmly fix a picture of it in my mind for future recollection, but just when I decided what I needed to do, the ancient symbol began to vibrate at a speed so fast that it appeared blurry. Then, just as a symbol on the great tablet had previously done, it fragmented into tiny pieces. Rather than spiraling into its own center though, it transformed itself into a translucent page of sprawling, three-dimensional, ancient writing, floating slightly above the book's cover. The entire page then immediately disappeared, literally dissipating into the book. In its place on the book's cover, yet not quite making contact with it, there appeared three interlocking rings of gold, each rotating inward upon itself.

The bracelet-size golden rings, though moving as one, indescribably turned both clockwise and counterclockwise at the same time while still remaining centered on each other. I watched with great anticipation as they continued to turn faster and then faded into an airy jasper mist that enveloped the book like a soft layer of morning fog on a Tennessee mountain lake.

The book slowly opened, as if an invisible hand was doing its bidding, and there, appearing in the same ancient script we saw on the tablet, a copy of the directives presented itself to us. The symbols, written in calligraphy of gold lettering, fleetingly raised themselves about an inch above the page. As the letters settled back down onto the luminous page, however, they blazed like a red-hot branding iron and immediately turned the blackest black while translating themselves into modern English. It was quite a sight to see.

Joshua put his hands on my shoulders and gently turned me toward him. He looked deep into my thoughts, and in a slow and fatherly manner, he stated, "You have seen many things, and now your searching has brought you here to rendezvous with your destiny. Providence has guided you so the searching of others will lead them to discover the path *you* set forth."

After clearly getting my attention with that mind-bewildering statement, Joshua directed me with a gesture of his hand to focus my attention back on the book. I wanted to take some time to analyze and figure out what Joshua just told me. More importantly, I wanted to know exactly what he expected of me, but my eyes took over control of my thoughts, and all I could do was stare at the mystifying writings in sedated silence. A warm rush of peace and tranquility instantly filled my body.

Compelled to close my eyes, I transitioned into a meditative state. I remained completely alert, however, and became acutely aware of the divine presence all around me.

In this introspective state, a voice, which I'm sure was the voice of the Creator, echoed through every segment of my mind. The voice came from a faraway, unreachable place, yet it felt like it emanated from the core of my being. I reverently listened to the words, and they carried me to an eternal location of solitude deep within my own inner sanctuary.

In that sacred place, all the beings of light gathered before the presence of pure light to receive the promise of comfort and love that would accompany us on our journeys. We knelt in front of the crystal pedestal in silence, holding a single bright candle. The Archangel Michael, carrying a large, glowing, white book in his powerful arms, approached us, floating as gracefully as an eagle riding a mid-autumn breeze. He placed the radiant book upon the pedestal. We knew it to be the book that holds the secrets of divine thought, the Book of Eternities, the God's book.

Michael took a step away from the book, folded his mighty wings back, and assumed a stance of guarding, as the voice of our creator addressed our gathering and echoed benevolently throughout the assembly.

"*In my own image,*" the Creator began, "*we created the human races so that our children everywhere would be one in spirit with all that dwell within the realms. Through the sanctified light of truth, experience leads to knowledge, and knowledge becomes wisdom.*

"*I sent my spirit to be with all creatures, great and small, known and unknown, so they would carry in their souls the protection of divine love. Surely, I say to you, all the Earthly children are blessed, but you, my beloved, are the chosen ones.*

"*In these realms, you will be guardians of a covenant sealed at the very beginning of the age. As proclaimed in the book, all will be remembered. Witness and partake in all that is within your perception while remaining faithful to your charge.*

"*Receive the understanding consecrated in this oath and personified through me. It marks the beginning and the end of eternity, the freedom and imprisonment of immortality, and the finality of infinity. For these words hold the covenant to the ceaseless atonement of time.*

"*These directives, given by my hand, will provide the strength and enlightenment through which all my children will return to the source of all knowledge. This declaration will guide you to a love and understanding which will be instantaneously recognizable and always available within and throughout your Earthly endeavors.*"

I couldn't tell how much time had passed after the silence began; the inner peace felt so complete that nothing else mattered. When I did finally open my eyes, I felt transformed and refreshed, as though awakening from a long, much-needed sleep. I found myself numbly staring directly at the glowing page containing the directives until my mind caught up with my emotional state. Looking up at Michael, I smiled profusely.

"I think I just experienced that very moment when the directives were first given to us."

"Look at the words in the book," Michael stated with an acknowledging smile. "What you see is written in your native tongue, on a level of understanding that is comfortable and meaningful to you. However, since the Creator is the author, these words will be seen and understood by whoever reads them at their own level of understanding."

Michael looked deep into my eyes.

"Is this clear to you?" he asked.

"Yes, it is," I deliberately replied.

"Then embrace your commission and commit to memory that which is before you," he commanded.

"But always keep in mind," he added, "it is not your duty or privilege to question or interpret what you see. You have been brought to this point and time only to bring the directives back to those who have forgotten the source of their own thoughts and the true dynamics of the power they possess."

The Archangel Michael leaned closer and concluded, "Describe fully, every detail you perceive, making clarity and completeness your paramount concern. You must convey this message of love and remembrance to the lost, as well as the enlightened, bearing in mind the directives are a gift to all the children. Many who hear the words will only remember and understand at the level of awareness to which they have grown accustomed. Most, out of fear and self-doubt, will choose to remain spiritually asleep and willfully unaware. You must awaken the spiritual phoenix within them!"

Joshua added, "This is your calling, Jeremiah. You are the chosen one commissioned to be the messenger of this celebrated revival. The extent of truthfulness and completeness depends on you. All who search for the truth and are willing to accept it will find themselves spiritually transformed by your words."

I stood silently staring at the book, my mind racing through incomplete possibilities as I tried to lock onto one that would capture the enormous responsibility they were giving me. *So, this is where all these deep meditations were leading me?* I thought. I looked back at my companions and nervously joked, "I sure hope you guys have a backup plan."

My comment had been an obvious attempt to cover up my fear of failure with humor, but I'm sure they could detect the apprehension and uncertainty in my voice. Joshua and Michael only smiled at me without addressing my pleading remark.

"Portray the details of the book to us as it is revealed to you," Michael directed, "and we will help you understand on a level that is comfortable for you. Remember that others who study your words will only see what you see clearly, *if* your descriptions allow them to do so."

I looked at the two pages facing each other and, with a long sigh, started to read the first sentence.

"Okay, it says—"

"No, Jeremiah," Joshua interrupted abruptly, "you must describe *everything*. Do you think any part of this sacred document could be trivial? Everything the Creator has authored is by design; that which you may think inconsequential could be of profound importance to another. Start again and leave nothing out."

I studied his solemn look; he never blinked. Re-examining the book, I began again.

"Centered at the top of the first page ..." I suddenly needed to stop talking and involuntarily slammed shut my eyes as memories and images from an unknown source began flooding my mind, diverting reality away from my cognitive grasp. This time, however, it filled me with more than only pictures and sounds. All the quickly changing images came accompanied with a complete understanding of the meaning behind them.

An untraceable period of time must have passed before my thoughts maneuvered themselves back to the consciousness of my surroundings. I felt recharged with a newfound confidence and ready to accomplish this privileged task. Looking back down at the book, I continued to express what I saw. I, however, clearly no longer steered the course of my own words or ideas. My total responsiveness seemed channeled through a divine reality I could not begin to explain or understand. All the thoughts streaming through my mind instantaneously collated and manifested themselves in a live, three-dimensional scene before us. I know that my enhanced ability to clearly explain everything I witnessed so flawlessly came directly from this elevated state of presence and consciousness. Even my own voice took on an enhanced overtone.

"Centered at the top of the first page," I began in an enlightened manner, "is the symbol chosen to represent all the human races. The symbol shows the divine blessing of humankind with the duality of living in the flesh while having an immortal, eternal soul. This gift from our creator reminds us, and all the human races yet to come, that we are protected by divine grace."

As the raised symbol transfigured itself before us, thoughts and words filled with a primordial knowledge of a profound truth entered my mind. I felt deeply privileged for the insight given me to convey its meaning to my companions and myself.

"It shows that there are at least seven levels of grace, given specifically to all the human races, which are reflected in auras around each and every individual. They are spiritual layers of impenetrable armor forming a divine shield around the sacred thoughts that are the framework of our being. At each deepening level of grace, the revelation of a greater divine presence is present. This gift accompanies us throughout and beyond our Earthly lives.

"A divine gift of grace," I now understood, "that *only* the Creator has the power to give or take away."

Directly under the symbol, I read the story Ariana revealed to Joshua and me through the great diamond orb. It portrayed the events of the sacred crystal precisely as we witnessed them, but on a much more personal level. Starting with the words, *"My beloved children,"* the pictures and words conveyed the message more like one from loving and concerned parents.

I read aloud the story of the purge of humanity and the agreement made with the ancient ones to restore it. It still ended with the destructive cleansing of the great flood. However, following the story, the book revealed this solemn promise:

"From this time to the end of the age, not one of the divine children will ever be alone or forsaken, for the spirit of your creator will be with you always. On every level of existence, divine love will abound, and grace will keep you ever in its presence. It is in the fulfillment of this pledge that you have been given these Directives of Love."

I read aloud the last passage to my companions, knowing that they were hearing, as I was, the wondrous words of our creator. In that instant, we found ourselves removed from time and whisked away to a place that existed before the separation.

The three of us stood in a clearing on a mountaintop. I immediately recognized it as the same place where Metatron and his two companion angels had taken me to witness the prophetic images in the crystal orb through the eyes of Daniel and John. An endless multitude of angels gathered all around, including the Archangel Michael, Joshua, and me. We all stood in total silence and listened to the voice of the Creator as it echoed through our gathering.

"Throughout your journeys, divine presence and love will be glorified in all that you are and all that you choose to be. The knowledge of your true natures, both physical and spiritual, will be with you always. The will to accept or reject this truth rests with you alone.

"If you keep your spirit free from limitations, the fulfillment of your hopes and dreams will be forged along the pathway of truth through experience, wisdom, and time. Trust in the conviction of your soul and remember that nothing is so unless you choose it to be so.

"Remember to be pure of heart while in pursuit of your ambitions, for only those who fervently desire to remain devoted to the full presence and grace of divine wisdom will understand the inner strength required to do so.

"Maintaining the conscious balance of your dual natures will be greatly challenged by the desire for human experiences. This then must be your charge: strive for the greatest levels of understanding and discernment, knowing that you will be granted all that you seek, yet never more than you can grasp."

I looked up at Joshua and Michael as they both silently nodded and smiled. I joined them in wholehearted agreement as the divine words took on a more personal urgency.

"Be diligent in your efforts, for only a few will reach the highest level of awareness. Some will celebrate the reaching of false levels, and many will, by choice, remain lethargically ignorant to any higher realms of spiritual wisdom ... thus, this prophesy is written."

I looked again into the faces of my companions. Their expressions clearly reflected the same feeling of awe that I felt.

We once again found ourselves in the sanctuary that housed the Book of Eternities. I felt sure that being in the company of these two heavenly beings, they must have already been familiar with what we just experienced. Perhaps to allow me time to comprehend the significance of these powerful words, or maybe out of reverence for the divine author of them, neither spoke for several seconds.

Then Michael broke the silence.

"For all of us, a new day is at hand," he said in a soft tone as he nodded toward the book for me to continue. "Tell us about the directives."

The whole reality shift happened in such an unreal way, I could not say for sure whether we ever really left or perhaps just experienced some kind of ultra-real flashback, like reliving a forgotten memory. I again found myself in exactly the same position as before, looking down at the Book of Eternities without knowing what would happen next, but I knew in my heart and deep in my soul it would be an unforgettable experience of a lifetime.

CHAPTER 14

THE DIRECTIVES

"GO ON, JEREMIAH," JOSHUA SAID as if he had been patiently waiting for my response. "Continue to tell us what you see in the book." I looked back down at the gently glowing pages before me with a newfound confidence.

"The opposite page," I explained, while giving Joshua a quick glance just to be sure, "contains the directives themselves, as pristine now as they must have been when they first came into being at the beginning of the age. They are underlined but are not numbered, and in all, I count ten."

Memories of the emotional fulfillment and immense honor I felt when I first experienced this divine gift began to saturate my thoughts and pull me once again into a reminiscent reality. Michael leaned in close to me, whispering my name.

"Jeremiah."

He leaned back to an upright position, and, softly smiling, he stated, "They are not numbered, as the priority you place on each of the directives coincides with your own state of understanding and the degree of spiritual recognition you are prepared to accept."

"The directives were preordained to stimulate your soul, as well as your thoughts," Joshua added. "Each one will rekindle a profound spiritual awakening in everyone who sees or hears them and truly understands their meanings. They will bring forth divine reminders, in unfamiliar ways, of a simple but delicate balance found in the duality of human existence. For this reason, each directive will be interpreted and understood in the most personal way your comprehension can accept."

"You must keep this in mind as you share your testimony with others," Michael said cheerfully, "so they, too, can fulfill their innermost spiritual needs in terms that will bring them to the level of enlightenment and balance they desire to attain."

He paused and studied my face, I suppose to evaluate my understanding of what he meant. He obviously assumed I understood because he then smiled and requested, "Please read for us the first directive."

Standing close but making sure I did not touch the book, I glanced over at Joshua, thinking he might want to impose some final thought-provoking words of wisdom before I continued. He remained silent and unassuming, so I refocused my attention on the softly glowing pages.

"This is the first directive:

"Choose freely your own destiny, touching the essence of those that precede you, respecting the realms of those that have not."

I looked up at Joshua, eager to hear his thoughts, only to find myself looking into a full-length mirror. As my focus widened, I discovered the mirror, in actuality, consisted of three very large, full-length mirrors joined together in front of me. In their reflection, I could also see three mirrors identical to them behind me.

The mirrors in front of me reflected the images of the mirrors behind me in such a way that I saw within them countless reflections of me looking into the mirror. The effect could best be described as looking down a very long tunnel made up of progressively smaller copies of myself until my own image became too small to see. I turned around and looked behind me, then turned again and looked back in front of me. Since both sets of mirrors appeared to be identical, I saw exactly the same images regardless of how I faced them.

The clearly illuminated tunnel of images in the center mirror, directly in front of me, looked the same for the entire length of the reflections. However, the replicas in the mirrored tunnel on the right started out with abundant bright light but progressively darkened until the reflected images could no longer be seen. Instead, in its center, I saw only a tiny, black spot.

The mirrored tunnels of images on the left expressed exactly the opposite. They started out dark and barely visible and then progressively got brighter until they gathered into a single point of very bright light.

I found the visual sensation to be both chilling and fascinating. Then Joshua's voice spoke to me.

"In which image before you do you find truth?" he asked. "Do you see life's journey in the reflections that begin without light but at journey's end have become one with it? Or, do the reflections of life begin pure in light, free of all shadows, only to then grow in darkness until the light is no longer found?" He paused. "Perhaps, you would choose the middle mirror, which continues to be as it is and has always been, experiencing no lasting influence from the darkness or the light, ending precisely as it began."

Joshua stopped talking while I thought about the riddle he presented to me. Suddenly, he appeared alongside me, yet only *my* reflections were visible in the mirrors. He looked earnestly at me and explained, "Many images lie in front of you, and just as many lie behind you, yet the reflections are all your own."

I looked intently at the figures in the mirrors, and then Joshua continued, "Much can be learned from the experience of another, even when that other person is *you*."

I turned and faced him as he continued, "In the same manner, you must respect those whose experience is not yet known, either to themselves or to others. The secrets they uncover on *their* journey may be the very lessons *you* are charged to understand." He looked into my eyes and heightened the sincerity in his face.

After a brief pause, he continued, "Remember, you have been given the gift of life, and you must remain in control of it, rather than allowing it to control you. When you feel you are losing control and life's circumstances are getting the best of you, *that* is when you must find comfort and direction from those whose paths you cross as well as the teachings of the mirror. In doing so, you will find that the lessons you are facing are reflected off lessons of the past and are further directed back at the lessons yet to be learned. To look elsewhere, you will find only the reflections of others."

Joshua gave me only a few moments to think before interrupting my thoughts.

"Continue. Read for us the second directive."

In the time it took to hesitate, I found myself back in the Hall of Angels in front of the crystal podium and the Book of Eternities, with Joshua remaining at my side and the Archangel Michael still standing opposite us, smiling. I couldn't say for sure that he or I ever really left each other, but I was glad to be in their presence once more.

Both of my companions, without comment, gestured with their expressions for me to continue reading from the book. Beaming with youthful excitement, I hoped each directive would carry with it its own personal mind trip, if one could call it that.

I smiled and read aloud from the Book of Eternities.

"Understanding of your creator and of yourself must be recognized from within before fear of the unknown can be vanquished.

"Offer only counsel and guidance to those who have not yet reached your level of awareness and realize spiritual acceptance is often confused with emotional fulfillment."

I no sooner finished reading the last word when I looked up to find the most incredible view in front of me. With Joshua still standing alongside of me, we found ourselves atop a huge, flat rock on a snow-covered ridge overlooking a glistening, blue mountain lake. The ridgeline enclosing the lake suggested that we were now standing on the crest of a crater, perhaps belonging to an extinct volcano. Far below us, the calm, mirrored, deep blue water reflected the cloudless sun, making it almost blinding to look at.

"What is this place?" I asked as I scanned the majestic landscape before us. "It's absolutely breathtaking."

Joshua remained silent. He stood peacefully facing the lake with his eyes closed. Enjoying the full magnificence of the panoramic view before me, a study of the natural beauty all around us revealed a quite distinctive topography. From hardwood forests to desert to a frozen tundra, the mountainsides encircling the lake displayed every imaginable type of terrain. I witnessed sections completely barren of all vegetation right alongside others with a thick canopy of jungle growth.

Each area, like the individual wedges of a pie, joined with the next, fitting into a masterfully orchestrated ecological puzzle around the perfectly circular lake. Each distinct area offered its own unique characteristics to the whole, rendering it complete. I immediately noticed one thing in common with each pattern of the terrain; the presence of many, perhaps hundreds, of rivers, creeks, and tributaries winding their way down the mountain's sides to the picturesque lake below.

Without opening his eyes, Joshua addressed me.

"Study the profound complexity and simple beauty of all that is before you and consider precisely this one small piece of creation multiplied by the depth of the universe. Tell me, Jeremiah, what is the source and magnitude of its existence?"

I looked all around at the splendor before us and took great pleasure in the solitude of our surroundings. Of course, I had absolutely *no* idea what Joshua just asked me or how to respond at all to his perplexing question. However, before I could ask him what he had just said, he opened his eyes and simplified the question.

"Where does all the water come from?"

Since the section directly below where we stood represented one distinguished by a covering of packed snow, the answer to his question seemed rather obvious.

"It comes from the melting snow," I blurted out with confidence.

"And the snow?" he continued. "What of its origin?"

"Well, I am pretty sure it comes from the clouds that form as the water evaporates off the lake," I quickly responded, recalling memories of my high school Earth Science classes.

"There is truth in what you say," Joshua stated.

Finally, I thought to myself, quite elated, *he acknowledged my answer without turning it into a question. I think I may be finally keeping up with him!*

Joshua continued. "Each drop of water that travels down the mountain to the lake is only returning to where it started its journey," he said, with accompanying hand gestures. "It will then leave again, and again, always finding its way, in the end, back to its own origin. With each new journey, its pathway home is different. It may find its way quickly or it may linger, at times becoming stagnant. It may evaporate along the way and rejoin the clouds to start somewhere new. It may take a path that is straight and direct or one with many turns, falls, and obstacles. Yet it always, inevitably, returns to its own source, its own creation."

Joshua paused and gazed into my eyes.

"What of the lake itself?" he asked. "If all of the drops of water are created by the lake, and the lake is created by all the drops of water, then what is the origin of the water itself? If you believe in a God and believe that God is the Creator, would not that God then be the origin of the water?"

Before I could respond, Joshua asked, "What does this tell you of your own existence?"

He looked at me earnestly, reassuring me that his question was not rhetorical. Since I couldn't think of anything intelligent to say, I just gave him a clueless look and said nothing at all.

Maybe I'm not quite as ready to keep up with him as I thought, I silently admitted, waiting for him to continue. Joshua smiled.

"Every one of us begins our journey in the presence of the Creator," he stated. "When life's journey comes to an end, each will return to the place where they began, in the presence of their creator. This fate of mortal existence pays no regard to the degree of power, wealth, notoriety, or beliefs held by any person, which humans value so highly.

"Just as a drop of water will, in due time, complete its cycle, so too will each one of us find our way home. However, making the journey on its own, the drop of water often finds the passage down the mountain to be very slow and tedious. It is only when it joins the path of others and unites with them as one that the combined energy and strength of the whole are able to minimize and overcome many of the obstacles along the way. Together, they attain their final destiny with greater confidence and purpose. With each successive journey, learning from others that follow the same path, the way becomes clearer and the conviction of the journey itself ever deeper. Eventually, a well-established, free-flowing river forms.

"Does this great force, made by so many, mean it is the best or most correct way to finish the journey? Would you perceive it to be the easiest? Is it better to create your own path or spend the entire journey being carried along by the others? The numbers of pathways are endless, and their courses may be steady or ever changing. They may branch off into smaller streams or combine with others to continue with a single design. But you see, Jeremiah, in the end they will *all* become one with the same lake, the same source, the same creator."

I stared into Joshua's determined eyes and tried to understand the meaning he attempted to convey. I believe he wanted me to think about life's journey and the many choices we have to experience it, perhaps through one of the several different spiritual beliefs or religions. My thoughts took me back to my own search for the true meaning of God and religion.

Years of superficially delving into different church doctrines left me with fragments of ideas and experiences. My shabby rubble of virtuous interpretations filled my head with unresolved questions. However, when I recalled what Joshua just attempted to teach me, the complex yet simple example of the lake may have been confusing at first, but the basic analogy with religion surprisingly seemed relatively simple and actually made sense.

"Why does the whole idea regarding the vast differences between one set of beliefs and another seem not so different after all when, throughout my entire life, it was precisely because of those differences that the others seemed so threatening?" I wondered to myself.

"Sometimes it is difficult to see beyond the next bend when we limit our path to only that which lies directly in front of us. However, from here, the highest point on the mountain," Joshua explained as he scanned the horizon with his eyes and his outstretched hand, "we not only see where our journey will take us, we are also capable of seeing and understanding the pathways of others as well. To realize where your journey is heading and to see the paths it will cross along the way, you must view it from a higher perspective."

Joshua looked at me with loving, fatherly eyes, and I looked back at him with a slightly awakened sense of limited understanding. He shifted his glance to something over my right shoulder, so I instinctively turned my head and found myself staring into the unwavering face of the Archangel Michael. We once again had returned to the Hall of Angels containing the Book of Eternities. I smiled at Michael as he spoke.

"Have you been shown the strength of belief or the power of faith?" Michael asked.

It sounded like a great question for which I had no great answer. In fact, before I could think of any answer or even clarify in my mind what the question was, Joshua stated, "If your wisdom is channeled through your beliefs, and your beliefs are sound, your faith will be strong."

Then Michael added, "If your faith is the wisdom behind your beliefs, a great personal understanding will be the force that guides you."

I just stood there motionless and silent, staring at this remarkable archangel, wondering if I looked as confused as I felt. Then I turned my attention back toward Joshua in hopes that he would rescue me from my bewilderment. Instead, I found him looking at me and smiling while nodding his head in agreement with Michael.

Have you ever gotten the feeling that something should be really obvious, but you just don't get it? For an extended pause, which seemed like hours, no one spoke.

Then Michael broke the silence by saying, "Jeremiah, please read for us the next directive."

"The next directive," I blankly repeated, realizing I was lost in my own thoughts. I reoriented myself on the Book of Eternities.

"The next directive states:

"**Seek enlightened awareness through balanced judgment, invoking counsel from the elders, for they teach from wisdom.**

"**Born of a dual nature, perception and understanding often come cloaked in discontent or despair.**"

Looking up from the book, I found myself standing in a wooded area at the edge of a clearing. Standing alongside me and staring at me as if he had been waiting for me to wake up stood an older, wise-looking Native American Indian. He wore straight, shoulder-length, white hair, braided twice on his left side, with each braid containing a single large, black feather with a downy soft, white base. The feather hung upside down, held in place with three alternating red and turquoise beads. He looked at me with his hands cupped in front of him and a welcoming smile in his eyes. He introduced himself as Silver Wolf, the tribal medicine man.

About twenty-five feet in front of us, several young girls, probably ten to twelve years old, could be seen gathering bark, nuts, and red berries on the other side of the clearing. They spent as much time playing around and eating the berries as they did gathering them.

Clothed completely in white buckskin, Silver Wolf stood well camouflaged among the tall, white birch trees. My jeans and navy blue T-shirt, however, made me stand out like a blueberry on a marshmallow. Since none of the young maidens even looked our way, I do not believe they were aware of our presence.

As we watched the carefree playfulness of the girls, Silver Wolf turned to me and foretold, "The berries they eat will turn inside them like a raging river. For three nights, they will carry with them the heat of the summertime sun while visions of angry spirits fill their dreams."

As he spoke, his hand and arm gestures confirmed to me that eating the berries would make the girls very sick.

"If the berries will make them sick, why don't you stop them?" I questioned.

"For many winters to come," Silver Wolf responded in a slow, paternal manner, "these young women will gather the food and build shelters for their tribe, their family. They must learn about all the bountiful gifts our Mother Earth has given us, as well as those that she has kept for our animal brothers and sisters or for herself. We survive as a people only as long as we respect the ways and teachings of our creator, our ancestors, our land, and ourselves."

"But they are only children," I said.

"They have been given to us as a gift by the Great Spirit to learn the ways of our people and their ancestors," Silver Wolf affirmed. "They must be taught how to grow strong in body and spirit if they are to understand this gift of life."

Silver Wolf looked up at the sun and stated, "The journey begins with the first sunrise, and each new day brings new lessons to be learned. Only fools who walk with their eyes closed or keep their thoughts lost in a cloud of self-importance will let a day pass without asking what wisdom it carries with it."

He faced me and continued, "All that our Mother Earth has to offer and teach us is both understood and cherished by the smallest of creatures, except by those who claim superiority over the others.

"As people continue to destroy the treasures and beauty of our Mother Earth without remorse, to kill without purpose, and to claim as their own the gifts meant for all of creation, they travel further and further into the darkness of the forest until the once clear paths disappear beneath briars and twigs. If they ignore the light of wisdom passed down from our ancestors, it will be forgotten and leave them lost in the shadows to follow only their own footprints."

He looked at me with saddened eyes and declared, "The Great Spirit has given us the sun, the wind, the earth, and the rain so we would always find food and clothing while living in harmony with our brothers and sisters. Our ancestors taught us that we once walked with the Great Spirit. They have shown us much of our creator's wisdom in their ways and their teachings. We must always carry the Great Spirit within us. If we forget how to live in harmony with our world, we will become a stranger to it, one that is no longer welcome. Like a newborn fawn without its mother, we will not know which path to take, and we will stumble through the forest in fear, weak and hungry and alone."

Deeply moved by the words of Silver Wolf, I wanted to thank him for his wisdom, but he and everything else in my view suddenly faded away. In his place, I found myself again alongside Joshua, facing the Archangel Michael.

"Only seconds ago, I was standing in a wooded area talking to a wise, old medicine man," I exclaimed.

Michael only smiled at me. I looked at Joshua.

"Read the next directive, Jeremiah," he remarked without expression.

CHAPTER 15

MEANING, WHOLENESS, AND A GIFT

I PAUSED, TOOK A DEEP BREATH, and looked back down at
The Book of Eternities. "The next directive states:

**"In all things, search for meaning beyond what you perceive.
Only with this understanding can you teach, guide, and learn
from all that will follow.**

**"Inner growth through self-awareness allows knowledge to
become wisdom, and faith, absolute freedom."**

As I finished reading the last word, I looked up as quickly as
possible in hopes of witnessing the transition I knew would take
place. Instead, I found myself still standing at the crystal podium
in front of the Book of Eternities. Somewhat disappointed, I
turned toward Joshua, only to find myself completely alone. I
continued turning all the way around, hoping to find Joshua and
Michael standing behind me, but instead I found myself facing
an endless flat terrain covered with pure white sand.

"What do you see?" asked Joshua, now suddenly standing
alongside me.

"I see a land of beautiful white sand," I responded.

"What else do you see?" Joshua asked.

I looked out to where I believed the horizon would be but saw no mountains, trees, rocks, or even small plants, only sand. I looked up and found the sky was also white, making any distinction between it and the ground almost indiscernible. I slowly turned completely around, observing the same view in every direction. "I see only a white sand desert and white sky."

"This is all you see?" Joshua questioned again.

It seemed obvious that he wanted me to see more, so I searched far and near in every direction, but there simply wasn't anything there. "I still see only the sand and the sky," I repeated.

"Then, what understanding does this reveal?" Joshua asked.

I looked out again at the vast white expanse, then back at my teacher. "Is it the understanding that the universe is so immense? Or that the Earth and the sky are very similar in appearance but are not the same?" Joshua offered up no response or even bothered to look at me. Instead, he stood perfectly still with his hands folded in front of him and his eyes closed.

"Can you give me a hint?" I asked rather impatiently.

Joshua didn't respond. I searched again in every direction but saw only the bright white sand and sky. I looked back at Joshua and waited for at least a minute, hoping he would grow impatient and help me, but he remained quiet and motionless with his eyes closed. So, breaking the awkwardness, I asked, "Do you want me to close my eyes and meditate on the question?"

"No!" he said sternly, briefly opening his eyes. "I want you to look with your eyes and tell me what you see and what understanding it brings to you."

I looked out again over the bright white blanket of sand. Then, throwing my hands up, I looked into the distance as far as I could while moving my head from side to side.

"There is nothing here except a barren desert that reaches out, as far as the eye can see. I have near perfect vision, and unless what you expect me to see is as white as the sand, I think I would be able to spot it. Of course, if you gave me some idea of what you *expect* me to see, it would be a lot easier." Clearly frustrated, I said this with significant sarcasm in my voice, but apparently not enough to get a reaction from my stubborn companion. I looked back at Joshua, but he annoyingly stood there expressionless, his eyes still closed. So, I continued, "Okay, now I am looking in this direction, and I see … nothing! Oh wait, I do see something … *white sand.* In addition, over there I see *more white sand!* Let's see, did I miss anything? Sure did! There it is … a white sky!"

I stood there looking defiantly at Joshua for the longest time until he opened his eyes and looked sternly at me, saying, "What do you say of a man who talks just to relish in his own words?"

I said nothing.

Joshua sat down on the ground in a yoga-looking position and commanded, "Sit."

I immediately sat down across from him with my legs crossed as he gently reached into the fine, white sand and picked up a few grains between his fingers. He leaned toward me, took my left hand, and placed a single grain of sand in my palm. I brought it up very close to see it clearly.

"Close your eyes," Joshua said, "and seek the true meaning of the grain of sand." I did as he requested. At the same time, he touched my wrist with two of his fingers, pushing my arm down slowly until my hand rested in my lap. With my eyes closed, I listened intently to the words of my teacher.

"Even though it is small in size," Joshua proclaimed in a teaching tone, "each grain of sand is a creation of the universe, just as a butterfly or a dewdrop or the sun and clouds. *All* things in creation have meaning and purpose. Do you know the purpose of the grain of sand?" he asked, pausing slightly before he continued. "Do you think it has any less or greater meaning than a rainbow ... or a dream ... or a leaf being carried by the wind?

"If searching for the meaning of life, or inner light, or your God, would lead you to the intricate pattern of a spider's web or the colorful delicacies of a coral reef, what miracles could the Creator of the heavens store in the tiny crystal you hold in your hand? What universe of its own could its secrets reveal?"

I opened my eyes and again examined the tiny crystal granule. Then I looked up and into Joshua's eyes. They gleamed from the reflection of the brightness of the sand, enhanced, I believe, by his wisdom. He looked back down at my hand, prompting me to look back down at the tiny crystal in my palm.

Then he asked, "Do you find any significance in something so small? In such a vast desert, would removing this single grain of sand have any consequence? Any meaning? In which reality is there significance in size? That which you see before you, or the countless stars in the sky above you? Is there a difference?"

Joshua told me to close my eyes again and to visualize the grain of sand in my mind's eye as he continued. "Imagine it as only one of the billions of stars in the heavens which you hold in your palm, or one seedling in a great forest, or one tiny creature in the ocean, or one soft voice in a crowded stadium," Joshua paused and added in a slower, more deliberate tone, "or one prayer sent out to an infinite universe? What then, would be its significance?"

I opened my eyes to find Joshua looking deep into my soul. He raised my hand with the grain of sand up to our eye level and concluded, "What if that one star in the infinite heavens was your sun? Would removing it then make a difference? Do you not see that everything is as unique as one, as one is uniquely part of everything, part of the same creation? One design ... one purpose ... one being.

"As we are one within ourselves, we are also one with each other, with the universe, and with our creator. To comprehend anything without first understanding *this* is like cupping your hands together in a storm and believing that you have captured the wind."

When Joshua stopped talking, I briefly closed my eyes again and tried to visualize all the images his words created. Multiple layered thoughts danced through my imagination. I couldn't really say how much time passed, but when I finally opened my eyes, I found myself once again standing in front of the podium on which the Book of Eternities rested.

The Archangel Michael, standing firmly behind the podium, smiled at me and said, "Creation carries within it the miracle of its own existence. You must come to this understanding through your own recognition of it. Therein is found the beginning of all that is and of all that is to be, as well as the purpose that makes it so!"

After a brief pause, Joshua smiled, nodded his head, and stated, "The profound meaning of this directive is not one that your human nature will easily grasp or accept. Yet, when you are ready, the mystery of life and the true completeness of the universe will reveal itself to you."

I looked at my spiritual friends for a few thoughtless seconds before refocusing my eyes back on the book. I could only hope that I would be able to spend plenty of time with them in the future to delve deeper into the complexity of this, as well as the other directives. And, more importantly, I needed to figure out what bearing all this might have on where my life was going.

Joshua put his hand on my shoulder and said, "Tell us the next directive."

I looked back down at the directives, and when I saw the words, a big smile came over me. I looked back up at Joshua, still smiling, and nodded. Looking back down at the book, I read aloud.

"Center on the light during all temptations and tribulations. Through this centering, you will find wholeness and peace.

"The light is truth and purest love. Without it, there is no balance, and fear will disrupt the spirit—disorder awaits opportunity."

Center on the light, I thought. That little phrase immediately brought back memories of the first thing Joshua tried to teach me. The thought of it threw a clownish grin on my face as I reminisced about our first, very unusual meeting. I closed my eyes and pleasantly recalled the whole "center on the light" memory.

However, a sudden, somersaulting, sinking feeling quickly disintegrated my pleasurable reflection into the urgency of my present situation.

I opened my eyes wide but found myself blinded by total darkness. I knew I was falling, very fast, and totally out of control. I tried not to panic, but that battle was already lost, and an overpowering sense of doom all but consumed me. In only moments, at this speed, I knew, without any need for visual clues, the impact would be fatal, and nothing I could do would save me from it. Shock stifled all my senses, and fear took control of my brain as I slammed my eyes shut. It didn't help!

My muscles froze in place, leaving me quiet and motionless in my self-induced darkness. Straddling the void of space and time, not knowing what would happen next or even what had just happened, I *knew* my obvious outcome and nothing else. In that instant, as my mind cried out, "Oh God …," everything … including my thoughts … plummeted into slow motion. I knew, or at least sensed that everything I thought to be true promptly vanished beyond my control. The anxiety had grabbed me like someone squeezing out a wet sponge. Then, suddenly, I found myself totally at peace, safe, and reassured in a protective, uncharted place deep within my being.

I felt like God had heard me and suspended time itself, and, in doing so, offered me all the time I needed to understand what was about to take place. Through the darkness, my life nonchalantly pranced before me. As the images and their memories passed by and I examined all the facets of my life that I believed to be *me,* I reluctantly had to accept the understanding that right here, right now, none of it mattered, and I had to question if it ever really had.

I calmly opened my eyes wide and found myself placidly suspended in time and space. Though void of any physical references, the darkness gave way to the presence of a soft but focused light illuminating the area behind me. Intrigued, I slowly turned my body around, hoping to observe the source of the light. However, as I turned, the light turned with me, keeping its position safely tucked behind me.

Focusing forward instead, I somehow found myself face to face with my shadow! In complete amazement, I witnessed a spectacular display of dancing, fiery rays as I watched an aura of rainbow light fully highlight the outline of my shadowy silhouette. I somehow knew that if my shadow had not been there to shroud my view, I would be looking straight into the intense illumination of my soul!

I briefly closed my eyes again in undeserved remembrance as a familiar, warm, deep peace reverberated through me. While being reminded of the true source of the spiritual nature each of us possesses, I realized that, through the light and the love that brings it forth, the intricate balance of creation is as unwavering as existence itself.

I opened my eyes again, still facing the shroud that kept me from seeing my eternal soul, but with renewed strength. Through a core-level understanding, I knew with total certainty that this life force, my soul, was indeed part of me. Or maybe, it was all of me, and I was only part of it. In either case, despite the fact that I could not peer directly into it, I didn't have to because I knew it was there! Always there! And that's all I needed to know to reassure me and make me complete, possibly even immortal.

I may not know where it all starts or where we go from here, but I now knew for sure that we really do possess a spirit, a soul, and it is eternal! I smiled and turned slowly back around. Again facing only darkness, I once again closed my eyes. My mind filled with the peace of knowing. Through the deepened sounds of silence, I could hear a voice, my own voice, saying to me, "You can never wander into complete darkness because the light is too great."

I opened my eyes, facing the Archangel Michael, who continued my own thoughts, saying, "The truth is pure love, and it knows no bounds; even your thoughts are captive to it. The splendor of life is but a glimpse of the fellowship we share in the light. You must understand that, within this truth, your every need has already been fully satisfied. Remember that the separation was of the flesh. Unlike your temporal existence, the truth is eternal and has no bounds. In that respect, you have never been separated from it."

I felt deeply transformed. Insight and awakened perceptions flowed through my mind, and I recognized that I had just been given a life-changing gift. One that allowed me to connect with the deepest, most profound beginnings of all the thoughts and memories that defined my very existence. At the same time, I consciously became very much aware of every part of my conscious being that separated me from myself.

Joshua added, "In your heart, you called out, and in your soul, you found answers. Do you think you are ever alone? You are not! When others around you are happy, are you not happy? When they feel sadness and grief, do you not feel their pain? Why stumble through life confused, blinded only because you have closed your own spiritual eyes? Open your eyes, Jeremiah, and keep them open if you want to observe the fullness of life!"

After giving Joshua a steady puzzling look to ensure him I *did not* get the whole meaning of his last statement, I refocused my attention back on the Book of Eternities and asked, "If there are no further words of wisdom, would anyone like me to read the next directive?"

Michael smiled, almost to a polite laugh, and commented, "You will understand in time, Jeremiah. For now, find comfort in knowing you will always find love, strength, and reassurance among the communions of souls." Then he nodded for me to continue.

I paused, took a slow, deep breath in anticipation of whatever experience might accompany the next reading, and then read aloud.

"You have been given the gift of reasoning and emotion. With this gift, your dual natures empower you to transcend all mortal limitations while still remaining within them."

"Close your eyes," Joshua commanded, "and tell me what you perceive to be real."

I did as my teacher instructed, assuming Joshua would be leading me through another lesson. Instead, I found myself transported back through time to re-live one of the most vivid and emotionally charged dreams of my entire life.

I was fifteen years old at the time and still living at home with my family, which included my Grandmother Busia. The dream I now recalled occurred three days before her death. A day or two before the dream, she meticulously sorted through her small jewelry box and shoebox full of mementos and arranged everything in explicit piles on top of her 1950s antique, white vanity. She gave the collection of things to my mom with instructions for her to pass them on to each of her grandchildren after her death.

Then, on the night of November 18, shortly after I went to sleep, I dreamed, with very vivid realism, of Busia standing inside a beautiful garden filled with an abundance of flowers, shrubs, trees, ferns, and a variety of vegetables and herbs. A perfectly manicured, thick, neck-high, soft green hedge encircled the garden.

I stood on the outside of the hedge pleasantly talking to her as she stood on the other side. She looked so happy that her infectious smile brought a smile to my face just to see her that way. Not only did she clearly have no pain, her entire demeanor was almost giddy and childlike.

She told me all about her new garden and how happy it made her feel. Gardening had always been her passion, and she seemed so pleased and proud of this one. As we talked, we slowly walked all the way along the garden hedge while she cheerfully described which different plants grew well together and which ones, especially the herbs, had medicinal properties. In addition to the time-tested, old folktale cures for colds, bee stings, rashes, and such, she also added wonderful, emotionally filled stories gathered from a full lifetime of hardships and happiness.

As we continued to walk around the entire length of the lush green hedge, I kept looking for a way in, but I couldn't find one. I remember Busia looking a little saddened that I was not able to come in and walk hand in hand with her and see her garden up close and that made me feel sad too.

Once I finished walking completely around the perimeter of the garden, and I realized I could not get in, the dream quickly faded away, and I woke up. It didn't take me long to fall back to sleep, and I woke up for school the next morning, just like I did every school day, with the exception that I recalled the dream completely and in full detail. The next night, I had exactly the same dream in every aspect from beginning to end and with such realism that it seemed much more to me than merely a dream.

On the third night, I again had the same dream. It came to me every bit as real and vibrant as the two preceding nights and the same in every detail until the end. This time, after I walked all the way around the garden and realized that I could not get in, Busia gave me a very warm and loving smile, told me how much she loved me, and said she would always be watching over me. Then she walked into the center of the garden and out of sight.

The next day, her heart gave out, and she passed away!

Her heart attack came without warning, and yet I absolutely believe that somehow Busia knew exactly when she would die, and because she knew, I truly believe she felt at peace at the time of her death.

Did God send her a message in a dream or premonition that her time had come and that she would be all right? Could it be possible that when it is our time to die, even if it is sudden, that God will send an angel to comfort us and help us through the transition? Or perhaps our own spiritual self collects our soul and carries it safely to the other side. I could only wonder. I wish I knew.

That dream, as vivid and real as it was, did not answer these questions for me, but it sure made me question the answers I thought I already had.

I never forgot any of the details of that dream. It allowed me to peek beyond the curtain of life and transformed my way of thinking forever. Busia played a very significant role in my life, and it should have been very traumatic for me when she died. Because of that dream, however, as much as I missed her after that, whenever I thought about her being gone, I knew, with absolute certainty, that whether it's called heaven or something else, Busia was in her spectacular garden, and she was very happy.

I thought often about Busia's preparations for her death and the dreams that became such a source of mystery and comfort to me. Over the ensuing years, I filled my head with many questions about the meaning of life and death. Moreover, I began to question some of my core religious beliefs and found myself on a lifelong quest for spiritual understanding. This quest only became more intense as I grew older. I felt now that Joshua seemed to be offering me answers to the very questions I had been searching for most of my life.

I know what you are trying to help me understand, Joshua, I thought as I left this treasured memory and returned to my present place and time. I kept my eyes closed, but I felt Joshua was near and could hear me.

"If God or angels or some sort of divine intervention can help us deal with death by showing us what awaits us beyond this life, why could they not help us in dealing with life itself, as it is happening?"

"You are learning to ask pertinent questions," Joshua stated.

I opened my eyes to find myself still standing in front of the crystal pedestal that held the Book of Eternities.

"How do the answers to these questions affect your quest for truth and your perception of the meaning of life?" Michael asked.

"The answers?"

Of course, I didn't *know* the answers to these questions, so I blankly looked at both of them for a long time. Finally, I responded, "I'm not sure which questions are even the ones I should ask. I am sure, however, that I do *not* know with *any* degree of confidence the answers to any of them. After all that you've shown me though, I'm beginning to wonder if perhaps finding the answers is far less important than being able to ask the right questions."

Michael smiled and spoke, his voice full of compassion, "Let these directives guide you and be your source of strength and comfort. In so doing, with their help and your ability of expression, your sharing of this gift of hope will be demonstrated in your words, charged by your commitment, and emotionally transformed into an even greater strength and comfort for everyone who is touched by your message."

Michael's words probably implied a much deeper meaning, but I think his intent was to tell me that anyone spiritually wrestling with the ultimately fundamental questions about life and death could look to the directives as *the* source of spiritual answers and understanding.

Before I could ask him to clarify his statement though, he instructed me to go on to the next directive. So, with my head and my heart filled with new questions, I continued reading from the beautiful, luminous, white book in high hopes that at least some of the answers would be forthcoming. I wasn't disappointed!

CHAPTER 16

A POWERFUL
TRUTH REVEALED

THE MORE I STUDIED THE amazing book, the deeper I felt my spiritual awakening grow. My angelic guides kept reminding me that I was merely a messenger, taken on this incredible journey to learn and remember all that I could so I would be able to share my experience with anyone that would listen.

That may sound easy enough, but the problem is they are not *just* stories; they are also a full range of indescribable emotions, as well!

Michael interrupted my deep thoughts.

"Please continue with the next directive."

I looked at him, and he smiled. I smiled back and read the next directive to myself from the Book of Eternities. Then nodding in confirmation to where my thoughts had already taken me, I looked up at Michael, then over at Joshua, and stated in a firm voice, "The next directive says:

"**Seek guidance and intervention through fellowship with the divine. Learn from your decisions and experiences, for all that you are and all that you become will be with you always.**

"Unaffected by time, each passing moment is remembered with or without your understanding of it."

I looked up from the book to find a very unusual assembly of people in front of me. The group, made up of both men and women, seemed to contain a lot of clergy and looked like it was made up of many different cultures and denominations. A few looked familiar, but there were many I didn't recognize. Besides the dozens of distinctively dressed religious clerics, there were many more in regular street clothes or business attire. As I scanned across this old-world diversity from left to right, I realized, as I reached a point over my right shoulder, that Joshua was silently standing at my side, staring at me.

"Who are all these people?" I quietly inquired.

He quickly pointed out Greek and Russian Orthodox clergy, Jewish rabbis, priests and missionaries carrying the Book of Mormon and others witnessing the word of Jehovah, Mid-Eastern and Western Muslims, Catholics, Wiccans, Scientologists, Hindus, Zoroastrian priests (which I never heard of) in long white robes and veiled faces, Shinto priests with their overflowing white robes and cool black hats, Buddhists of all types, and even members of Amish and Mennonite communities as well as a few Native cultures in colorful ceremonial attire. Surprisingly, I even saw what Joshua referred to as sorcerers and practitioners of voodoo and witchcraft (most of them with very distinctive hairstyles). Even though the bulk of this gathering of perhaps two or three hundred consisted of just regular people, it must have included representatives from almost every major tribe, nation, and religion known.

"Watch. Do not speak," Joshua commanded softly just as I was about to inquire about the stage and the highly unusual audience.

Everyone in the room focused silently on the scene taking place on a stage, to my left, in front of them.

On the stage, a thin, young woman with short, dark hair and a tanned complexion, probably in her late teens or early twenties, dressed in a bright white hospital gown, was at that very moment giving birth as we all silently watched.

Having experienced the birth of my first son and actually delivering my second, I found it very surprising that not only did the woman not make a sound, but her entire demeanor radiated a very peaceful look.

A beautiful, golden-haired angel with her back to us received the baby and held it up for all to see. We watched in shock and awe as the newborn took its first breath, and in that same instant, the mother took her last, giving us the sad opportunity to witness in this scene both the miracle of birth and the certainty of death.

As the umbilical cord unexplainably faded away, the angel handed the newborn to one of the women in the front row. That is when I noticed all the people in the room were coupled man and woman, and all the women held newborns. After observing many of the new parents for several minutes, I concluded that each mother held, cuddled, and cared for her infant in her own traditional way and spoke to the baby in her own language. The fact that all the people stood together as couples seemed odd to me because it seems that many children born today, at least in America, are not born to couples.

When I looked back over to where the deceased woman and the stage should have been, I found, to my surprise, that not only was the same woman still alive, but she was now all alone in a completely different and disturbing setting and had not yet delivered her baby! A quick glance to my right and left confirmed the fact that now Joshua and I were the only onlookers.

I briefly looked over at Joshua, standing on my right, then back at the drama playing out in front of us. Once again, we would witness this woman giving birth. Her innocent face, light brown skin, and short, black hair left no doubt she was indeed the same woman we observed only moments ago. This time, however, she was not only all alone, but also clearly in a lot of pain. She was lying on her back in a dirty, tattered gown on a filthy, worn out, torn-open mattress. Her face was blank and rigid as she stared at the single dim light bulb in the ceiling and whimpered a deep, painful cry.

Aside from the dirty mattress lying in the corner on the filthy floor, this small room with its broken windows, smell of mildew, and strewn piles of trash only contained a small, dark brown wooden table holding what remained of a white candle lying in a hardened puddle of wax. Two matching wooden chairs, both without backs, were near the table, one of them propped against the wall due to a missing left rear leg. Through the broken window, I could hear the sound of construction machinery, leading me to believe that this was probably an abandoned building.

The woman's anguishing moans refocused my attention on her suffering. As her newborn attempted to enter the world on its own, the young mother screamed out in obvious pain and despair. Her white-knuckle grip on the sides of the mattress further amplified the tears streaming down her pain-stricken face as she cried out, "Oh, God, make it stop!"

I wanted to help the poor woman in some way, but I quickly realized that I could not move any closer or speak out to her. I could only be an observer. I felt her pain, and it broke my heart that I couldn't help.

"Tell me, Jeremiah, what is prayer?" Joshua asked quietly.

With my eyes wide open and filled with compassionate tears from the shock of what we were witnessing, I turned my head and looked at Joshua without speaking. He was observing the woman like someone contemplating a unique piece of sculpture in a museum. Several seconds passed. Then, still without saying a word, I looked back at the young woman on the mattress. To my utter surprise, all movements were frozen in time as if we were watching a movie and someone hit the pause button. The room remained deathly silent. I looked back at Joshua and in a broken voice asked, "What?"

"What is prayer?" he calmly repeated.

Trying to regain my thoughts after glancing back at the time-frozen scene, I finally replied, "Prayer is asking God for help through difficulties in life."

"Is it?" Joshua replied. "Then did this woman just pray to her God for help?"

I studied the intensity in Joshua's eyes without answering the question. Then I looked back over at the woman. In that instant, we had returned to the original version of the mother in the clean, white hospital gown giving birth on the stage. Only this time, when the angel handed the newborn to the woman in the front row, it became clear to me that the young woman accepting the baby was, in fact, the baby's mother. I quickly looked back up on the stage, but the golden-haired angel stood there alone.

Joshua faced me and looked earnestly into my eyes, stating, "Throughout our lifetimes, we experience many things, good and bad. Each of these experiences can teach us valuable lessons about our mortal nature and the complexity of the emotions that play such a vital part in our lives. Often we are motivated, consciously or subconsciously, by perceptions, which can limit our view of reality. Often we can see only what we believe we can see. For some, however, there is an inner personal drive, a voice of conviction that seems to be more powerful than anyone or anything, including the very laws of nature."

Joshua looked patiently at me, I suppose in the hope of me asking some profound question, but I said nothing, so he continued.

"Have you ever wondered how Olympic athletes can continue to break endurance records each time the games are held, going well beyond what anyone thought to be humanly possible? Or why every few years you hear about a child genius that is graduating from college before he or she even reaches puberty? Did you ever wonder why some people get cancer or rare diseases and others seem immune? Or why many people die from simple illnesses or freak accidents while others are the recipients of 'miracles' that are beyond the explanation of medicine or technology? What about everyday heroes like nurses and doctors, police, fire, and military men and women displaying unexplainable stamina when they are physically, mentally, and emotionally exhausted? How do you explain the stories of elderly couples dying within a few days or hours of each other for no medical reason other than a broken heart? How about the countless stories of people 'knowing' that a loved one far away has died or been physically or emotionally hurt?"

Joshua paused the way he does when he wants me to think through what he is trying to tell me. Then he continued, "Keep this always in your thoughts, Jeremiah. Everything that happens is by design. Never forget, however, that the Creator's foremost gift to all of creation, beyond the gift of life, is the gift of free will. Would it make sense for humankind to be blessed with a dual nature, one being embodied and the other spirit, if *both* were not able to exercise that free will?"

Joshua smiled at me and said, "People exercise spiritual free will through prayer. However, they can only express that prayer in a way that articulates their beliefs within the context of their lives and state of mind. Sometimes, Jeremiah, it is in the most fearful moments of our human existence that we allow the emotional barriers that keep us from our own spiritual freedom to be conquered. And when we free our spiritual selves, the limits we set on our physical being can also be overcome.

"Those who have not yet learned, accepted, or understood the power of prayer or the magnitude of their own spirituality are not any less bestowed with the blessings of their creator; they just haven't reached the level of awareness they are capable of to recognize and embrace those blessings. Sometimes, they only need to be *reminded* that they are spirit as well as flesh and that each is equally a part of who they are."

"How are they reminded?" I asked.

"They are reminded through faith, Jeremiah, and the testimony of others. Find your own personal resilience in this belief, and through it, your testimony too will enlighten and empower others to find their own spiritual convictions and resolve. Countless others will be inspired when they witness your ability to apply what you have learned through these directives and the dual natures of life when you are able to express it in *your* daily life."

"Always remember, the Creator's children are never alone or forsaken," the Archangel Michael added, alerting me to the fact that we once again had returned to the Hall of Angels.

"Use the power of prayer, uncompromising belief in yourself, and meditation to look beyond your own physical capabilities and limitations. Focusing on and understanding your dual natures will enable you to explore the depths of your human experience. And," he emphasized by raising the volume of his voice noticeably, "if you remember that a divine guidance is always within your reach, you can find clarity, wisdom, and understanding in *everything* you choose to do."

Michael finished his statement with the assurance, "When it seems like *nothing* is going right and none of your plans are working, remember, the divine plan is *always* in effect."

As Michael spoke, I turned and faced him. He maintained his protective stance a couple of feet in front of me, directly behind the crystal pedestal, with Joshua standing in his usual place alongside of me on my right.

"Please read the next directive for us, Jeremiah," Michael requested with a brief smile.

I continued with the next reading.

CHAPTER 17

THE POWER OF LOVE

66 **L**OVE IS THE MOST POWERFUL **force in all of creation, as it originates from the source and is always with you.**

"The presence and power of love are eternal. It is the essence of your soul: the source of your wisdom, strength, and understanding, as well as your beacon home."

I looked up from the book as quickly as my eyes could shift to catch the transition and ... nothing changed! I looked up at Michael, and he smiled. "What does this directive mean to you?"

"Read it again," Joshua instructed.

I re-read the directive to my companions, and again Michael asked, "What do these words mean to you?"

"Well ..." I hesitated as many different thoughts climbed through my mind. To answer the question, I needed to know if Michael meant it as a general question or a personal one. Either way, it seemed pretty straightforward, so I answered, "It means that love is always with us."

"Is this true?" Joshua asked. "What then is love?"

Love is such a big word. The more I thought about it, the more I realized answering what seemed like a very simple question was not so simple after all. However, since the very first thing I thought of was how much I loved my children, I answered from my heart.

I closed my eyes, and a lifetime of memories with my boys flooded in. I guess until now, with all that had been happening to me, I hadn't realized just how much I really missed them. I couldn't hold back the tears as I weaved through the emotional memories.

I remembered how nervous and excited I got when I witnessed each of their births and how sad and helpless I felt anytime they were sick. I recalled the excitement and joy of Christmas mornings when they would drag me half-asleep into the living room to see what Santa Claus left for them and how their little faces beamed with pride when I told them how much I loved the drawings and projects they brought home from school. I remembered the fear and anguish I felt when my oldest son injured himself in a serious bicycle accident and they took him away in an ambulance. My heart shattered when I saw how hurt he felt when his pathetic Little League coach would not let him in the game so he could play his own son instead. I barely controlled my anger.

I am sure that I stood out as the proudest father in the world when my youngest son outperformed all the other kids in his elementary school as the lead singer in the Christmas play and my oldest played his viola in the high school all-county string quartet.

Moreover, I've shown dozens of perfect strangers pictures of my boys and bragged about their induction into the International Honor Society after making the dean's list and president's list every semester at their college.

Pausing in deep thought, I opened my eyes.

"These are exceptional memories and make me so proud whenever I think of them, but right now they are only painful because I miss my boys so much and love them more than anyone could ever understand."

I couldn't hold back the tears. My heart ached for a chance to be with my boys and tell them how much I missed and loved them. Without any clear sense of time, I had no idea how long I have been away, but it suddenly felt like an eternity.

"Peace be with you, Jeremiah," Michael said tenderly.

Drying my eyes with my hands, I took a deep breath and felt more composed.

Joshua compassionately put his hands on my shoulders and just as compassionately asked, "You know that your love and your children's love will always be a part of you?"

"Yes, of course it will!" I said, defensively.

"Then is this the love that the directive speaks of?" he asked softly.

I re-read the directive again in my head, and after applying it to all my memories, I said, "There are times when I've been angry or disappointed with my children. And I am sure I've made plenty of mistakes as a parent that caused them to be angry or disappointed in me. But, deep down, we love each other very much, and there is *nothing* that could ever change that! So yes, I have no doubt that the love we share will always be with us."

"What about before you had children? Did you feel loved then? What about people who do not or cannot have children of their own?" Joshua asked.

This question hit me as a sobering one and helped me refocus my thoughts on understanding the directive. But frankly, I had a hard time answering Joshua's question, because, after raising my children from infants to young adults as a single parent, I actually had a hard time coming up with very many clear memories of the time before they became the focus of my life. A different thought came to me, however, so I stated, "Well, I am not sure about the people who cannot have children of their own, but everyone has a mother, right?"

Michael and Joshua both gave me an encouraging look to go on with my thoughts, but I didn't really have a follow-on statement to accompany the first one. I have always known how fortunate I am to have come from a very close family, growing up with two parents and a grandmother, all under one roof, who dearly loved all of us. Though my grandmother and parents are no longer with us, the love and respect they instilled in me as a child is still, very much a stabilizing force in my life.

These thoughts made me recall a teenage friend of my son who used to hang out at our house all the time. Because his single-parent mother died from complications of a supposedly routine operation when he was still in elementary school, he spent much of his adolescence as an angry young man, shuffling in and out of foster homes and halfway houses. He had already experienced a few minor run-ins with the law when we first met him, and, in my opinion, he should have been treated for depression, not delinquency.

I felt compassion for him and tried to treat him the same as my own children, but I found it hard to understand how he must have felt, dealing with so much at such a young age. Fortunately, my son kept him as a friend, against my initial better judgment, and he grew up to be a very well-mannered and caring young adult, despite his circumstances. I know now that all he really needed was to trust that someone actually cared enough to believe in him.

Then I thought about all the children and young adults that no one seemed to want, the ones who spend their entire adolescence bouncing from one correctional facility to another. I wondered, too, about homeless people and those who are clinically depressed or suicidal. What about those individuals who constantly try to hurt themselves or others? Do they have any love in their lives? Would they recognize it if they did? And could it be strong enough to overcome their anger and despair?

I knew that Joshua and Michael could read my thoughts, so I asked, "What about people like that?"

"What does the directive tell you?" Joshua asked.

I re-read the directive to myself:

"Love is the most powerful force in all of creation, as it originates from the source and is always with you.

"The presence and power of love are eternal. It is the essence of your soul: the source of your wisdom, strength, and understanding, as well as your beacon home."

"It's true, Jeremiah, love *is* always with us because the Creator is love and a part of each and every one of our spiritual beings. It doesn't matter what your concept or belief in a creator or God is. That doesn't change what is real; it only changes an individual's perception of what's real. Every one of the people you mentioned *is* loved and can *feel* loved every moment of their lives if they so choose, but to do so or not must be their own personal decision," Michael explained.

I tried to comprehend the meaning of this directive, but it seemed to me that it could be taken in so many different ways and levels. How could someone whose heart is filled with hate be interested in or even open to the love of anyone—even themselves?

"The directive says love is always with us, but if people in tragic or bitter, lonely situations do not *feel* loved, then how can these words help them?" I questioned.

"That is precisely why you must remind them of all the directives!" Michael exclaimed.

"I understand the others are just as important. But just to make sure I understand *this* directive," I said, "is it saying that because love is always with us, and the Creator or God is love, then God is always with us because God's spirit is part of our spirit and, therefore, we are part of God? And even those people I mentioned and others, such as hardened criminals or individuals who are totally rejected by society or themselves, can experience real true love if they would only open their hearts and minds up enough to accept it?"

"Yes, Jeremiah. This is the understanding you must carry with you," Michael asserted. "There is abundant love to fill their lives and transform them without the slightest hesitation. Moreover, the wonderful part is that this divine love is abundant and free for the asking, always there, a gift from their creator. No one has to do anything to get it. All they have to do is accept it, and it is theirs."

"Tell me then, how can I get people to believe in this directive if they have already given up on ever finding or believing in love?" I asked.

"Through your writing and the personality you present to others, you will teach them by your actions and words, and they, in turn, will do the same. Then, the cycle of learning and living with love will continue until the clarity of the directive is unmistakable."

"I would very much like to do that, and I understand what you are saying, but I am only one person, so how much of a difference could I possibly make?"

"This directive does not *only* mean that divine love is always inherently with us. It also means that, because of our dual natures and spiritual connection to each other, there will always be others all around us that will pass on the compassion we express to others. They, in turn, will then pass it on to still others and so forth until it touches the souls of people far removed from us, from every walk of life. When you show genuine caring and love, you will have an impact even on people you will never meet," Michael said.

"Have you not seen and heard of this over and over again in stories all around the world? Strangers helping each other in tragic situations while taking extreme risks and ignoring their own safety?" Joshua asked.

"But if this is true," I responded, "then why have I, many times in my life, often felt unloved and alone, even though I know deep down that my family loves me very much? And if everyone is capable of showing all this love, why does there appear to be so much hate and apathy in the world?"

"Holy texts throughout the world teach us to love our neighbors as we love ourselves," Michael stated. "The sad and distressing truth about people is that most of them are doing exactly that! How can people love their neighbors if they do not accept or know how to love themselves?"

There was no room to disagree because I knew he was right. Sadly, I think I have spent a lot of my life as one of those people.

"Many people of the world," Michael continued in a sobering tone, "not only fail to *love* themselves, but often they don't really even *like* themselves. They dislike their jobs, their spouses, their families, where they live, how they live, where they have been, or where they are going. They barely tolerate who they think they are, surviving day to day wishing they were a different person, or somewhere else, or with someone else, or dead. They may be capable of demonstrating deep passion and emotions to others but reject accepting it for themselves. Rather, they carry this false image of who they superficially believe they are inside, and in reaction to that image they created, they never allow themselves to say honestly and without reservation, 'I love who I am.'

"Once they lose their passion, or fail to believe they deserve it in the first place, it's easy for the mind to convince the heart that dreams are unachievable. These lost souls subconsciously, or often consciously, feel they are inadequate or flawed in some way and continue outwardly moving through life but inwardly believing they are failures. This is emotionally too painful for most people to accept. So they either internally steer their lives onto a self-destructive course or defensively project it onto others around them."

Joshua added, "Can you imagine how much easier and stronger we could love one another if we could first develop the compassion it takes to love ourselves? Is that not how it felt before the separation? How it should always be?"

I didn't have to be convinced because I knew his words rang true. I read the directive over again to myself and smiled. "Yes, that *is* how it should always be!"

"Good," Joshua said. "The last two directives will show you what you need to make it so, Jeremiah. When you read them, you will rekindle the innocence of trust and belief you knew as a child. Never retreat from this state of being. It summons the inner peace and emotional fortitude that enables you to reach beyond what you think you can and embrace what you are truly capable of."

"Would you like to know the Creator's greatest gift to all of humanity?" Michael asked.

"Yes, of course," I replied.

"Then please read for us the next directive."

CHAPTER 18

DIVINE LAW

I FELT, WITHOUT A DOUBT, confident in my new level of spiritual intuitiveness, and it filled me with a feeling of ... empowerment! I brought my attention back on the Book of Eternities and read the next directive.

"You have been entrusted with the greatest act of love, commitment, and fulfillment in all the kingdoms—that of creation itself.

"As I am always with you, and you will always be my children, so too must you recognize on a core level of understanding that your children will always be part of you, and you will always be part of them.

"This is my law and shall not be broken or interfered with."

As I read the last line, the words "interfered with" stood out plainly to me. I immediately thought of all the stories and debates in the news lately about human cloning and stem cell research. I've seen many of the recent movies about cloning, and I personally believe many of those ideas could be a reality in the very near future or, for that matter, already exist.

"So, does that mean that God condemns the whole idea of cloning?" I asked, looking first at Michael and then at Joshua.

"I mean does the directive refer only to human cloning? What about the cloning of animals, such as sheep and cows? I thought the whole idea behind the original Dolly Project revolved around coming up with a way of mass-producing sheep and other 'food' animals as a means to feed the entire world's hungry. How could God be against that?" Again, I looked briefly at Michael and then began turning my head toward Joshua when ...

I found myself in a heavily wooded forest facing a wall of fire and billows of thick, gray and black smoke. In a panic, I turned around to make my escape, only to discover the same heated situation behind me and to my sides, as well. Apparently, my angelic guides felt the need to place me in the middle of a forest fire!

I looked all around for a way out but found none. The massive circle of fire crept slowly toward me from every direction. I spotted a small clearing with very little underbrush, about the size of a standard hotel room, only a few feet to my left, so I crouched down and hurriedly ran over to it. I quickly discovered the air closer to the ground to be much clearer, so I sat down at the base of a large oak tree just inside the perimeter of the clearing and used it as a shield with my back to the approaching flames, facing the clearing. I continued to frantically scan beyond the edges of the encroaching firewall, searching for a way out, but the unrelenting wall of flames left me with no escape and continued to grow more intense.

My mind shifted into survival mode without ever allowing me the time to stop and analyze the reason for my predicament. Fear quickly exceeded my need for rational judgments when a familiar voice spoke to me. I looked up and found Metatron standing in front of me in an almost transparent form, surrounded head to toe in a brilliant auric bubble of bluish-white light.

"Peace be with you, Jeremiah," he said. "Do not be troubled; you will not be harmed. You are only here to bear witness to the truth."

As soon as he said this, he faded into a thin layer of whirling smoke. I guess the distraction of the brief visit by Metatron and the crackling of the burning underbrush masked the entrance of several forest animals that now joined me in my small bastion of safety.

Over a period of the next few minutes, three deer, a buck, doe and fawn, a raccoon, a mother fox and her two cubs, a couple of rabbit families, and a young black bear occupied my small but temporarily safe, fire-free clearing. Predator and prey alike gathered with no apparent quarrel amongst them over being together in this small area. Of course, they too only wanted refuge from the flames.

The wall of fiery doom grew more and more intense. As the fire closed in on us, I realized that neither the smoke nor the flames affected me, confirming my role as only an observer, just as Metatron had promised. However, it became readily apparent that none of these poor forest creatures were given the same privilege and probably would not survive their ordeal.

What I witnessed next could only be described as incredible. As the temperature increased to the point where the ground cover of oak leaves and pine needles began to smolder, but moments before the fire or smoke actually incapacitated any of the animals, they all calmly gathered in the middle of the clearing and, lying down close to each other, they seemed to go into a deep, peaceful sleep.

Then, from each of them arose a tiny angelic form with two sets of wings each. These very small, delicate-looking beings wore sheer gowns that draped below them, giving each one the appearance of a curiously long torso, resembling ghost-like characteristics. Their silvery, translucent wings made them seem fairy-like and gave them a distinctly different look from the angels I had recently grown accustomed to seeing. They wisped off into the sky, I guess to heaven, but as I watched them gracefully escaping the dancing waves of flames and smoke, I noticed out of the corner of my eye that something else had happened.

Shifting my glance briefly to the background of the raging fire, I found that the flames, smoke, and everything around me now moved in very slow motion. Time apparently slowed itself down almost to a stop, and the only things not affected by it seemed to be the little, translucent angels and me.

I watched these delightful beings continue to fly away at what I thought to be a normal speed, and then I realized by the movement of their wings that my first conclusion was incorrect. Time *did* indeed slow down for them, but their movements were so fast that in "real" time, these tiny angels would have probably been much too fast for any human eye to see. It made me realize I was given a unique opportunity to witness a part of nature that few have probably ever seen.

"I wonder how many actual angels are all around us every day that are barely out of reach of our normal human senses," I said to myself. Then smiling at the thought of it, I watched the last little angel leaving as normal time caught up with us, and it immediately faded into the smoke along with everything else in my view.

In the next instant, I found myself no longer in a burning forest but back in front of the podium with Joshua standing beside me and the Archangel Michael still firmly positioned at our front.

"People and places sure come and go quickly around here," I declared.

"What people and places are you referring to?" Joshua responded.

With his straightforward look, I could not tell if he intended that to be a joke or not, so I just looked at him, thinking about his unique personality, and smiled. He then asked, "What have you seen?"

"I've just figured out," I said after some deep thought, "that apparently *all* members of the animal kingdom, not just humans, have souls, or at least Guardian Angels, and transcend this mortal realm when they die."

Michael knew I understood that all living creatures *are* sacred in the eyes of their creator, and he added, "The dolphins have long been the guardians over all the dominions of the seas, but the human races have been charged with the stewardship of all the lands and its inhabitants of the Earth, including the plants and animals from each realm.

"Many types of plants cover the planet to provide nourishment, healing, beauty, comfort, protection, and breathable air for many life forms, including humans. The Creator has permitted certain animals to work with or for humans. Others play their part by serving as nourishment for the others. These animals serve their creator in this way, and they understand and accept their place in the divine plan.

"However, the torturing, destroying, or manipulating of plants and animals for pure greed without this spiritual acknowledgment or an inspired purpose never goes unnoticed and will not go unpunished."

"What else does the directive reveal to you?" Joshua asked.

I looked down at the incredible book and read the middle part of the directive again:

"As I am always with you, and you will always be my children, so too must you recognize on a core level of understanding that your children will always be part of you, and you will always be part of them."

As a dad, I love my children very much, and I know no matter what they do, and no matter how upset, frustrated, or disappointed I may be with some of their decisions, I could never, ever stop loving them. However, I felt like this directive, by saying, **"your children will always be part of you, and you will always be part of them,"** probably referred to those distinguishing physical characteristics and mannerisms, like their hair, their noses, their build, the way they talk and smile— all the unique similarities between me and my boys and the rest of our extended family that would make even a stranger say, "You can sure tell he is your son!"

Therefore, I inquired of Joshua, "The directive is talking about heredity, right?"

"Is it?" Joshua asked back.

"Well, I know that all people, and for that matter, all animals and probably plants as well, obtain their physical individuality from the genes they inherit from their parents. Therefore, from a physical point of view, this directive would remind us of that. Am I right?"

"If the other directives are rules that you may choose to follow or not follow, how then would heredity be placed within the same perception?" Joshua inquired of me.

He made a valid point. Heredity is not something we have much control over, at least not yet.

"But if it isn't talking about heredity, then what?" I asked myself. I read the directive a third and fourth time but kept coming up with heredity. I re-read it again, slowly, hoping to dissect a different meaning out of it, but when I tried to tap into my mind's resources, I found it to be empty. So I looked at Joshua, shrugged my shoulders, and said, "I think I need a little help on this one."

"Are the puppies all the same?" Joshua immediately responded as he looked past me toward where the crystal pedestal *should* have been.

When I turned my head back toward the front, I found myself seated and looking at a movie screen. Joshua and I were now comfortably sitting in the front section of a Cinerama movie theater watching *101 Dalmatians*.

"Cool!" I said. By now I had grown so accustomed to the idea that, at any moment, I could be anywhere in any situation. I also noticed that my mind was adjusting to these changes much quicker than when this all started.

"This is one of my kids' favorites," I declared. "And mine too."

"Are any of the puppies exactly the same?" Joshua repeated as he reached into the large bag of buttered popcorn now resting in my lap and pulled out a single piece coated with butter.

"No!" I said, with a chuckle because of the unexpected environment I was thoroughly enjoying.

"They might be similar in a lot of ways," I said as I crammed a handful of popcorn in my mouth, "but I am pretty sure no two are ever *exactly* alike."

"And your children, are they the same?" Joshua asked as he closely examined the kernel of popped corn before smelling it and then putting it in his mouth.

"Oh heck no," I remarked while giving him a weird look in response to his equally weird behavior.

"As a matter of fact," I continued, "I have always tried to raise both of my boys with the same rules and expectations, and in everything we did together, I always tried to do it exactly the same for both of them so they would never feel I was favoring one over the other. Yet they still turned out to be completely different individuals," I stated while grabbing another big handful of delicious popcorn and stuffing it in my mouth.

"So they have completely different personalities, likes, dislikes, habits, and mannerisms. Yet you still love them both equally?" Joshua questioned.

"Of course I do!" I exclaimed firmly between chews.

"I'm their dad, I love being their dad, and I will always love them the same no matter how they turn out or what they do in life."

"And this is because of heredity?" Joshua asked in a matter-of-fact sort of way. As he asked his question, he gingerly picked out several pieces of popped corn one at a time from the bag with his right hand and delicately placed them in his left hand.

The answer of course was no. However, I wanted to figure out a way to word it for Joshua so he would concede that it at least played a part, but he interrupted my thoughts with a new question.

"Do you think you or any other parent could feel the same degree of love for a child if he or she were a stepchild or adopted?"

"Of course they could and do," I said with almost certain conviction. Only then did I notice that the movie in the background now displayed scenes from *Cinderella* and then *Annie*.

"Then does the directive speak of a physical love or an emotional one?" Joshua queried while eating the popcorn from his left hand one at a time and chewing it much longer than normal people do.

"Well, both!" I stated after considerable thought.

"You can't really separate the two, can you?"

As the scenes on the movie screen again shifted to clips from *The Jungle Book* and *The Lion King,* Joshua looked at me in a more serious tone and asked, "If this is so, do you think this emotional love still exists between a parent and child that is abused or abandoned?"

I felt confident the movie on the screen shouldn't have any effect on my answer, but it shifted my way of thinking enough that I remained silent and let Joshua continue.

"Would one of these children be physically or spiritually less a part of their parents? What about children that are born without the capacity to ever know their parents or themselves? Or those not allowed to be born at all? Is that natural love between a child and a parent different from what you feel for your children? Do you think the origin of that love is different?"

I am sure with the seriousness of this line of questioning that there must have been a noticeable shift in my entire demeanor, so Joshua gave me plenty of time to answer. However, I did not know what to say, so I quietly watched the movie for a little while, and then I closed my eyes and reflected on how blessed I've been to have such intelligent, healthy, loving children.

I opened my eyes when Joshua asked, "Do you recall the young woman who gave birth on the stage?"

Since, in that instant, we found ourselves back at the scene with the actual stage birth taking place, it would have been pretty hard not to remember.

"What have you learned about love, life, death, and creation through the directives, Jeremiah?"

As Joshua asked this question of me, he gestured for me to turn around. In doing so, we were given the advantage of observing the young pregnant woman both in the setting of the dirty, abandoned building and on the stage with the angel all dressed in white. I watched in wonderment as it suddenly dawned on me what Joshua needed me to understand.

In the first scenario, the young woman clearly died at the moment of the baby's birth. In the second one, the woman did not die—but the baby did! Yet, in the end, the same young woman turned out to be the one holding and loving the newborn.

"Joshua, I figured it out."

"Quiet," Joshua snapped. "Look. Do not speak."

I looked over the entire room filled with couples from every nation, nationality, and culture. Every woman held a new baby. I studied them intently as a silent observer, scanning the room from the front to the back and from one side to the other. Then, the most spectacular thing happened.

A pinpoint of twinkling light, surrounded by a flaming aura, appeared on the stage. It started out about chest high, where the birthing woman had originally been, and grew to about the size of a large adult. Of course, we all shifted our attention toward the stage, and silence filled the room. Beams of multicolored plumes danced from the light's expanding center and radiated out in every direction. The extravagant light show lasted for several seconds before the lights consolidated into solid golden rays. Then, in one fluid motion, like someone turning on a giant magnet, the splinters of golden rays gathered themselves together and transformed into the shape of a woman. She further refined her form into the stunning, heavenly being we knew as Ariana. Her beautiful red hair of gold draped her shoulders like a shawl of divine fire.

Ariana's radiance so captivated me that when her eyes locked onto mine, my consciousness surrendered to the trappings of her intense beauty. I could do nothing but stare in motionless awe as she came closer and closer to me. When she stopped moving, we found ourselves face to face, mutually smiling, and only about two feet from each other. With both arms outstretched, she silently motioned for me to turn around. As I turned my head, my body slowly followed. That's when I realized that Ariana had not come to me; I had gone to her. Floating several inches above the center of the stage, to match Ariana's height, we together looked out over all the couples with their newborns as she stated in a near whisper, "Behold the wonder and compassion of the Creator!"

At that moment, I felt and witnessed the most astonishing display of divine presence that anyone could probably handle on this side of heaven. Around every person in the room, I saw an amazingly vivid display of fantastically colored auras. I counted seven different levels of the beautifully painted energy that made it look like each person wore their own personal customized rainbow. I felt privileged beyond description.

"*This* is divine love," Joshua said softly into my right ear. I didn't need to turn and acknowledge his presence because I felt the depth of what he meant. As I looked from couple to couple, I realized that the color of the seventh layer of light emanating from each of them and that of the baby they held matched in every couple. The other colors varied in different degrees between the three of them.

From one couple to the next, the color arrangement changed both in hue and in magnitude, but within each family unit, for every man and woman and their baby, the color of the seventh layer identically matched.

"Are all these couples the natural parents of the babies?" I asked.

"We are all united through the divine love of our creator as well as the love we share with each other," Joshua responded.

"Then I think I understand," I commented with compassion. "The question isn't a biological one; it's an emotional and spiritual one."

"The divine love you have been shown is as precious now as it has always been, Jeremiah. The Creator's image of humanity and the seven divine levels of grace you are witnessing are consecrated in each new child as he or she enters their world. When true love binds a child to a parent, they are blessed with a confirmation the Creator has bestowed upon the human races, a privilege of knowing that divine love is eternal and all encompassing," Ariana declared.

"Do not take the creation of life lightly. In the spiritual realm, the physical joining of two beings to make one brings into that new life a joining of the essence of both parents. This is the reality of your physical being, but the directive speaks of divine decree, not human intervention. Remember what you have learned of your dual natures," Joshua stated.

"This physical realm of existence will pass, but the spiritual bond of grace and divine love endures forever," Ariana proclaimed. I turned to face her as she concluded, "The Creator's love is eternal and free, but most of all, it is abundant and has been entrusted to all of us."

Joshua put his hand on my shoulder and as he spoke. I turned to face him and found myself once again standing in front of the Book of Eternities. "The Divine gift of creating a new life is one that has been given to you with the ultimate privilege of sharing it with each other. But make no mistake Jeremiah. **The sanctity of life is divine law; it is the Creator's greatest gift to all of humanity. Those who disregard it will be fully accountable to the Creator.**

"Do not ever mistakenly believe that just because a culture, society, individual, or group of individuals says it's okay to take the life of another as a matter of choice or duty or loyalty or any of the many other excuses blindly acceptable to humans, that this makes it also being acceptable to God—because it does not."

"Each and every person **will be judged** for their actions," Michael sternly warned with an intensity he had not shown before.

As he emphasized these words, Michael's wings appeared, semi-extended, and his aura got extremely fiery and bright in a frightening sort of way. I figured out immediately that this is what a mighty archangel looks like when he portrays a heightened emotion, and I would definitely *never* want to be on the receiving end of it!

He just as quickly calmed back down to his usual gentle demeanor—but I got the point. Still a little bit shaken emotionally, I nodded my acknowledgment of his words and turned my head slightly toward the direction of Joshua for moral support.

"*Now* I understand what this directive is really about," I said without any further comment.

"Good!" Joshua exclaimed in a non-expressional but still serious tone. "What is the next directive?"

"There is but one directive left to be remembered. It is one you should be quite familiar with by now, Jeremiah," Michael said while smiling at me and nodding. "Please read it for us."

I looked down at the sacred book and read the directive silently to myself first, to see what Michael meant by his joyful remark. I should have known!

CHAPTER 19

THE FINAL DIRECTIVE

S MILING, I CLOSED MY EYES to remember. Then, opening them wide, I extended my smile to both Michael and Joshua and gratefully read the tenth and final directive.

"When the peace of another can find them not, say to them, 'Peace be with you,' beseeching their spirit to comfort them from within, renewing the balance of the dual natures they possess."

I turned to Joshua and Michael and said, "So all those times since we first met that I suddenly felt so peaceful and relaxed by everyone's greetings, it wasn't some special power that heavenly beings possess over humans, but rather it's the divine authority of these special words put into place to help realign our spiritual nature with our human one."

"Very well put," Michael said. "With these words, even the rage of an incensed spirit will be quieted, for they have been spoken by the Creator into the very fabric of our souls to ensure that peace and balance are never more than a breath away from divine consciousness." He smiled and added, "You have come a long way since we first met in understanding the purpose and necessity of the dual natures of humankind."

"Thank you," I responded.

I looked once more at the sacred text and discovered that the page containing the directives had turned, revealing a new proclamation. I quickly looked over the page to check for any special symbols or other markings to ensure I would not miss any important details. Not spotting anything obvious, I proceeded to read the new passage to my companions.

"Always remember, my beloved, before the thought that shaped creation, there was unconditional love—that which has no origin and beyond which infinity fades. Therein you will find the secret of your immortality reflected in the essence of these directives as well as the consciousness of origin. Keep hallowed the vessel which carries this love, and enlightened destiny will be sanctified within."

I looked up at Michael, then at Joshua, and said, "The directives were given to us as a guide, to help us understand and deal with the ever-changing arena of humanity. They permeate our souls with a source of inspiration, comfort, and security." I looked very sincerely at the two of them and quietly added, "I understand why we were given the directives and how significant they should become in all of our everyday lives, but now that I have this knowledge, how exactly am *I* supposed to use it?"

"You have been shown many things, Jeremiah. We have guided you to cultivate within your own spiritual recognition all that you need to fully remember and understand. As you have discovered, these are not only the words and the meanings of each directive, but their divine origins, as well. Few have known the travels you have journeyed, the visions you have witnessed, or the gift of experiencing the words of their creator. You are here because of who you are. You possess talents you are yet unaware of, but you must remember, Jeremiah, you are only tasked with sharing what you have learned, which must be proclaimed unaltered and complete.

"All you are asked to do now is to remember and accurately record everything we have shown you and to share it with all of creation," Joshua reiterated earnestly and without hesitation.

"Peace be with you, Jeremiah," Michael declared. "In the same manner that you bring awareness back to this sacred document, others will interpret and share its meanings throughout your Earthly realm. As these words speak to their hearts and minds, they will then share their experience with others who wish to discover their own personal level of enlightenment.

"Take this to heart, Jeremiah. Where there is love, there is light, but in the absence of light, there is only fear!"

Michael took a step closer to me and continued, "You will bring awareness back to the directives so long ago abandoned. However, since you are *only* the messenger, be always mindful that your responsibility is only to share what you have been shown. All that you hold to be reality and truth are real and true only within the realms of your perception. Your capacity to understand this truth is on a level commensurate to your own reality."

"Remember the grain of sand!" Joshua commanded. "From the simple grain of sand to a full understanding of the cosmic meaning of life, unconditional truth can come only from the one true source that is all knowledge and infinite wisdom.

"However, for any concept, thought, or idea to be accepted as truth, it must first be recognized as true without reservation within your own state of being. It must make sense to you within the framework of your conceptual and emotional reality."

"In other words, Jeremiah," Michael added, "if you do not first believe in and love yourself, all of your other values will be shadowed in doubt. If the visions you share with others leave them doubting the message *or the messenger,* then you have not fully realized the fulfillment of your destiny."

I wanted to say *something,* but all my thoughts at that moment seemed trivial, so I remained silent.

Joshua stepped closer to the crystal pedestal and said, "It is time for you to understand why the Book of Eternities is called God's book."

Michael and Joshua looked at each other, smiled, and then they both looked at me as Michael stated, "You have done well reading from the book, but to truly understand the extent of its magnitude, you must experience the book itself. Only then will you truly comprehend who you are and where you came from."

Joshua leaned in close to me and whispered, "Reach out and touch it."

"You have been granted a privilege very few have known. Are you ready to take on such a responsibility?" Michael asked.

I nodded my head slightly and very briskly rubbed my hands over my shirt several times to ensure they were dry and oil free. Then, with the last couple of rubs on my jeans, I smoothly extended my right hand toward the glowing pages beneath it. I focused intently on just the tips of my fingers as I brought them closer and closer to the sacred book.

With my hand still inches away from the luminous pages, I could feel the energy they possessed. The closer my fingers moved toward the book, the harder the effort to move them became, like trying to push two powerful magnets together. My heart and breathing challenged each other with anticipation as my fingertips neared the sacred manuscript.

I am not quite sure if I actually touched the Book of Eternities, or exactly what happened next. All I know is that whatever happened, it could not compare to anything I have ever experienced before, not even here!

CHAPTER 20

TIME REVISITED

I'M NOT SURE IF I ever actually touched the sacred Book of Eternities, because the moment my fingertips may have touched the book, time and reality immediately vaporized all around me, and I was instantaneously propelled into the middle of a spectacular explosion of lights and colors streaming all around me and spreading out in every direction. A fiery, explosive flurry of millions of microbursts shot forth in an unconstrained cosmological dynamic wave that could best be imagined as if you were standing next to a giant can of shaken soda-pop as it was opened. A kaleidoscope of sparkling energy painted the heavens as far as my vision could take me.

My first impression was that I had been placed in the clear night sky amidst a colossal fireworks display during the grand finale, but then I realized that it wasn't up-close fireworks that I was seeing, but rather, I was witnessing the birth of billions and billions of stars, from nearby to light years away. They blanketed the universe all around me but originated from only one central location as if someone had shot them out of a giant cosmic leaf blower. The magnitude of it was beyond breathtaking, and just when I decided this was the most amazing thing I could ever possibly witness—it got even better!

When I realized that I was completely weightless, like an astronaut, only without the cool space suit, I slowly spun myself around in a clockwise direction to get a panoramic 360-degree view of what was taking place all around me. Just as I completed one full turn and was once again facing the direction I started from, everything stopped, briefly frozen in an electrifying pause in time as if the universe wanted me to remember the unmeasurable scale of the phenomenon.

Then, without any input from me, and, in fact, contrary to my own intentions, I slowly started to spin around, this time in a counterclockwise direction. Since I was no longer in control, and the view was so incredibly awesome, I decided to enjoy the ride and absorb as much as my perceptibly limited human brain could handle. After completing the reverse 360-degree spin, I once again was back where I started. This time, however, the spectacular explosion of lights and colors I originally witnessed streaming all around me and spreading out in every direction did just the opposite. These expressions of endless energies pulled themselves back together in an implosive whirlwind of celestial ribbons, twisting inward first, forming a double helix, then further compacting into an almost solid-looking, tightly curled ribbon, and finally into a single point of incredibly clear, white light. If ever there was a sight indescribable in human terms, this had to be it.

Except for that one point of light, there was nothing left, only an eternity of empty space! I knew I was in the middle of the entire universe, but I could have just as easily been in a small, closed room. Other than the single point of light, which I believe was God, there was only an absolute void of complete and utter silence and darkness.

What I had seen was, as I said, indescribable, yet even this paled in comparison to the deep understanding I was given explaining it all.

In that breath of creation, that instant of time-before-time, a deep fullness stirred me with the inspiration that this source of unspeakable glory I had been given the unearned privilege to witness was merely *the thought* from the Creator that created *everything*! It was the creation of creation!

And, in that same thought, the authority and power that immortalized our souls gave birth to the source of infinite knowledge which all that followed would be built upon. The creation of not just the entire universe and everything we have ever known to exist, but a countless number of worlds, dimensions, realms, domains, and realities we have yet to attain the capability of even perceiving.

In the very next moment … or maybe even in the same one … without any cognizance of the passing of time, I focused intently on just the tips of my fingers as I brought them closer and closer to … the face of Ariana. Just when I believed my fingertips might have touched her delicate skin, I found myself standing on a pristine, polished, white stone floor amidst an infinite gathering of bluish-white tongues of fire assembled in perfect unison around an eternal light, gently floating downward. Captivated by the calming sensation of the colorful wisps, I found myself focusing on one of them and tracing its fall as it descended like a blazing snowflake on a breezeless winter morn. When it got to about knee level, I saw that the solid floor had evolved into a relaxing, silky layer of a very emotionally charged, vibrant, translucent hue that wafted above the floor like a lightly whipped frosting. It looked so dreamy soft that my first thought was to just fall into it, as one would fall onto a big overstuffed mattress.

As I followed the descent of the fiery entity, I watched as it and all the others disappeared into a sparkly, velvety layer, melted into a multicolored, shimmering, ethereal bubble and transformed into cotton-candy-looking, smoke-like wisps. Each one of these dreamy wisps instantaneously materialized into full-size, two- or multi-winged angels that ever so gracefully ascended into the heavens. There were countless multitudes of them. I had witnessed their creation, and it was spectacular!

The emotional feeling that came over me, along with the impact that accompanied it, left no doubt that all these heavenly beings became, and will always remain, living portraits of divine love, conceived and dedicated to the devotion and glorification of their creator. I had been given the indescribable privilege to witness the miracle of their transition, from inception to completion, in the same divine breath.

Again, in the very next moment ... or maybe even in the same one ... without any knowledge of the passing of time, I focused intently on the tips of my fingers as I brought them closer and closer to ... the inner wall of the archway. Just when I believed my fingertips might have touched the smooth, white stone, the invisible authority that shielded it transformed what should have been solid a rock into a silvery, mercury-like liquid coating with a single point of light emanating from its center, no bigger than a laser point.

In that precise instant when my fingertip would have touched that same point of light, the liquid coating started spreading outward in every direction, as if something was rapidly spilling out of that point. Then, in an instant, the whole process reversed itself, sucking all the silvery liquid back into the point of light while sending waves of a rainbow-colored film out to envelop the entire arch. Instead of stopping when it reached the edge of the arch's wall, however, the multicolored, now sparkling wave continued, pushing the physical edges along with it as it expanded, until the supernaturally transformed view in front of me became one of looking through a room-size picture window that had no perceivable boundaries. The actual arch was nowhere in sight.

Through this magical portal, experienced from the point of view of a celestial onlooker, I observed a majestic view of the entire dynamic universe. It immediately drew in closer and closer, like I was looking out the window of a speeding space ship, hurling toward the center, until our galaxy, through the Milky Way, closed in on our solar system and centered on the third planet from the sun. I stood in awe as all movement slowed to an effortless stop, and I witnessed the molding, transforming, and populating of the planet we call home.

At first, all I could see was a thick, billowing mass of gloomy, poisonous clouds that seemed to envelop the entire planet. Underneath this cloud layer lay the dark, empty void of cold, deep waters. Then the light of the sun broke through, and the light was good. It transformed the clouds of death into facilitators of life, and as the sun began burning holes through the dense clouds, daylight spread across the planet, revealing the immense diversity between the land and the seas.

The single, large land mass separated into smaller ones and spread across the planet. Thriving waters, teaming with animals, plants, and trees began to diversify and spread throughout the new world. The sun and moon traded turns watching over the fledgling planet, and the human races began their quest for knowledge and enlightenment.

As I looked on with wonder, the emergence of this new cosmic participant, now ablaze with color and life, I witnessed as well the very methodical alignment of the rest of the planets, moons, and star systems as they expanded and set in motion the heavenly horizon.

An absolute certainty was implanted into the core of both my natures. Not only are we *not* alone in the great expanse of the heavens, but what I was witnessing inside the tiny perspective of our own galaxy was simultaneously happening in countless other worlds in that same instant. An even greater predestined realization confirmed that, within all those creations, all those worlds, all those star systems, dimensions, domains, realms, and dominions, there is present an unimaginable number of other life forms that all fall under the same watchful eye of our creator. The majesty and fullness of the divine plan was only beginning to unfold.

In the very next moment ... or maybe even in the same one ... without any perception of the passing of time, I focused intently on the tips of my fingers as I brought them closer and closer to ... the crystal pedestal that held the Book of Eternities. Just when I believed my fingertips were about to touch the pedestal, an electrified, pulsating sensation reverberated through my entire being, forcing my eyes shut and rendering me completely motionless. I could see my body reflected in my mind's eye. My feet stayed positioned shoulder width apart, and my arms fell straight, extended forty-five degrees from my sides with my fingers pointed downward.

I could feel and sense the location of every internal and external part of my body as if each one was, at that very moment, being correlated with a corresponding point in my brain and spinal cord, while being simultaneously energized from unknown power centers throughout my core. This full-emersion stimulation overpowered my emotions, resulting in an uncontrollable, rapid cycle of passing through one emotion after another, until my entire body went limp from sheer exhaustion.

Some time passed, and I forcibly managed to open my eyes, but just long enough to capture a fleeting physical view of my surroundings. I found myself centered beneath the crystal pyramids of the archway, with all the crystals glowing exceptionally bright.

As my sensory sensations returned and intensified, I could feel the force from the crystals pushing down, on, and through me as if I had been standing under a huge, warm fan, once again forcing my eyes shut. In my mind, I saw angels, thousands and thousands of them, all kneeling around the beautiful crystal pedestal, which held the Book of Eternities. Each angel held a single, very bright, white candle.

Suddenly, the angels all disappeared, and I found myself all alone, surrounded by nothingness. Everything was dark and still. In a mild panic, I forced my eyes open with my fingers, only to find that I was now standing atop the high spot in the floor, between the crystal fountain and the archway. However, I felt like it wasn't really me, not physically anyway, only my consciousness. The feeling was very strange and too difficult to put into words—I felt emotionally void and ghost-like.

Across the room, directly in front of me and high above the floor, I found myself focusing on one of the twelve huge, triangular-shaped, colored windows—the indigo-colored one. Other than its shape and color, the window contained no other features. I saw no windowsill, frame, or opening device that would typically be associated with a window, just a single pane of lightly colored glass filling an equal-sided, triangular opening. I looked over to my right at the archway and then to my left at the fountain and realized that my position atop the white mound, as well as the window high in front of me, put me precisely in the midpoint, between all three of them.

An overpowering sentiment of deep inspiration came over me, directing my unsuspecting thoughts back to the archway. Centered in the opening of the arch and suspended halfway between it and the floor, I could see a blurry silhouette of a small human figure made purely of a clear, glistening substance, kind of like an electrified, clear gel. It looked over at me, then up at the glowing crystals, and blasted up straight into them like a dust bunny being sucked up by a powerful vacuum.

Suddenly disappearing into and then exiting the top of the arch, now in the shape of a soccer-ball-size sphere of golden-blue electricity, it zoomed straight to the indigo-colored window at the speed of lightning. It then either hit the window and changed into a golden beam of light or went through the window, triggering the beam. Whichever the case, a very bright shaft of light blasted directly down to the center of the tree inside the fountain.

Even though this entire event happened so fast that it only took a second or two, at the same time, a soft but clear voice from somewhere deep within my unseen consciousness said, "Peace be with you. Go with love."

Of course, as soon as the golden light beam shined on the tree, I immediately shifted all my focus there. The tree, completely encased in a protective shield of bluish-white light, when penetrated by the golden beam became lavishly drenched in a spotlight of expanded violet light, which accentuated the entire tree, as well as the crystal fountain surrounding it.

Standing within this light, straddling the center trunk with a foot on either side, stood a completely clear, glass-like shell of a small, featureless child. The beam could no longer be seen.

As the water from the tree flowed over the feet of the small human figure and started rising inside it, it continually grew brighter, as if it was electrically charged by the light beam. An overwhelming feeling of immense love came over me. The concentrated mental, emotional, and spiritual sensations rushing into all aspects of my mind and body reached far beyond mere human feelings or descriptions. And the fact that I was experiencing them as I watched the life form being filled with this illuminated energy left no doubt in my mind that the being experiencing the divine nourishment of the sacred water and I shared some sort of intimate spiritual union with each other. Even though I continued to view it from the vantage point of a position outside of the fountain, I felt myself experiencing every sensation through the figure in the tree. I can't explain how or why, but at that moment, we were one and the same.

As the spiritually charged water filled us from our feet up, three other phenomena simultaneously took place. The figure in the tree steadily grew in size from that of a child to the size of an adult man. As I felt the power of the liquid mystically traveling up my own body, specific areas became intensely stimulated in me and perceptibly brighter on the figure in the tree.

These areas were in the regions of my groin, below and above my navel, my chest, my neck, my eyes, and the top of my head.

The other kind of spooky but fascinating observation I made was the fact that while all this took place, a barely visible human face appeared on the figure in the tree. It presented itself in an almost phantom form, progressively transforming from that of an infant and child, through young and full adulthood, to that of an old man probably in his mid-seventies. Then it faded back into its faceless state.

Lastly, I witnessed one other astonishing point, which I almost missed because of being so focused on the transition taking place in the tree. One of the dozens of angelic shoulder-to-shoulder figures forming the protective ring around the tree, also in perfect unison with the figure in the tree, filled up to the top with the same energized water, going from a colorless, clear crystal to a beautiful, clear blue crystal.

Because of the magnitude of this incredible experience, I needed to take the time to explain it thoroughly, but I also need to point out that all of it took place not only in a dream-like fashion, but also, if there had been any sense of time (which there wasn't), in the span of only a matter of seconds.

When the watery energy reached the top of the heads of both the figure in the tree and the angelic guardian, it burst outward and upward in a cone-like pattern, filling the room in a supercharged, cloud-like fashion, then gathered almost immediately as if it was going through an invisible, clear funnel into a single point of very bright, golden light about the size of a golf ball, directly over the center of the tree. This mega-energized ball of light suddenly disappeared and reappeared only inches in front of my face at eye level. Because of the brightness, I could not look directly at it, so I blocked my eyes with my right hand and reached out with my left to try to touch it. I focused on my fingertips as I cautiously reached for the ball of energy.

Before my fingers could reach their objective though, it simply faded away.

For several seconds, with my hand still fully extended, I continued focusing intently on just the tips of my fingers and realized I was bringing them closer and closer to … the giant crystal presented to us by Ariana. The one transformed from the enormous diamond.

As an emotionally heated wave of energy from the massive orb blasted me with its paralyzing authority, I closed my eyes and waited patiently for what it had in store for me. I found myself suddenly drenched in a tidal wave of inspirational memories as they broke through all my defenses of logical thinking and captured my subconscious.

I tried to keep up, but I was inundated with an endless barrage of colors, shapes, sounds, thoughts, recollections, stories, ideas, and designs. I could feel the unbridled power as my mind and soul witnessed that exact moment at the dawn of existence when we humans were given the ability to imagine and to dream, to envision ideas that know no bounds, to store memories that could last a lifetime, and to develop feelings and beliefs that could turn any creative thought into a life-changing event or a physical masterpiece capable of altering the course of human existence. Our connection to our spiritual selves and to the very source of our existence just became a living reality!

When the torrent of streaming possibilities slowed down to a manageable level, I opened my eyes with the full knowledge and appreciation for the depth of capability and power I (we) now held in our minds and in the full capacity of our inner-most thoughts and desires. I brought my hands up in front of me and examined them with a newfound gratitude.

In the very next moment … or maybe even in the same one … with the whole concept of time now as obscure as everything else, I focused intently on the tips of my fingers as I brought them closer and closer to … the windshield of my car in that expanded moment following the accident just before I lost consciousness.

During that timeless interval, my every thought gathered in a place void of all thoughts and sent me searching for an answer that had no question. A total peace came over me, and someone's hand firmly grasped mine and escorted me from the inner darkness to the opening of what first looked like the entrance to a somewhat blurry tunnel filled with bright light.

Entering the tunnel, I could see both physically and spiritually that both the tunnel and I were simultaneously creating each other as we transitioned through what actually resembled three golden rings of light joined together in perfect unison with whatever internal force was moving me gracefully through to the other side.

I passed through the first soft ring of golden light, and I immediately recognized the familiar architecture of the archway containing the twelve crystal pyramids. However, only things in my immediate view were clear. Everything else stayed just out of focus.

As the reassurance of the crystals wrapped my existence in a blanket of indigo light, both my physical and nonphysical perception of reality ceased as I basked in a transitional cocoon of protection and love. A clearness of purpose and resolve came over me as I experienced my own conception and birth.

I emerged into the light of humanity and witnessed an in-between instant when the veil dropped behind me and I could no longer recall my own pre-existence.

At once, I passed through a second soft ring of golden light and experienced my entire life as it unfolded before me. However, I did not see my life from my own perspective. I only saw it from the viewpoint of every person whose life I had touched or been touched by throughout this human presence.

Passing through the third and final ring of soft golden light, I found myself being pulled up onto the ledge by Joshua. When I first saw his face, I knew beyond any doubt that I was looking into the face of someone who truly loved me. In that instant, with that realization, I knew that everything, every moment, all that life encompasses, had been guided by love, down to the minutest detail. I also knew in my very soul that even though the understanding of it may have been just out of reach, everything was as it should be.

Now standing securely on the ledge, Joshua let go of my hand, closed his eyes without saying a word, and just stood there for a few moments as if he were waiting for something. I noticed a faint, white mist all around us, so I naturally looked down at the ground to check it out. The mist instantly dissolved, and we were once again standing in the wagon-wheel-shaped circle of stones in front of the building Joshua referred to as the Tabernacle of Souls.

Am I really standing here or just imagining it? I thought as I tried to get some sort of grasp on reality.

"Close your eyes," Joshua said softly without opening his. I did like my teacher directed and waited for further instructions. Almost immediately, I felt somewhat numb but acutely aware. My whole body turned slowly in a clockwise direction, but in a sleep-like state. I wanted to open my eyes, but they rejected the idea. I was very unsuccessfully analyzing my situation when Joshua spoke.

"Come," he commanded.

I opened my eyes (without any difficulty) and found myself sitting cross-legged in the stone circle. Joshua sprang to his feet and quickly walked away from me in the direction of the beautiful, ornately constructed mansion.

I got up and ran to catch up with my mentor, wondering if we had been sitting in the circle all along, and everything I just experienced, including the directives could have just been some sort of celestial trance or dream.

As we approached the temple, I wondered excitedly what I would see once we entered the structure. Joshua stopped in front of it, so I thought he would wait for me. However, with barely a hesitation, he proceeded to the edge of the building and disappeared around the corner.

"Hey, wait for me," I called out, scurrying to catch up with him.

Rounding the corner, I found that my speedy companion had stopped again about halfway down the side of the wall and stood quietly staring at the building. I stopped next to him, acting as if I was admiring the beautiful structure, while in reality trying to catch my breath.

I wasn't running that hard or long, so I couldn't understand why I got tired so quickly. I bent over with my hands on my knees to catch my breath. In the process, the reason for my sudden lack of endurance became clear. Apparently, my *free ticket* to the Fountain of Youth had expired. My current appearance and stamina once again reflected my actual, slightly overweight and out of shape, forty-three-year-old body, rather than the energy-filled, youthful body I borrowed most of my time here in this miraculous place.

After reluctantly accepting my re-transformation, I looked up to check out this side of the building only to discover that it looked the same as the front, with four enormous, spectacularly carved, angelic pillars, including the ends, and three more of the incredible crystal pyramids in their own unique colors and, of course, their accompanying black-glass-looking symbols. However, I still saw no apparent door, so it did not surprise me when Joshua, without even looking at me, darted around the corner like a graceful gazelle, again shouting, "Hurry," as he went.

Rounding the next corner, I observed the same scene—more pillars, crystal triangles, and the ancient black symbols, but still no door. So, as I again expected, only this time giving me no time to rest, Joshua continued around the third corner and disappeared from sight with me scurrying behind him. I caught up to him and, still winded, said, "Thanks a lot for waiting."

In the middle of the fourth wall, we found the beautiful indigo-colored, crystal pyramid that stood out each time as our main focus of interest in previous encounters. I looked down both sides of the building and still did not see any doors or other openings. Then it occurred to me that, instead of going completely around three corners of the building to the right, we could have gone around just one corner to the left. I wondered to myself if, by chance, Joshua intended this to be some sort of hidden teaching adventure or if he, in fact, had to search for the entrance himself.

Perhaps he just wanted to remind me that even though the indigo-colored crystal apparently coincided with the creation of the human races, there were still eleven others of equal significance, whatever that might be, I thought.

"Did you forget where the door was or did you just feel like taking the scenic route?" I asked, smiling, still breathing hard.

Joshua stood silently in front of the crystal with his hands folded in front of him as if he were admiring its beauty. He did not answer me. I moved close by his side, mimicking my teacher's stance. We quietly stared at the huge, embedded gem for at least a minute. I took advantage of the chance to rest.

As my heart rate started to return to normal and my patience for staring at the wall gave way to my curiosity of what awaited us inside the building, I gently leaned toward Joshua, and in a tone only slightly above a whisper, I asked with mounting excitement, "How do we get in?"

Joshua turned his head barely enough to make eye contact out of the corner of his eye and smiled in a deviously curious way, lifting only one corner of his mouth. Then, with the speed of a startled rabbit, he leapt toward the crystal as he yelled over his shoulder, "Jump!" Then he disappeared into the wall.

"Okay, that was pretty cool," I said to myself. A bit taken aback at first, but by now, ready for anything Joshua could throw at me, I covered my eyes with my arm, just in case, and threw myself at the colorful gem protruding from the side of the building.

The feeling that came over me next could probably best be described as floating through air thick enough to hold me suspended indefinitely, like invisible Jell-O. I uncovered my eyes barely in time to catch a quick glimpse of the most incredible place I've ever seen.

I saw a city with futuristic architecture, made of polished gold, passing beneath me as if I were flying over the city like Superman. The buildings were ablaze with luminescence that easily rivaled a highlighted diamond in a jeweler's display. I wish I had been able to view it longer and share the details more vividly, but my restricted glimpse ended quicker than my mind could wrap a memory around it, changing everything from my view to a camouflaging, foggy, blue mist.

The next thing I knew, I clumsily landed on what seemed to be a very large and unnaturally smooth stone block. I quickly realized that I was actually on a large stone staircase. By large, I am referring to the steps themselves. They were maybe five or more times as high, wide, and deep as normal stairs. I stood up and looked around, but I couldn't tell where the stairs led because the bluish-white mist that now filled the entire room concealed everything except the actual step I stood on and a partial view of the steps above and below it.

"Hurry!" Joshua said from somewhere above me.

"I'm right behind you!" I shouted as I completed the climb onto the next step above me. Even though Joshua didn't wait for me, at least he let me know which direction to go, and I was pleased to find him still with me, since, at this point, I could no longer see him. Because of the unusual size of the steps, I felt like an infant trying to climb them.

The mist faded away as quickly as it came, and to my surprise, the stone staircase seemed to start on the step I was on and extended upward for as far as my eyes could discern. Joshua, like a little giant, stood defiantly watching about six or seven steps ahead of me, letting me know that he hadn't left me behind, but at the same time rushing me to hurry up and catch up with him.

"Hey, if you hadn't noticed, I'm not as young as I was before," I shouted up to him.

I looked over the side, not really knowing what to expect. Still, after all I had been through, it managed to surprise me a little when I saw nothing! I mean absolutely nothing! I climbed another step, this time a little quicker and easier after figuring out the best leverage positions for my hands and elbows. I looked back down at the two steps I had painstakingly climbed and discovered that the staircase now went on indefinitely in both directions.

After ascending a couple more of the oversized steps, I stopped to take a quick break and again looked up to see if I had gotten any closer to my mentor. He was still several steps ahead of me, impatiently staring down at me with his arms folded. For some foolish reason, I thought I might be capable of catching up to Joshua since I was at least four or five inches taller than him. Instead, when I again looked up, I noticed that he now had gained the lead on me by at least fifteen or more steps!

"Hurry!" he shouted down to me while smiling and waving his arm to emphasize the point.

"Oh yeah, right," I shouted back up at him while I continued my climb up the mammoth staircase. "You're telling me to hurry, and you probably *flew* up there," I mumbled under my breath, pulling myself up onto the next step.

"Yes, I did." Joshua chuckled.

He now stood on the same step I just pulled myself onto and genuinely seemed to be enjoying all the exercise I was getting.

When I got back up on my feet, I stood facing Joshua. He displayed a childlike glimmer in his eyes and a big smile on his face that exemplified true happiness. At first, I thought he was just gloating over making me struggle, but then he turned his body, allowing me to see past him. We most definitely no longer needed stone steps. The indescribable view all around us froze me in awe and nearly took my breath away.

CHAPTER 21

THE GAME OF LIFE

I N THAT INSTANT, WE FOUND ourselves centered on a clear, crystal, round disc probably about ten feet in diameter and appearing to be as thin as a sheet of window glass. There were no stairs above or below us, or any other structure for that matter. We stood all by ourselves, just Joshua and I, in the center of the entire universe, looking at the breadth of all of creation. I could only describe it as a sight beyond imagining. The stars, moons, and planets faded outward into clusters of sparkling celestial diamonds and massive, kaleidoscope-looking, multi-colored clouds. Even though the depth of our privileged viewing spanned light years, the sheer magnitude of their numbers opened up mind-boggling possibilities that could not be denied. This was surely a gift of divine magnitude. To even casually imagine what secrets and treasures those billions of other worlds might hold left me hoping and praying that just one of them would be revealed in my lifetime. I slowly turned in all directions to admire the totality of this heavenly masterpiece.

Joshua didn't say anything, nor did he need to. The view presented to us spoke for itself. For several minutes, the two of us just stood there, together admiring the inexpressible handiwork of the ultimate master artist before Joshua quietly interrupted the deep silence.

"The wonders of the Creator are more numerous than all the heavens you are capable of imagining." Joshua extended his arm in front of him. "Yet, each and every one of the divine children is equally loved and watched over throughout their existence."

I turned my head and looked at Joshua with the deepest gratitude.

My teacher then looked eagerly into my eyes and asked, "What is your favorite sport?"

"My favorite sport?" I repeated. "What a bizarre thing to ask now!"

I looked into his eyes, and he looked like a little kid who was about to reveal a big secret.

"Well, I like baseball and soccer, but for the sheer determination and strategy, I guess my favorite sport is football."

"Have you ever heard anyone refer to life as the Game of Life?"

"Of course I have, Joshua," I said, turning my body toward him. *But life is much too serious to think of it as a game*, I thought to myself.

Then I glanced over Joshua's shoulder, noticing that the stunning display of the heavens no longer surrounded us.

Instead, we now found ourselves standing in a sports announcer's booth, of all places, overlooking a stadium with a football game already in progress on the field below. Joshua, still facing me, continued speaking without missing a beat.

"To understand the meaning of life, you must understand the purpose of living. Think of it in terms of a football game in which the Creator is the head coach of *both* teams. The one you believe to be the Son of God is the quarterback of one team, and

Satan, the one you call the devil, is the quarterback of the other team. Because one of the Creator's greatest gifts to all the players is the gift of free will, you are free to choose whatever team and position you want to play in the game. All the members of both teams, whether they are offense or defense, have an important role to play. In addition, in this championship-level game, every player will participate.

As your life progresses from play to play, sometimes you will make great strides toward your goal, and sometimes you will lose ground. Since many people go through life without realizing what their goals are, or if they really exist, it is the head coach's job to make sure you keep going in the right direction until that realization becomes evident.

Each time you try a new play and it works well for you, you will remember and learn from that experience. Then, every time you use it, you build on its success. As your experience grows through the success or failure of new plays and old ones, you become wiser in the knowledge of what makes a play good or bad, what helps you to move toward the goal and what does not. As the game progresses, you pass on what you have learned to new players—your children, co-workers, friends, family, neighbors, and strangers that you meet, no matter how briefly, along the way."

Joshua paused and looked at me as if he thought I might have something to say, but I did not, so he continued.

"Throughout the game of life, sometimes it is obvious that the Son of God is winning, and sometimes Satan seems to have the upper hand. What you *must* realize is that if there were no challenges or adversities in life provided by the other team, there could be no game!

"To put your mind at ease, Satan is only a player too. When it seems like he is winning, it is just another play. The Creator is always in complete control of every aspect of the game. Everything that happens or has ever happened since the first thought of creation is part of the divine plan. A plan so astonishing, so colossal, and so miraculous, you or I could not even begin to comprehend it.

"Go ahead, Jeremiah. Ask me the questions that are filling your thoughts," Joshua insisted.

"Okay, Joshua," I replied, ready for some deep answers, "if God is in complete control and Satan is only another player under that control, then why does God allow all the pain and suffering and killing to go on without ever lifting a finger to stop it?" I waited long enough for him to answer, but without speaking, Joshua only nodded. Without analyzing his response, I continued.

"Why do bad things always seem to happen to good people, and why do bad people seem to get all the breaks? If God is really in control, then why is there so much evil and wickedness in the world? Why not just get rid of it altogether? Why does there have to be both good and evil? There would still be adversities in life without the devil, wouldn't there?"

Because I have always felt that this is one of the most important questions I have wanted to find the answer to in life, I hoped that he would give me a meaningful response. After everything I'd been privileged to see and feel through Joshua's teachings, as well as those of the archangels, I felt sure I could accept and handle whatever he would tell me.

"I'll tell you why, Jeremiah," Joshua began. "The landlord of the Earth realms is Satan, exactly as the Creator designed it.

This is his home field. He is a formidable opponent, and he loves to win. Satan has powers, resources, and persuasive measures beyond anything you could possibly imagine. However, they are all within the parameters of the game.

"Through spiritual growth and personal experiences, life is an opportunity to comprehend and appreciate the magnitude of your God. Satan and all his Earth angels, as well as the angels of heaven, understand this and *trust* in the divine plan. This is faith, Jeremiah. Faith in the divine plan *is* the foundation upon which life, all life, is built. Therefore, to this end, all the members of both teams know and play their parts.

"In the Game of Life, as in any game, it is only through playing a worthy opponent that you are able to grow in strength, wisdom, and self-confidence. You must develop strategies that work by trusting your abilities, believing in yourself and your teammates, and having faith that the choices you make can and will make a difference, not only in your life, but in the lives of those you touch, as well.

"You must know, without any doubt, that Satan is not only real, but is masterful in understanding human psychology. Consequently, he is often successful at making people believe he is winning, so that they will just quit trying. He appears to break all the rules and is an expert at pitting the players against each other. If you see through his deception by staying focused on your inner light and your goal, however, you can take him on and beat him, because in the darkness, he calls the plays, but in the light, he too is a divine child of the Creator."

That last statement caught me a little off-guard, but I didn't say anything. I just continued to listen attentively to Joshua's words so that, when he finished, I would hopefully understand his true meaning.

"The wiser, stronger, and more confident you are than your opponent," Joshua continued, "the bigger the players Satan will send against you, and the harder he will try to keep you from making a successful play. Better yet, if he can convince you that you would be happier and enjoy a more fulfilling life with him calling the plays, he will entice you to join his team by using wealth, fame, popularity, or whatever else it takes to win you over to his side.

"His goal is to make you think you do not need the Son of God's team at all. For him, that means there will be one less opposing player to worry about. For you, however, it could mean a life of spiritual confusion and emptiness, as well as emotional starvation and depressive loneliness. Keep this in mind, and remember that because you do have the gift of free will, *every* choice you make in life is always of your own choosing, even those in which you feel you have no choice."

Joshua's words made sense to me because of the many stories I've heard over the years about millionaires, entertainers, lottery winners, and people from all walks of life, who seemed to have everything they could ever want, killing themselves either outright or through drugs or alcohol.

Joshua let me finish my thought, and then he continued.

"As long as you persist in striving to reach your goal, with all your mind, heart, and soul, you will continue to move toward it. However, in doing so, you must never forget those who help you along the way. You are part of a team, and when the team, or any player on the team, moves you closer to your goal, no matter how minute you may think it is at the time, you must be thankful to those others, as well as to yourself. If you choose not to show your appreciation to your teammates and believe you can do it all on your own, your play will turn into an empty victory, and ultimately you will feel like you have failed in the other aspects of your life, leaving you unfulfilled and living with regrets."

Joshua grabbed me firmly by both shoulders and stared hard into my soul, affirming, "Love is the key to life, but gratitude is the key to happiness."

He made sure his statement had time to sink in, and then he lightly smiled and concluded, "When the game is over and your life is complete, you will be given the privilege of looking back at each play of your life. From this perspective, you will realize that it really did not matter how your final game turned out, because only the Creator has the wisdom to understand that. Likewise, only *you* and your God can evaluate how successful you think you played your position on the team. If you thought that you did not make a difference for someone else, or that your life carried no meaning beyond yourself, or in the end, that your life did not accomplish anything that mattered, then not only would you have been wrong, but you would have missed the point of the whole game.

"You must understand that *every* aspect of your life is interwoven with facets of everyone else's! Just by virtue of being in the game, you have influenced yourself, the world around you, the other members of your team, the members of the other team, the result of each play, and finally, the outcome of the game itself."

I never really thought of life as a game of any sort, but the analogy Joshua used really got me thinking. I guess as a parent, like all parents, my biggest goal in life has been to make a positive difference in my children's lives and to leave them with the knowledge and skills they need to be successful and happy. But in this big picture of life that Joshua talked about, my role outside of our little family seems so insignificant that I doubt I would be considered much of a contributor.

"I can see how some of the people that we interact with could have some long-term effect on us, such as our parents, significant teachers, or close friends. In addition, others might have a short-term impact, like a coach or a neighbor, but personally, I've never been lucky enough to have more than a handful of close friends or family at any particular point in my life. So it seems to me that in the big scheme of things, there are a lot more people—in fact, most of the people we meet in our daily lives—that have absolutely no consequence on our lives, or us on theirs."

"Do you?" Joshua asked. "Name one!"

"Name one? Are you kidding? I could name dozens!"

I considered my answer to be pretty obvious, so why did Joshua give me such an easy challenge? He seemed to be offering me an excellent opportunity to finally beat him at his own game, but why? What was he really up to?

I needed to make my answer foolproof. So, even though it seemed like a no-brainer, I decided to give it some serious thought before answering. If all he wanted me to do was name someone, anyone, that I probably would only meet once and would almost surely never see again, that seemed too easy. Of course, it had to be a complete stranger that I would have absolutely no influence on at all and vice-versa. Piece of cake!

"Okay, just to make sure I understand the challenge, all I have to do is name any person I come in contact with that doesn't influence me, and I don't influence them. And if I do, then I win—right?

Joshua didn't say anything, but he did break into a big smile and slightly nod his head.

"Well then, I got it! I am going to use a checkout person at a busy grocery store." I paused, thinking about how Joshua would probably respond, and quickly added, "While on a road trip, far away from home, in a little town I will never visit again."

"Are you usually cordial or harsh with that person when they check you out?" Joshua asked.

"Well, we all have bad days, but by my nature, I always try to smile and be kind to everyone, including, of course, the checkout people in any store," I responded.

"Is it not possible that the kindness you show could be just that little bit of cheering up the checkout person needed right then to change the way she might be feeling, or help her forget some unhappy or unkind thoughts running through her mind, perhaps from the customer before you? Maybe all she needed was a kind word and a genuine smile from a stranger to change her state of mind just enough to help her let go of a depressing thought that could have led to continuing or re-starting an addictive habit or a destructive, desperate, or painful act when she left work that day.

"What if, because you *were* having a bad day, you turned out to be *that* customer that came across rude or belittling to the unsuspecting checkout person? You may have only been angry with yourself, but not knowing that, she felt it as being directed at her. As a direct result of something you said or did, or even just a perceived mean look, you become the last straw that makes that person say, 'I can't take this anymore.' Perhaps you are that final stressor that makes her quit her job. What then?

"Because of *your* actions, this stranger, whom you will never encounter again, may make desperate choices with disastrous results that affect her, her family, her neighbors or co-workers, and many other lives. On the other hand, what if, because she quit her job due to the words or actions of you, a stranger, she then finds herself in a position to take a much better job that allows her to discover her innermost talents, and consequently she builds a career that positively and significantly impacts thousands?

"You see, Jeremiah, without knowing the state of mind or intimate thoughts of another, you have *no way* of knowing how some little thing you do or say will impact the lives of the people around you, whether they are friends, loved ones, or perfect strangers you will never meet again. Every thought you turn into an action or fail to act upon, every play you make in the Game of Life, has consequences one way or another. Some you will see, but most, you will not."

As Joshua continued, his thought-provoking scenarios not only made me ponder all the different possibilities, but touched my heart, as well.

"What about infants or young children that unfortunately die at birth or within the first days or months of life? Do you think they could have much of an impact on anyone else's life outside of their family or play a role in the way others look at life?" Joshua asked.

"I know they do," I stated sadly. "The types of unexpected, tragic deaths you speak of profoundly impact the lives of not only the parents and family, nurses and doctors, volunteers and support personnel, they usually affect the entire local community. In fact, recently in my church, we were asked to pray for a couple, people I never met before, who recently buried their three-month-old baby girl. It made my heart not only reach out to that young family in their time of grief, but really appreciate and thank God for the health of my own children. Dozens of families reached out to them with cards, and food, and flowers, and even though most of us did not know them personally, we were all emotionally affected by their loss."

After a lot of deep thought, I said to Joshua, "So, are you saying that no matter what direction we choose in life, or how good or bad our lives turn out, in the end, the most important point is that we participated in the Game of Life? And that whether we realize it or not, we influence and are affected by each and every person whose lives we touched or whose lives touched ours, no matter how significant or trivial it may seem at the time?"

Joshua didn't have to say anything. He just continued looking deep into my eyes and smiling until he knew I understood.

"So *that* is the essence and meaning of life!" I stated, knowing that I finally got it.

"When we first met, you said you wanted to understand life's true meaning. Is it really more complicated than you thought? Or, if you truly examined your questions from within the confines of your soul, did you not always possess the answers?"

I felt deeply inspired by Joshua's words and had been looking intently into his eyes. So I hadn't realized our return to the Book of Eternities in the Hall of Angels.

Once again, we found ourselves standing in front of the crystal pedestal with the mighty Archangel Michael standing guard behind it. I looked up at Michael with my newfound knowledge and said, "So, it really doesn't matter what particular religion or beliefs anyone chooses to follow, or how dedicated they are to the teachings and doctrine of any one church, does it?"

"Remember *all* of your lessons, Jeremiah," Michael cautioned me. "You have been shown that one of the core elements of life is found in all those who cross your path. You have also seen that people who choose to pass through life without seeking strength and guidance from the light, or wisdom from the teachings of others, will not rise to the level of passion required to enlighten their path enough to fill their spiritual needs. Those who fail to comprehend the sanctified gifts within their own souls will be too naïve to fully experience the true meaning and glory of being in fellowship with divine love. They will miss the opportunity to fulfill their lives with the blessed understanding their creator intended."

Joshua looked at me and nodded in agreement. "The directives are not meant to be a list from which you choose. They are each a part of a single song. If any part is left out, the song is not complete."

Then Michael added, "As you have been shown, the angels, *all* the angels, play an important role in the divine plan, Jeremiah. It is precisely at this juncture in the course of human events that the Creator's directives will lead us back from the edge of a spiritual abyss and toward the one true source of light and love. But the time is short, and the souls are many.

"The directives will help people to comprehend what is *real* in their daily lives, to look beyond their financial worries and job-related pressures, to reach out beyond their materialistic and superficial, self-imposed stresses, and to focus once again on the true meaning of life and love. With this divine gift, *everyone* has the potential to be an inspiration to themselves and everyone around them, if they so choose, to make the plays that really make a difference."

He continued, "All you really need is faith and love to understand that life's journey happens just as the Creator planned it. However, the self-restricting nature of the human psyche is quite comfortable dwelling in the temporal cloud of laziness and confusion of purpose. Always remember that it is the *depth* of experiencing love and life that is our greatest reward on this journey."

Joshua, now standing very close to me, whispered, "This is where your training begins. When you discover the seven divine gifts, you will be able to comprehend and appreciate the perceived boundaries and unobstructed possibilities of your humanity."

Michael nodded his head slightly as he confidently smiled and said, "You have seen many things that have not yet been explained to you. You have been allowed to see briefly beyond the veil, and you, Jeremiah, have been commissioned to bring hope back to the human races. There will be much strife and hard times ahead. Many will question the very presence of a God. Be steadfast and assured. All is as it should be to fulfill that which has been foretold. The pathway you have chosen is a noble one, but it is only the first step of your personal journey down your road of enlightenment."

Michael looked over at Joshua. They smiled and nodded in unison almost as if they were cueing each other for something special to happen. Then Joshua, still smiling, continued with these instructions: "Demanding times are forthcoming, unlike any in recent human memory. Bear in mind all the questions that sent you in search of your own spiritual identity and help others to find a path that will lead them to the answers they seek, as well. Through your example, many will follow as interpreters, teachers, and disciples. Their journeys will begin as others end, and the cycle of light and love will never be broken."

Michael added joyfully, "Your words will charge the souls of many and change lives in ways you cannot imagine, including your own. As people discover the true potential and innate abilities bestowed on all God's children, that knowledge will unbind their true natures. Once freed, the spiritual treasures bequeathed to us all will strengthen our conviction within. This, in turn, will be manifested through the power of divine love."

When I looked back at Joshua, he lovingly smiled at me with a bigger grin than I've ever seen on him and said in a whimsical sort of way, "If you think this adventure was an exciting one ... wait till you see the next one!"

Then Michael stepped around to the front of the podium directly behind Joshua. He spread his now fully visible, massive wings wide and raised his golden sword in a victory-style salute. They both looked at me with love, nodding their approval. Then, right before my eyes, the mighty archangel and Joshua melded together as one, and Michael simply faded away, leaving Joshua standing there alone.

Joshua stepped back over, close to my side, as I looked into his smiling eyes, trying to grasp what had taken place. Out of the corner of my eye, I noticed the next page in the Book of Eternities began to slowly turn itself. I glanced down at the glowing page but then immediately looked back up at Joshua when he leaned forward and gave me a loving fatherly embrace. As I hugged him back, a lonely, heartbreaking feeling swept through me because I knew he was saying good-bye, and I did not know when or if I would ever see him again. I came to not only respect, but to love Joshua very deeply through our adventures together.

He slowly leaned back away from me, but he kept his hands firmly on my shoulders. A heavenly glow radiated all around him. I stared deeply into the caring eyes of this elderly Asian man who stepped into my life to become my most profound teacher, and as I did so, right before my eyes, his entire personage transformed into that of my own father.

I looked passionately into my dad's loving eyes as they revealed a warmth and love that fulfilled my deepest hopes. My eyes instantly filled with tears, as did his, and he said to me, "I will always be with you, my son."

With a proud and gentle smile, he faded away, leaving me alone with the book. I stood motionless for several seconds and then slowly shifted my gaze and looked down at the page that had turned. With a tear running down my cheek, I smiled when I saw that the page was blank, for I knew it was yet to be written!

EPILOGUE

I STARED AT THE BOOK and silently wept while the memories of Dad and Joshua and Michael and Metatron and all the amazing things I had been shown flashed back and forth across my mind and ...

Knock. Knock. Knock. I heard it in that subconscious way you hear things as you are awakening from a dream.

"That's odd," I said, drying the tears from my eyes. There seemed to be a metallic knocking sound coming from the Book of Eternities.

Knock. Knock. Knock.

"Hey, buddy, are you all right?"

I sat back, opened my eyes, and turned my head just in time to have the bright light of a flashlight beamed into my face. As I shielded my eyes from the light, the person shining it directed it downward. I mentally tried to put the pieces back together as I slowly rolled the window down.

"Sorry 'bout that. Are you hurt?" the stranger asked.

I looked past the mostly shadowed man standing next to my car and concentrated my view on the wrecker's rotating amber light while I gave my mind a chance to catch up with my situation.

"Do you need an ambulance?" the man asked as he looked toward the front and rear of my car, assessing the situation.

I looked myself over and painlessly stretched out my arms and legs.

"No, I think I'm okay," I said, reaching up to gently touch the huge, very tender knot above my right eyebrow. I looked at my fingertips in the dim light. "No blood, that's good."

The man pulled open the driver's door and popped the seatbelt for me.

"Here, let me give you a hand."

He took hold of my right hand with his left, and reaching under my arm with his other hand, he lifted me out of the seat toward him.

"Hey, angel, shine the searchlight down here!" he shouted up the bank over his right shoulder. A pair of searchlights, one on either side of the truck, suddenly beamed straight up into the sky, and then the one on our side of the truck moved downward until it focused its beam directly on the ditch in front of my car. The wrecker man helped me up a shallow part of the bank and onto the road about ten feet in front of my car. He then led me over to sit down on the bumper of the truck. A silhouetted figure readjusted the light on to our side of the truck so that it lit up my car and the entire area behind it, and then they turned the other light off.

"Thanks, babe!" the man shouted as he let go of my arm and headed back down toward my car. The wrecker man, dressed in high-bib, blue coveralls and a baseball cap, looked like a pretty big guy in the dimness. He stood at least six foot tall and was very stocky, so I wasn't surprised when he didn't respond to my half-hearted offer to help. Talking over his shoulder, he said without stopping, "She's pretty good. Why don't you let her take a look at that bump on your head while I see what we can do about getting you outta here."

I turned my head back around just in time to have the wrecker man's partner, a woman, shine a flashlight on my face and forehead and start gently feeling around my goose egg until I pulled back with an, "Ouch."

"Sorry," she said barely above a whisper. "What's your name?"

"Jeremiah," I replied.

She passed the flashlight beam across my eyes a few times. "It doesn't look too bad, but you may want to have your doctor take a look just to be on the safe side. Do you hurt anywhere else, Jeremiah?" Even from my seated position, she too seemed unusually tall, probably close to six feet. From the residual light of the spotlight, I could see she wore jeans, work boots, and a dark-colored sweatshirt, but I couldn't really make out much else with the light in my face.

"No," I said. "I think my head got the worst of it."

"Shouldn't be any problem!" the wrecker man yelled up from the back of my car. I looked back toward the car and spotted him crouched down on one knee, looking and feeling under my trunk.

"I think the short block will do it!" he shouted without looking up.

I looked back to where the woman previously stood, but she had already scurried around to the other side of the truck to retrieve something from one of the side compartments there, so I got up and walked over closer to the edge of the bank, above my car, to observe what the wrecker man was doing.

I wonder how long I've been out, I thought. *It's still dark, so it couldn't have been too long.*

When I stood up, my head started throbbing, so, since I wasn't helping anyway, I decided to sit back down on the bumper of the truck. Just as I turned, the wrecker man's wife (I'm guessing) moved past me, carrying what looked like about a foot-long piece of a fence post. She squatted down on the top edge of the bank and tossed the wood behind my car, next to him.

With the searchlight now shining on her back, I could see she had on a bluish-green, hooded sweatshirt under her bib coveralls, but with a baseball cap covering her head and the hood down and covering her neck, I couldn't make out much else. The wrecker man shouted, "Okay," prompting me to look back down at him. Apparently, without me noticing, he already had the winch cable hooked up to the back of my car. He stood up, sidestepped over, and opened the driver's door while kicking some medium-size rocks out of the way with his boots.

"Excuse me, sir, do you know what time it is?" I asked.

"Sorry," he responded as he climbed in the driver's seat without looking up, "I haven't had a working watch in ages."

"Well, I've got three of them, still in their boxes," I mumbled to myself. "Okay, thanks anyway."

In the meantime, when I looked back toward his partner, she had already gotten up and headed to the cab of the truck. She switched off the searchlight and, by the sound of it, did something to engage the motor on the winch.

"Can't run them both at the same time," I barely heard her say over the rather loud grinding of the winch motor.

"You might want to stand back a bit!" the wrecker man shouted out in my direction as he climbed out of the driver's seat, closed the door, and reached in through the window. Without the searchlight, I was back to seeing only a moonlit silhouette of the wrecker man and the light from a small flashlight he was shining toward the rear of the car.

On the wrecker, the only light was the rotating beacon and a small, dome-type light in the outside center of the cab. The woman worked the controls on the winch as she looked over her shoulder down at her partner. I positioned myself safely in the middle of the road about twenty feet behind the truck. When he told me to stand back, I didn't know if he meant the cable might snap or what, but I wasn't taking any chances.

The cable reeled in slowly until it became taut. Then the woman stopped it, and her husband went to the back of the car, again got down on one knee, pulled a few times, and got back up and said, "Okay, baby, go ahead slow."

The back wheels slid toward the road about three feet, and then the whole back end came off the ground, lifting it up and over the bank, like a child picking up a toy from a sandbox.

While his wife worked the winch controls, the wrecker man, again reaching through the driver's window, straightened up the front wheels and steered the car until the rear end cleared the edge of the graveled bank.

So, this was all just a dream? I thought. *How could none of it be real? It had to be real; it was so clear, so amazing …*

"That's good!" the man shouted over the winch motor. "Have Dad pull it forward about ten feet."

Until he said that, I had no idea the wrecker still had another person in it.

"Pull ahead about ten feet," she repeated into the truck's window. The tow truck had been running the whole time, so as soon as she said it, the brake lights came on, and the gears went from some teeth-clenching grinding to a metallic thud. The engine throttled up, and the truck slowly moved forward as the wrecker man steered and his wife maneuvered the winch controls until the front of my car planted itself back on solid ground in the middle of the road. The brake lights came back on, and the truck stopped.

"Thanks, Dad," the woman said softly to the person driving the truck. She worked the levers on the winch until the back wheels once again rested on the graveled road. In no time, her husband had the cable unhooked and tossed the hook back toward the wrecker. While he finished up, I looked at the passenger side to see how much damage I caused and found, to my surprise, only minor surface scratches.

"Why don't you see if you can get it started?" the wrecker man instructed as he gathered up the piece of wood and a couple of chains. His wife continued slowly rolling up the cable and secured the end to the base of the winch.

"If not, we'll hook you up on the boom and tow it in."

I moved quickly to the car and tried to start it. I had recently bought a new, heavy-duty, expensive, high-amp battery after being thoroughly soaked and frustrated in the mall parking lot because I left the lights on and killed my cheap battery. So I knew, if nothing else, it had plenty of juice to turn over the motor. However, the starter wasn't catching. The wrecker man stepped over to the other side of the car and, talking through the passenger window, said, "Put the pedal all the way to the floor and hold it."

I did as he instructed, and after turning it over several times, it started to run, sputtered a bit, and quit. I turned the key again, and this time it sputtered, backfired, sputtered a little more, and cranked up. Once it kept running, it sounded great. I revved it a few times, let my foot off the gas, and it purred like a ferret. I looked up at my rescuer and smiled.

"These classic Cougars are hard to kill," he proclaimed, smiling back.

The searchlight suddenly came back on, and I realized the winch motor had once again fallen silent.

"Can't run them both at the same time," he stated, reiterating the words of his partner. "Too much of a drain on the system."

"We're ready to roll," his wife chimed in as she stepped around the back of the truck and readjusted the searchlight so it lit up the road between us. As she adjusted the light, I climbed out of my car, simultaneously reaching for my wallet in the back pocket of my jeans, only to find it missing. I often take my overstuffed-with-papers wallet out so I can be more comfortable as I drive, usually setting it on the console or passenger seat, especially on long trips.

"My wallet is in the car," I called out as I turned to get it. "I have a Triple A card. It's a little bit expired, but maybe you could try it anyway."

"You don't owe us anything, my friend. We're just glad you weren't hurt."

"Are you sure?" I asked, very surprised. I knew I only had a dollar or two in my wallet and maybe another two or three dollars' worth of change in the ashtray after putting my last twenty in the gas tank earlier in the day. However, I planned on giving them my name and number and taking care of the bill as soon as I could.

"Yeah, we're sure," the woman said as he hugged her close to his side.

"Thank you so much," I said very gratefully as I walked back toward the rear of the wrecker where the searchlight illuminated the road. I could finally get a good look at my rescuers.

They both appeared young, maybe mid-twenties, and ...

I knew them! I mean, I didn't *know* them, know them, but their faces looked so familiar.

The wrecker man reached out his very large hand, shaking mine with a firm grip, and smiled.

"Thank you so much," I said again as his wife leaned forward and also shook my hand with a very firm grip.

"You are very welcome, Jeremiah," she pleasantly remarked as she smiled and pulled off her cap, shaking down her long, golden-red hair. That's when it hit me.

I looked back at the wrecker man, who had also removed his ball cap, and found myself looking into the face of the Archangel Metatron. He smiled into a soft laugh and then winked at me and headed for the cab of the truck. I looked back into the beautiful face of his wife, Ariana, and just stood there half-smiling in shock, ready to burst into tears.

I didn't even realize I was still holding her hand until she put her other hand on top of mine and, tenderly shaking my hand with both of hers, she smiled with her eyes and joyfully said, "Peace be with you, Jeremiah." She let go of my hand, which remained extended, and moved quickly around to the passenger side of the wrecker. The searchlight faded out.

I looked up at the back window of the truck. When she opened the door, and the inside dome light illuminated, I wasn't at all surprised when the "dad," now sitting in the middle of the seat, turned and smiled at me. I glanced into the smiling face of Joshua, and tears immediately filled my eyes. Ariana closed the door, and the light went out, hiding the angelic crew in the darkness as they started to drive away.

I walked over to my car, plumped down into my seat, closed the door, and looked in the rearview mirror to find the road empty. Nevertheless, I heard Joshua's voice clearly and joyfully reminding me, "No one *ever* goes through life alone. Not ever!"

His reassuring words made me feel so peaceful and fervently satisfied—like everything was in its proper place and just as it should be. I felt emotionally serene, knowing that it wasn't all just a dream, but I also realized that I was much sleepier than I thought, and I knew I needed to get home to my awaiting family.

I turned on my headlights, put it in gear, and stepped on the gas before noticing that the reflection off the dash highlighted a plate-sized, shattered, spider-web-looking crack in the middle of the windshield where it had been struck by a rock. I reached up to feel if the safety glass had cracked all the way through. I lightly passed over the impact point and surrounding area with my fingertips ...

Just then, a shooting star shot across my view in the dark evening air, and it was one of those awesome, rare ones that actually displayed a long, fiery tail. It was so cool. I was able to watch it the full length of my windshield before it disappeared over the trees on the right side of the road. And, as an extra bonus, for a split second, it unexplainably even appeared to just stop! Of course, I knew that wasn't possible, so it clearly must have been my imagination or a direct result of my sleepiness. In either case, I have always enjoyed seeing shooting stars, and to this day, I'll admit I still childishly make a wish on them.

The windshield felt cold, but the warm air felt good on my hand. The blower was currently working just fine, so I rolled down the window, for the added stimulus of fresh air, and turned on the radio; I always left it set on the oldies station. I cranked it up and started singing along with The Byrds.

It was quite common to see several deer alongside the road at this time of the night, so I needed to stay focused and alert. The last thing I needed on my nonexistent budget was to end up in a ditch in the middle of nowhere. Singing to the oldies always helps. Besides, I reminded myself, in less than fifteen minutes

I would be snuggling up to an oversized pillow and a fleece blanket I brought back from overseas.

"To everything, turn! Turn! Turn! There is a season! Turn! Turn! Turn! ..."

All of a sudden, from out of nowhere, the suited, silver-haired preacher from my meditation appeared in the middle of the road, right in front of my car. My headlights lit up his deeply penetrating, reddish-purple eyes like lasers. I swerved to the right and slammed on the brakes, launching me into a skid on the loose gravel ...

CPSIA information can be obtained
at www.ICGtesting.com
Printed in the USA
BVHW081134221219
567499BV00001B/131/P